WITHDRAWN

PUBLISHING

a Jim Pattison Company

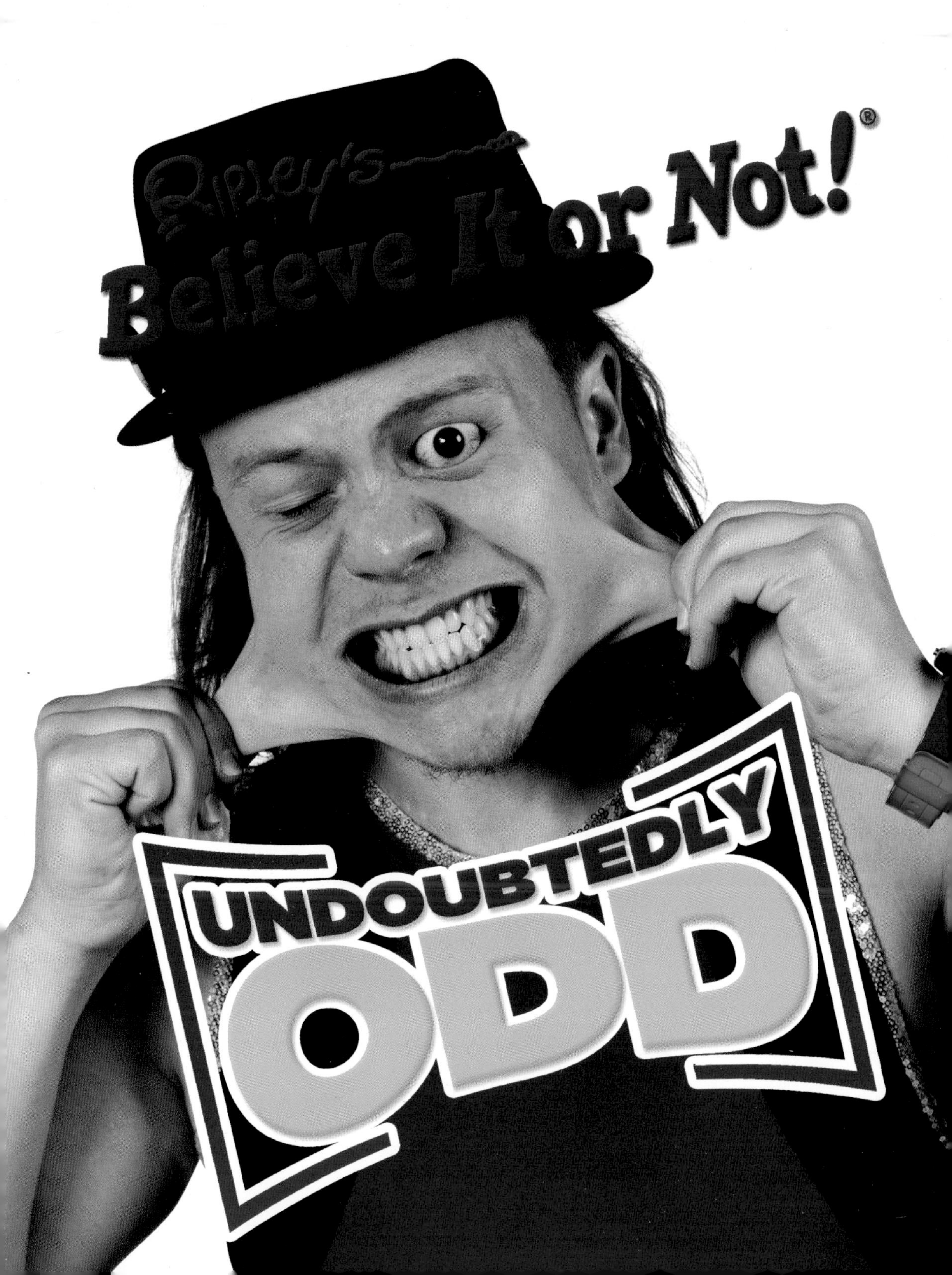
Ripley's
Believe It or Not!®
UNDOUBTEDLY
ODD

Executive Vice President, Intellectual Property Norm Deska
Senior Director of Publishing Amanda Joiner

Editorial Manager Carrie Bolin
Project Editor Jordie R. Orlando
Project Design Adam McCabe, Jordie R. Orlando, Sam South
Cover Design Luis Fuentes, Adam McCabe
Text Geoff Tibballs
Proofreader Rachel Paul
Indexer Yvette M. Chin

WARNING Some of the stunts and activities are undertaken by experts and should not be attempted by anyone without adequate training and supervision.

PUBLISHER'S NOTE While every effort has been made to verify the accuracy of the entries in this book, the Publisher cannot be held responsible for any errors contained in the work. They would be glad to receive any information from readers.

FRONT COVER IMAGE Jorge Iván Latorre Robles of Puerto Rico has Ehlers-Danlos syndrome, a condition that affects his body's production of collagen, giving him super-stretchy skin and incredible flexibility!

Published by Ripley Publishing 2018

Ripley Publishing
7576 Kingspointe Parkway, Suite 188
Orlando, Florida 32819 USA

1 3 5 7 9 10 8 6 4 2

ISBN 978-1-60991-205-5 (USA) | ISBN 978-1-78475-965-0 (UK)

Library of Congress Control Number: 2017956683

Some of this material first appeared in
Ripley's Believe It or Not! Eye-Popping Oddities!

Manufactured in China in December 2017
First Printing

For more information regarding permission, contact:
VP Intellectual Property
Ripley Entertainment Inc.
7576 Kingspointe Parkway, Suite 188
Orlando, Florida 32819 USA
publishing@ripleys.com
www.ripleys.com / books

Young Arrow
20 Vauxhall Bridge Road
London SW1V 2SA

Young Arrow is part of the Penguin Random House group of companies whose addresses can be found at global.penguinrandomhouse.com.

Ripley Entertainment Inc. has asserted the right to be identified as the author of this Work in accordance with the Copyright, Designs and Patents Act 1988.

First published in Great Britain in 2018 by Young Arrow

www.penguin.co.uk

A CIP catalogue record for this book is available from the British Library.

CONTENTS

ROBERT RIPLEY'S ENDURING LEGACY

Robert Ripley—artist, author, explorer, radio host, television and movie personality, and the man who coined one of the most famous phrases in the English language, "Believe It or Not!"—died nearly 70 years ago. However, he is still very relevant in our media-driven world as the founder of reality TV and social media as we know it today.

From his first Believe It or Not! cartoon at *The New York Globe* in 1918 until his death in 1949, Robert Ripley created a legacy that still has meaning and relevance today. By shining a light on the weird and wonderful people, places, and things he discovered around the world, Ripley showed us that being unique is something all humans have in common—and something to be proud of.

As pointed out in a PBS-produced 2015 television biography for the award-winning series American Experience, Ripley looked beyond the technology of his time to find ways to spread the reach of his popular syndicated cartoon. His ingenuity led to his successfully using what we would now call crowdsourcing: by encouraging readers to send him their own stories of the weird, he was able to more effectively use his time to seek out the odd in over 200 countries in a short 35-year period. As his mailbox literally overflowed with sometimes as many as two million reader submissions a year, Ripley's remarkable foresight allowed his fans to participate for the first time in the creation of both a cartoon they loved and what would become a global entertainment brand.

This incredible color photo of Robert Ripley was taken during his expedition to Panama in 1939.

Robert Ripley and his beloved friend and colleague, Li Ling Ai.

While working on the PBS biography, our researchers unearthed many rare photos of the 1940 New York Odditorium and its unusual performers, as well as new pictures of Ripley with his wife Beatrice and original photographs with his closest confidant during the 1940s, the wonderfully talented Li Ling Ai, who was not only the first person to win an Oscar for a documentary film (1941's *Kukan*), but also the first woman in America to host a weekly television show when she took the helm of the original *Ripley's Believe It or Not!* series after his death in 1949.

As the Ripley archive grows, so does the man's legend. Our fans' continuing desire to be part of our vast realm of "oddities" is proved by the many great photos and stories readers just like you have provided for this book.

Here, Robert Ripley is being greeted by Panamanian indigenous people in 1939, the first year full-color photography was readily available.

THE HUNT
FOR THE
UNUSUAL
AND
UNBELIEVABLE

Readers like you have always been a tremendous help in building our Believe It or Not! collection. We're constantly searching for new facts, photos, news, and videos to add to our cartoon and books—and we need YOUR help! Send in a photo or a source to help us verify your submission, and your ideas just might be in our next book. Bookmark our website—www.ripleys.com—to stay up-to-date on our latest contests and outreach programs.

RIPLEY'S BIZARRE
BUYING BAZAAR

In 2014, the *Ripley's Bizarre Buying Bazaar*, our traveling acquisitions road show, visited multiple locations across the United States. We invited anyone and everyone to bring us their oddities for an official Ripley odd-praisal and the opportunity to sell their unbelievable treasures to us for inclusion in our permanent Ripley collection.

We saw everything from Prohibition whiskey, to antique hair wreaths, to a priceless ivory German medieval bubonic plague prevention flea catcher. We even saw what may have been an ultra-rare Stradivarius violin—possibly one of only 650 in the world!

We'll hit the road again soon to visit more locations, so visit our website, www.ripleys.com, to find a stop near you.

This violin was brought to the Ripley's Bizarre Buying Bazaar. It may very well be an actual Stradivarius!

UNUSUAL MAIL

For the 2014 Unusual Mail Contest, fans were invited to send anything to us—literally anything—for a chance to win books from our vast library of titles. The only rule was that all submissions had to be received intact by regular post (no couriers), with no wrapping or packaging of any sort! The address and the stamps had to be placed directly on the object mailed.

We received inventive submissions from 27 different states and five different countries. Some entries were simple: postcards, playing cards, as well as small objects like toothbrushes and fridge magnets. However, our big winners all thought big AND strange!

This traffic cone was one of the more inventive submissions to Ripley's Unusual Mail Contest.

This life-sized rag doll was one of the largest entries we received.

This beautiful fan was one of the more unusual submissions. Note the postage stamps along the bottom handle.

STRANGE SHOPPING

Wherever we go, we get asked, "What is the weirdest, strangest, best thing you have acquired lately?" The answer of course is subjective, but there are always a few worthy standouts. Made of recycled metal, this life-sized Tyrannosaurus rex was created by artist John Lopez and is one of the latest Ripley's acquisitions.

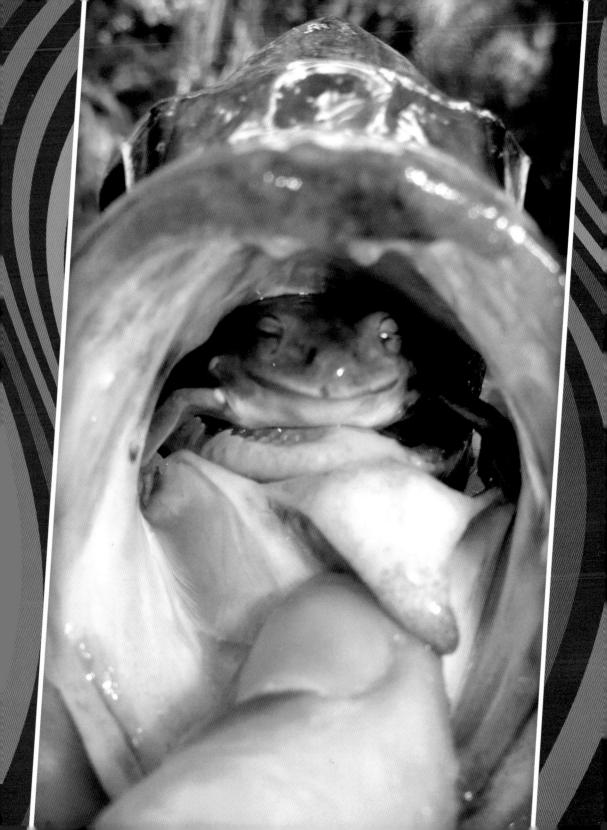

FIREWORKS SUIT!

Colin Furze, a plumber and inventor from Lincolnshire, England, built his own inflatable "Iron Man" suit that allowed him to stand inside a huge fireworks display.

Although he had giant rockets attached to his suit (turning him into a human firework) and nearly $1,000 of fireworks went off all around him, the homemade armor enabled him to emerge from the display without a single burn or even a scratch.

Turn the page to see behind the scenes of this crazy stunt!

Colin modeled the torso and limb armor piece by piece, and then welded the parts together.

FIREWORKS SUIT (CONT'D)

Daredevil Colin, who has previously built a 55 mph (88 kmph) toilet and a moped that fired 15-ft-long (4.5-m) flames from the back, used a process called hydroforming, which employs water pressure to bend and inflate steel sheets, so that the steel armor fit snugly around his body.

"Being able to stand inside a firework display is an experience I will not forget," he said afterward. "Seeing a lit rocket going off just six feet from your face is pretty epic."

Once he was inside the robot-like suit, his steel helmet was bolted on, leaving Perspex-covered eye slits so that he could see.

THIRD TWINS

Karen Rodger from Renfrewshire, Scotland, defied odds of 500,000 to 1 by giving birth to three sets of twins. Daughters Isla and Rowan arrived in 2013 to join four boys, 14-year-old Lewis and Kyle and 12-year-old Finn and Jude.

PEN PALS

Forty-one years after losing touch with her French pen pal Yvette Metay, Sue Ellis, from Staffordshire, England, found that they were living just 1 mi (1.6 km) apart. The girls had been randomly paired together as pen pals at their respective schools and visited and wrote to each other until 1973. Then, four decades later, Sue spotted her old friend in a local store and discovered that Yvette had moved from France in the 1980s, settling in Staffordshire in 2013.

LATE POST

A nine-page letter written in 1931 by Miriam McMichael of Houlton, Maine, to her mother Dollena 150 mi (240 km) away in Pittsfield was finally delivered in 2014—83 years later. Both women have since died, and ironically in the letter Miriam apologized for not writing sooner.

SAME FIRE

When 20-year-old Lunenburg, Massachusetts, firefighter Matt Benoit attended his first call—a house blaze in nearby Fitchburg—the first person he met there was his mother. Leominster Fire Lt. Audra Brown was exiting the house as Benoit arrived, mother and son having responded to the same fire from different fire departments.

STRANGE WEAPON

A man was charged with trying to rob a convenience store in Fort Smith, Arkansas, in April 2012 while armed with a pair of hot dog tongs.

TRAIN SMASH

In April 2012, a 31-year-old man from Pewaukee, Wisconsin, was found wandering around Canadian Pacific railroad tracks, unaware that he had just been hit by a 76-car freight train traveling at 48 mph (77 kmph).

BED TEST

Andrew Iwanicki from Los Angeles, California, was paid $18,000 by NASA to lie in bed for three months straight. He lay on a tilting bed at the NASA Flight Analog Research Unit in Houston, Texas, so that scientists could study the effects space has on bone and muscle.

EXTRA LEGS

A piglet owned by Mr. Tang in Sichuan Province, China, was born in August 2014 with two extra nonfunctioning legs and four extra trotters, or feet. The seven other piglets in the litter were completely normal.

DOLPHIN PROPOSAL

Alex Rigby of Merseyside, England, used a dolphin to deliver his marriage proposal to girlfriend Debbie Preston. She was in the water at Discovery Cove in Orlando, Florida, on a family vacation when the dolphin swam toward her pushing a buoy that said: "Debbie, will you marry me?"

NUMBER ONE

Currency collector Billy Baeder of Royersford, Pennsylvania, owns a $10 bill that is worth $500,000. The rare 1933 silver certificate bears the serial number A00000001A, making it probably the most valuable U.S. bill printed since 1929, when notes were shrunk to their current size.

MONSTER POOP

A 40-inch-long (1-m) alleged fossilized dinosaur poop, found in Washington State, sold for $8,500 in 2014. The monster coprolite—believed to be passed by an unknown species some 25 million years ago—was so long it had to be presented in four sections at the Beverly Hills auction.

BUG SWARM

In 2014, grasshopper swarms in Albuquerque, New Mexico, were so large they showed up as rainfall on local weather radar.

FORGER'S NIGHTMARE

The face of English composer Sir Edward Elgar was chosen to appear on the British £20 note for more than a decade because his distinctive, bushy mustache was difficult for would-be forgers to copy.

EXPENSIVE BED

A battered and chipped ceramic bowl that an elderly couple from Essex, England, regularly allowed their pet cat to sleep in sold for £108,000 ($170,000) in 2014 after it turned out to be a Chinese Ming dynasty piece dating back to the 15th century.

WEDDING GIFT

Mary and Ivor Waite from the West Midlands, England, are still using a vacuum cleaner made in 1925 that also paints, grinds coffee, and minces meat, and has never broken down. The German Piccolo appliance was a 1976 wedding gift from Ivor's aunt.

WOOLY AVALANCHE

While Pete Oswald was skiing on Hector Mountain on New Zealand's South Island, he saw what appeared to be a mini avalanche snowballing toward him—but then realized it was an injured sheep.

He managed to carry the 88-lb (40-kg) animal safely down the mountain on his skis before releasing it.

FAIRYTALE HOUSE

Artist Mary Rose Young has decorated her three-bedroom cottage in Gloucestershire, England, so that it resembles a full-size dollhouse.

The unique interior has bright, clashing colors, and is adorned with vibrant pottery pieces that she makes in her workshop. She has also sold her pottery to the likes of Ozzy Osbourne, Demi Moore, and Lady Gaga. Mary calls the cottage "an Alice in Wonderland sweet shop for adults."

I SPENT MY LAST £500
ON THIS BILLBOARD
PLEASE GIVE ME A JOB

EMPLOYADAM.COM

EMPLOY ME!

Unemployed university graduate Adam Pacitti spent his last £500 ($750) on renting a huge billboard in London, England, begging for a job.

He also set up a website, employadam.com, and the resulting publicity helped him receive more than 60 firm offers. Once he had landed a job with a top media company, he spent his first paycheck on another billboard to say thank you.

I SPENT MY FIRST
WAGE PACKET
ON THIS BILLBOARD
THANK YOU FOR HELPING ME

EMPLOYADAM.COM

Your Uploads

FOUR-EYED MOUSE

Katheryn Hung sent Ripley's this picture of an incredible four-eyed mouse that she spotted several times while she was on vacation in Destin, Florida. When she first saw it, she thought it was carrying a baby mouse, but later realized it was a strange mutant.

HOUSE SWAP

When his three-bedroom house in Detroit, Michigan, failed to sell in 2014, owner Nik Gindelhuber exchanged it for an iPhone 6 instead.

WRONG BIRTHDAY

Shortly before turning 100 years old, Evelyn Frost of Staffordshire, England, discovered she had been celebrating her birthday on the wrong date her whole life. When she applied for her birth certificate to register for the traditional 100th birthday letter from the Queen, she found that it listed her date of birth as April 16, 1914, not April 17 as she had always thought.

MISSING PERSON

A model drone helped authorities locate an 82-year-old man who had been missing for three days. When Guillermo DeVenecia disappeared near Fitchburg, Wisconsin, police dogs and helicopters scoured the area to no avail. When David Lesh, who was in the area visiting his girlfriend's family, offered the services of his drone, however, rescuers spotted the pensioner in a corner of a bean field in less than 20 minutes.

TV STATIC

The static on an untuned television set is partly caused by photon radiation left by the Big Bang 14 billion years ago.

FLYING PIGS

Farmer Sying P'an set up a zip wire as a means to stop his pigs from running off when he takes them to market in Weinan, China. He created a series of harnesses and pulleys to transport the 220-lb (100-kg) pigs through the air from his own truck straight into the truck of their new owner, without allowing their trotters to even touch the ground.

LICENSE TO STUDY

In 1990, 15-year-old student James Bond sat down to take his school examinations at Argoed High School, North Wales—and his examination paper reference number was 007.

25

STRANGE THINGS

BIRD BOMBS

Before releasing 10,000 pigeons for 2014 National Day celebrations in Beijing, Chinese officials examined the butts of every bird in case any one of them was carrying a bomb.

FIRST AND LAST

The first and last British soldiers to die in World War I, Privates John Parr and George Ellison, are both buried in St. Symphorien cemetery, in France, and face each other only yards apart.

BIONIC KANGAROO

Global engineering firm Festo has created a robot that exactly mimics the hopping jumps of a kangaroo. Bionic Kangaroo weighs just 15 lb (7 kg) and stands only 3 ft 3 in (1 m) tall, but it can jump 1 ft 4 in (40 cm) vertically and 2 ft 8 in (80 cm) horizontally.

HANDCUFF DAY

February 20 is National Handcuff Day in the U.S.A.—in honor of George A. Carney's revolutionary lightweight adjustable handcuff, which he patented on that date in 1912.

STRAW DRAW

Charles Piazza won a 2014 tied election for alderman in Waveland, Mississippi, by drawing the longer of two straws. Back in 2002, he had lost another tied Mississippi election on the toss of a coin. Local law calls for tied elections to be decided by a game of chance.

CRYSTAL BLAZE

A house fire in London, England, was caused by a crystal doorknob. Sunlight refracted through the doorknob and reflected onto a nearby dressing gown, setting it on fire.

KOO KOO THE BIRD GIRL

Koo Koo the Bird Girl, blind and toothless, with her small head, thin face, and beaky nose, was a well-known character on the circus sideshow circuit in the early 20th century.

Koo Koo's act, completed with fluffy feathers and oversized chicken feet, consisted of dancing strangely and acting the fool. She was born Minnie Woolsey in Georgia in 1880, and became a fixture for many years in the Ringling Brothers Circus sideshow. In 1932, her unique appearance earned her a role in the Hollywood movie *Freaks*, featuring an ensemble cast of bizarre sideshow workers, and she was performing as the "Cuckoo Girl" at the World Circus Side Show at Coney Island, New York, into the 1940s. Unlike many of her outlandish colleagues, Minnie was quiet and reserved away from the stage and did not draw attention to herself until dressed in her feathers. It's likely that Woolsey suffered from a type of dwarfism called Seckel syndrome, also known as "bird-

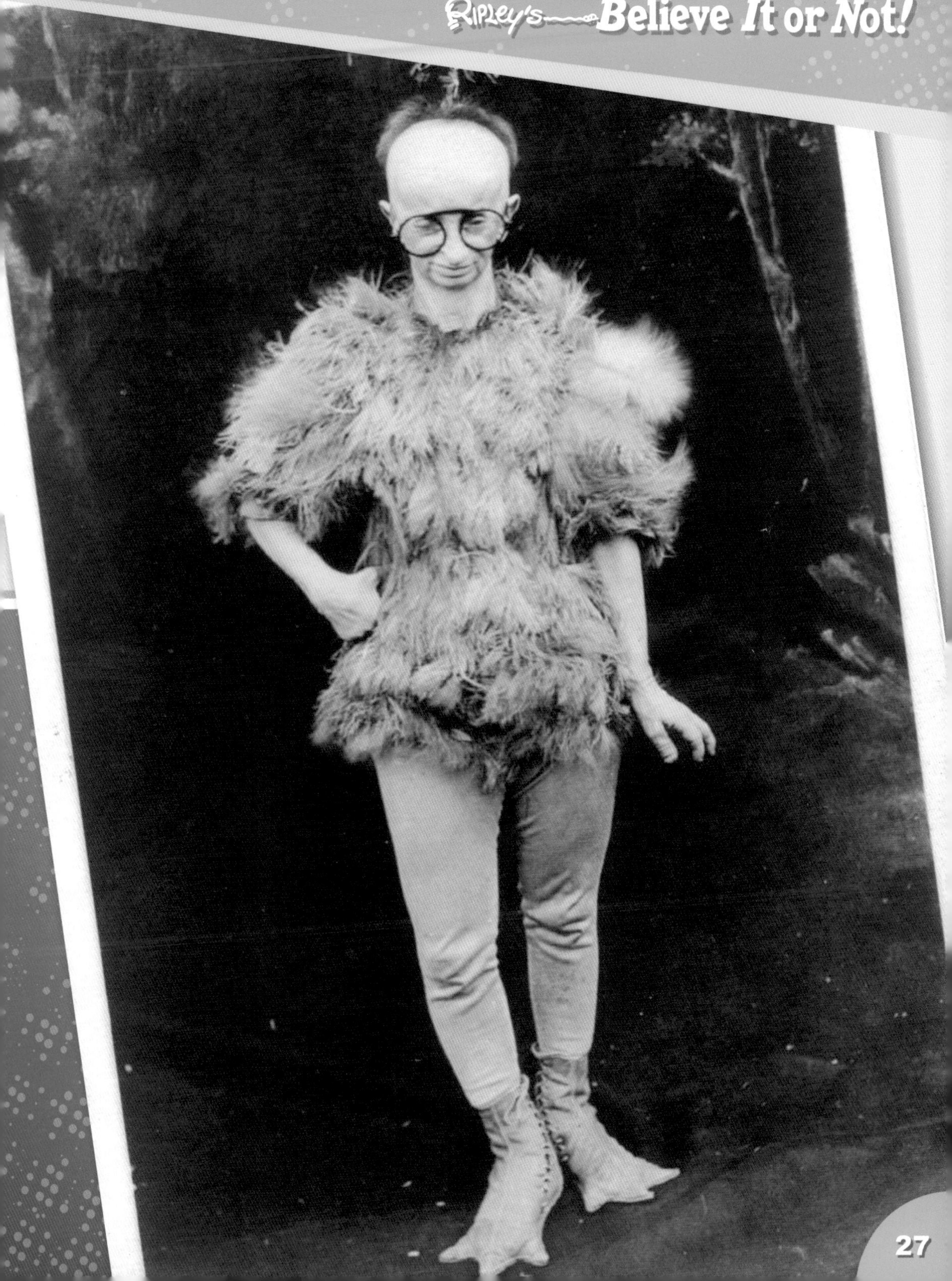

BEDPAN COLLECTOR

For 25 years Eric Eakin has been building up a collection of more than 250 bedpans—in porcelain, metal, glass, and even recycled newspaper—which he keeps in the basement of his home in Bay Village, Ohio.

The oldest pan dates from the 19th century and the smallest, designed for a dollhouse, is less than 0.5 in (1.2 cm) long. His collection includes beautifully decorated bedpans with Native American imagery, another in the shape of a guitar with barbed wire strings, and a novelty item with a little Richard Nixon head inside.

FART MACHINE

Plumber and inventor Colin Furze from Lincolnshire, England, built a 16-ft-high (5-m) "fart machine," transported it to Kent, and aimed it at France to see whether it could be heard 21 mi (33 km) away across the English Channel. People in France reported hearing a "faint rumble" from the machine, which consisted of a giant pulse jet engine housed in a pair of specially constructed buttocks.

LIVING PROOF

Sixty-eight-year-old Jean-Marie Sevrain was forced to obtain a letter from his doctor certifying that he was still alive after the French health service had refused to pay his medical expenses on the grounds that he was dead. When he applied for a $30 refund after renewing a prescription, he was informed that he was not entitled to one because, according to health service records, he had died four years earlier.

STORM NAMESAKE

Australian meteorologist Clement Wragge (1852-1922) was the first to name hurricanes—calling them after politicians he disliked.

PHONE SHIELD

A gas station clerk in Winter Garden, Florida, was saved from a robber's bullet by his cell phone. He didn't realize the phone had stopped the bullet until he took the shattered device from his shirt pocket.

Your Uploads

THUMBS UP

Paws, a cat owned by Billy Rice of Atwater, California, has extra toes that are separated from the rest so that it looks as though he has thumbs. He has quickly learned to adapt to his unusual condition and uses his "thumbs" to reach inside food containers for his favorite whipped cream.

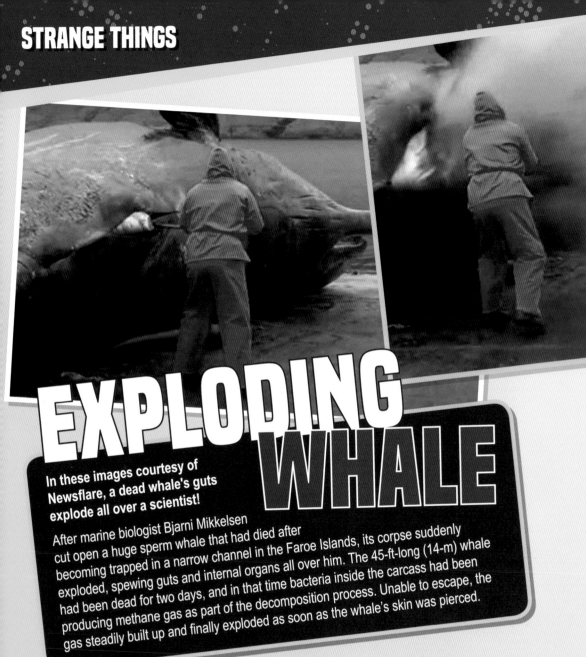

EXPLODING WHALE

In these images courtesy of Newsflare, a dead whale's guts explode all over a scientist!

After marine biologist Bjarni Mikkelsen cut open a huge sperm whale that had died after becoming trapped in a narrow channel in the Faroe Islands, its corpse suddenly exploded, spewing guts and internal organs all over him. The 45-ft-long (14-m) whale had been dead for two days, and in that time bacteria inside the carcass had been producing methane gas as part of the decomposition process. Unable to escape, the gas steadily built up and finally exploded as soon as the whale's skin was pierced.

NAME CHANGE
Melanie Ann Convery and her husband Neal James Coughlin from Holyoke, Massachusetts, successfully petitioned a court to change both of their middle names to "Seamonster."

BIGFOOT LAW
It is legal in Texas to kill Bigfoot if you can find him because he is not technically an endangered species.

PLANT HAUL
Thieves stole 10,000 carnivorous Venus flytrap plants, worth a total of $65,000, from greenhouses at a farm near Wilmington, North Carolina.

DRAFT MOTION

Eminent scientist Isaac Newton (1642–1727) was elected as an M.P. (Member of Parliament) to represent Cambridge University in 1689 and 1701, but the only time he spoke in Parliament was to ask for a window to be closed because of a draft.

FLESH SEATS

British furniture designer Gigi Barker has devised a range of flesh-colored leather sofas and chairs that look and feel like human skin. She started by tracing the outline of a man's midriff before modeling it in clay and then impregnating the leather with pheromones and aftershave to make it seem more human.

DUMMY FAMILY

Suzanne Heintz from Englewood, Colorado, has lived with a family of mannequins for more than 14 years and has traveled 10,000 mi (16,000 km) around the world with them. For an art project she takes pictures of herself at various locations with her plastic "husband" Chauncey, a clothing-store dummy, and a plastic teen "daughter" Mary-Margaret as if they were a real family.

BIG WEDDING

When a Sri Lankan couple, Nisansala and Nalin, got married in Colombo in 2013, they walked down the aisle with 126 bridesmaids, 25 best men, 20 pageboys, and 23 flower girls.

PERSONALITY CHANGE

After suffering a stroke, a 49-year-old Brazilian man underwent a complete personality change and developed "pathological generosity," where he could not help giving money away to strangers.

CRASH LANDINGS

In 1937, street sweeper Joseph Figlock was cleaning an alley in Detroit, Michigan, when a baby boy fell from a fourth-story window and landed on Joseph's head and shoulders. The collision broke the baby's fall and saved his life. A year later, Figlock was sweeping out another alley when two-year-old David Thomas fell from a fourth-story window and landed safely on him.

ROCKING WAKE

For her wake at a funeral home in San Juan, Puerto Rico, the body of 80-year-old Georgina Chervony Lloren was clothed in her wedding dress from her second marriage and seated in her favorite red-cushioned rocking chair. Her daughter Miriam said her mother specified that was how she envisioned her wake.

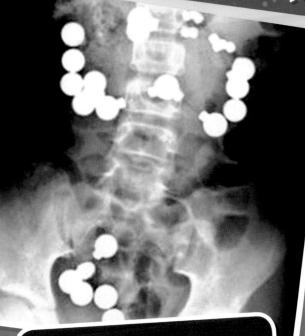

HARD TO SWALLOW

Doctors in Chhattisgarh, India, removed 431 coins, 197 fishnet pellets, 19 bicycle chain bolts, and three keys from a man's stomach. The haul weighed more than 13 lb (6 kg).

A woman in Thailand was found to have 199 nails in her stomach—some as long as 3 in (7.5 cm).

A 10-lb (4.5-kg) hairball was found in the stomach of a Chicago teenager who suffered from trichophagia, a habit of eating her own hair.

A 52-year-old woman in Rotterdam, the Netherlands, had 78 items of metal cutlery removed from her stomach.

Doctors in Hunan Province, China, discovered a 2-in-long (5-cm) thermometer in a woman's lung that she had swallowed 44 years earlier.

A 38-year-old woman from Galati, Romania, accidentally swallowed her boyfriend's false teeth during a passionate kiss.

A 62-year-old man in Cholet, France, swallowed 350 coins, an assortment of necklaces, and several needles, with a combined weight of 12 lb (5.5 kg).

FRIDGE MAGNETS

After studying this hospital X-ray, surgeons removed 42 tiny magnets from the stomach of a 16-month-old boy who had swallowed them at his home in Chelyabinsk, Russia. The child's mother had become alarmed when she noticed that all of the fridge alphabet magnets had gone missing after her son was alone in the kitchen for a few minutes.

FAMILY BIRTHDAY

Joshua Strnad of Ingersoll, Ontario, tells Ripley's that his fiancée, Sarah Mailloux, their daughter Olivia, and son Elijah were all born on March 9—in 1992, 2011, and 2012, respectively. Joshua's own birthday is exactly a week earlier than Sarah's, as he was born on March 2, 1990.

BAD START

The U.S. Secret Service, tasked with protecting the President, was created by Abraham Lincoln on the day he was assassinated.

33

EYEPOPPERS

Way back in 1928, Robert Ripley first learned about voluntary eyeball propulsion when he met a Cuban eye popper named Avelino Perez Matos of the Baracoa District of Santiago de Cuba. After featuring Avelino in his Believe It or Not! newspaper feature on August 3, 1929, Ripley decided to make him a featured performer in the very first Odditorium, to be held at the 1933 Chicago World's Fair. As the curtain went up in Illinois at the Century of Progress World's Fair, Avelino stole the show and was forever nicknamed, "The Human Eye Popper."

Since then, we have found a small handful of other people who can also pop their eyes out of their sockets—some one eye only, some one at a time, some both at once, and all incredible to behold. We think you'll agree that, however they do it, the results are definitely eye-popping!

Jalisa Thompson, a former cashier at our Atlantic City Odditorium, was herself an eye popper! She traveled to several Ripley's locations, demonstrating her unique skill.

Brothers Hugh (left) and Antonio Francis (right) of Essex, England, show that eye poppers can run in the family!

The medical condition that occurs when humans "pop" their eyeballs is called *exophthalmos*. This allows the person to dislocate and relocate the eye from its "orbit," or socket, at will without any discomfort or effort.

Avelino and Jalisa both had normal eyesight—neither wore glasses!

Avelino could pop his eyes a full 9 millimeters and hold them out for several minutes!

1939 photos of Avelino Perez Matos taken at the New York World's Fair.

HUMAN PENDULUM

Top animal trainer, Frank "Cheerful" Gardner, is seen here with one of the elephants that toured with the Hagenbeck-Wallace Circus in 1931.

Luckily, this isn't a vicious attack, but Cheerful's signature act—a trick known as the "head carry," or "human pendulum," in which the elephant would carry his trainer around the circus tent. It was said that a rival trainer once tried the same trick and ended up in hospital with a fractured skull. Cheerful was known as the "Dean" of elephant trainers, and looked after herds for several different circuses in a career that spanned decades. He proudly stated, "Elephants are the smartest and most lovable animals on earth," and that he had never been injured in his work.

CHEERFUL GARDNER

CERAMIC INFLATABLES

Pennsylvania artist Brett Kern creates ceramic models that look exactly like inflatable toys.

He is able to copy the precise wrinkles and shapes of inexpensive air-filled dinosaurs, rabbits, and astronauts, but his ceramic versions sell for up to $800. The series of artworks was inspired by an inflatable dinosaur he was given as a child.

GOD MYSTERY

A New York City man claims that a credit-rating agency refuses to acknowledge that he has a financial history because his first name is God. Russian native God Gazarov, who owns a Brighton Beach jewelry store, is named after his grandfather.

DECEPTION TACTIC

Colonel William Washington forced the surrender of more than 100 British loyalists during the American War of Independence without firing a shot, by painting a log to look like a cannon—a so-called "Quaker Gun."

THE STING

A thief in Leeds, England, was caught after he accidentally disturbed a nest of wasps while stopping to urinate in a bush during his getaway. Jamie Brown had made off with a £200 ($300) fish tank from a store, but was caught by police officers who saw him crying in pain after being repeatedly stung by the insects. He spent six hours in agony in a hospital before appearing in court.

PERFECT JOB

A specialist pharmacist at the Royal Cornwall Hospital in Truro, Cornwall, England, is listed as Mr. A. Pothecary. Andrew Pothecary first thought about studying medicine because he had a suitable name and, although he has enjoyed a successful career, he believes he may have been turned down for some jobs by employers who thought the name on the application form was a joke.

OLD PANTS

A pair of pants discovered in a cemetery in Xinjiang, China, is believed to have been worn by a horseman 3,300 years ago. Stripped from a mummy, the pants were made of three pieces of cloth—two for legs and one for the crotch. Nomads in Xinjiang originally wore pants just consisting of two legs that were fastened to the waist with strings. It was only later that crotches were sewn on to the legs.

GAME OPTION

In Taiwan, drunk drivers are given the option of playing Mahjong, a popular Chinese tile game, with the elderly instead of paying a fine.

DIFFERENT YEARS

Lindsay Salgueiro of Toronto, Ontario, gave birth to twin girls—but they were born in different years. Gabriella arrived at 11:52 p.m. on December 31, 2013, and her younger sister Sophia was delivered 38 seconds after midnight, so she has a birth date of January 1, 2014.

BODY POWER

Inspired by the fact that at any given moment the human body produces energy equivalent to a 100-watt lightbulb, 16-year-old Ann Makosinski from Victoria, British Columbia, has invented a flashlight that is powered solely by body heat. Requiring no batteries, it powers as soon as it is held in the hand.

DANGER KIT

The Gilbert Atomic Energy Lab, a 1950s science kit for children, included genuine radioactive uranium and polonium, and a Geiger counter!

GOAT DUNG

Artist and goat breeder Patrick Page-Sutter built this life-size sculpture of a goat entirely from pellets of goat dung collected on the family ranch in Natalia, Texas.

Your Uploads

EXTRA TOES

Kirstin Mercer of Orangeville, Ontario, Canada, sent Ripley's this picture of her cat Lilli who was born with 32 toes. Cats are normally born with 18 toes, so Lilli, who has a condition called polydactyly (or "many fingers"), boasts nearly twice as many.

FELT
STORE

Lucy recently made a felt bodega in New York City—filled with more than 9,000 handmade items—called 8 'Till Late.

Artist Lucy Sparrow from Bath, England, created a life-size grocery store in which all 4,000 items were made of felt.

It took her seven months and more than 250,000 stitches to make the display, which included fish sticks, cans of Spam, newspapers, toilet rolls, a cash register, and a pricing gun—all made from felt.

Please do not touch

HONEYMOON PRANK

Newlyweds Jamie and Emily Pharro returned home from their honeymoon to find their friends had covered the entire ground floor of their house in Lincolnshire, England, with 14,000 Post-It® notes. The yellow notes were stuck in neat rows to the walls, floors, furniture, cupboards, and the TV, and took 2.5 hours to remove.

STICKY SITUATIONS

To mark the 30th birthday of the Post-It® note, in 2010 American conceptual artist Eric Daigh built a giant 1,760-sq-ft (164 sq m) billboard at New York City's Grand Central Station with 112,640 brightly colored Post-It® notes.

Artist Yo Shimada created an entire city out of 30,000 Post-It® notes for an installation at an art gallery in Kyoto, Japan.

The animated music video for the 2012 track "If You Ever Need Someone" by Justin Web's Los Angeles band The Family Bones was filmed using 25,000 Post-It® notes. It took four months to make.

Jessica Biffi from Guelph, Ontario, made an award-winning evening gown in 48 hours using 3,000 Post-It® notes.

Pranksters covered Kansas City Police Detective Stuart Littlefield's car with 4,000 colorful Post-It® notes for his 50th birthday, in 2014.

Artist Rebecca Murtaugh spent six days and over $1,000 covering her bedroom and all the objects in it—including bed coverings, lamps, and rugs—with 10,000 Post-It® notes for an installation at Arcata, California.

Kaitlin Neary, a medical resident in Omaha, Nebraska, can stick 58 Post-It® notes on her face in one minute.

FROG IN THROAT

SKATEBOARDING COP

Joel Zwicky, an officer with the Green Bay Police Department, Wisconsin, patrols the streets on a skateboard with red and blue LED lights. The skateboard enables him to access more areas than in a car and is quicker than traveling on foot.

DELAYED MEDALS

Ninety-three-year-old Tom Harrison, of Salt Lake City, Utah, received seven military medals in 2011—more than 60 years after his service in World War II.

DREAM MONITOR

San Diego, California, company iWinks has invented a headband that can help people control their dreams. The Aurora measures brain activity and plays lights and sounds during REM (rapid eye movement) sleep to help people become aware they are dreaming even though they are still asleep. The idea is that this will enable them to take control of their sleeping brain and direct the course of their dreams.

COMPUTER ERROR

A computer error meant that grandparents Nigel and Linda Brotherton from Lancashire, England, received an electrical bill for £500 million ($850 million) and were told by their energy supplier that if they failed to pay it their monthly direct debit payment would go up from £87 ($148) to £53.5 million ($91 million).

This jungle perch caught by fisherman Angus James near Townsville in Queensland, Australia, literally had a frog in its throat.

When James opened the fish's mouth, he saw a live green tree frog staring back at him. He said: "As I was pulling my lure from the fish to release it back into the water, I noticed two little eyes looking back at me from inside the fish's mouth. The frog then leaped straight past my head onto the nearest tree. It was one of the coolest things I have seen in my life. This is one lucky frog!"

NEAR AND FAR

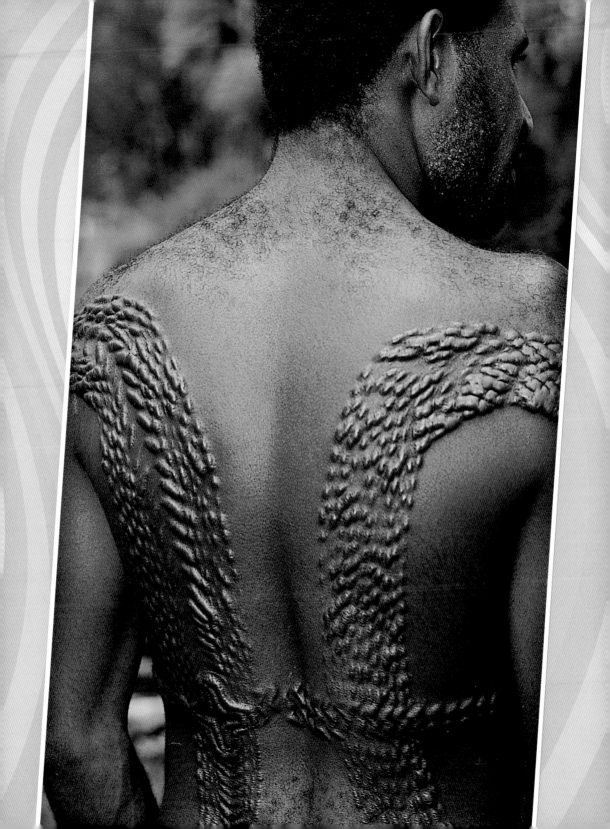

ICE CAVE

This incredible ice cave in the Kamchatka Peninsula of eastern Russia measures nearly 0.6 mi (1 km) long!

It was formed by a hot spring gushing from the nearby Mutnovsky volcano and carving its way through the glaciers. As these glaciers have been melting in recent years, the roof of the cave is now thin enough to allow sunlight to penetrate and create colorful illuminations inside.

CRANE HOTEL

An industrial dockside crane perched high above the ground in Harlingen, the Netherlands, has been converted into a luxury, $389-a-night hotel. Elevators take guests up to the living quarters, which are located in the crane's old machine room. From there, guests can climb a ladder to access a balcony.

TWO DESIGNS

Oregon's state flag features a picture of a beaver on its reverse side and is the only U.S. state flag to carry two different designs.

WATER RELEASE

Each year, a large oak tree can release 1,000-bathtubs-worth of water from its leaves into the atmosphere.

GARBAGE DUMP

The Jardim Gramacho dump outside Rio de Janeiro, Brazil, covered an area of 14 million sq ft (1.3 million sq m)—the equivalent of 244 American football fields—and was piled with garbage 300 ft (90 m) high. It received 9,000 tons of garbage a day, but closed in 2012, after 34 years.

SKULL CUPS

A ritual bowl called a kapala, used by Indian Hindus and Buddhists in Tibet, is made from a human skull!

The skulls are usually collected at burial sites before being ornately carved or mounted with precious jewels or silver. There are two types of kapala—those that use the whole skull and those that use only the skull cap or top half of the cranium. They often serve as vessels for holding food or wine, but some followers also allegedly drink blood from skull cups.

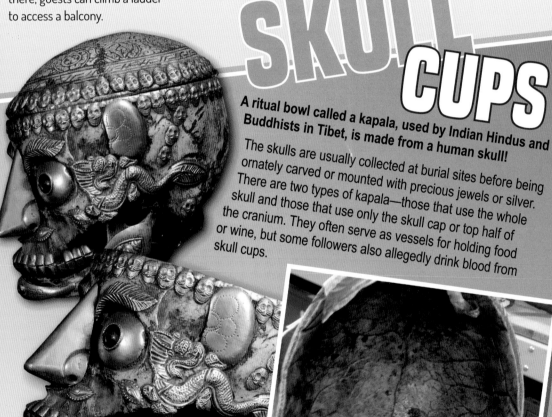

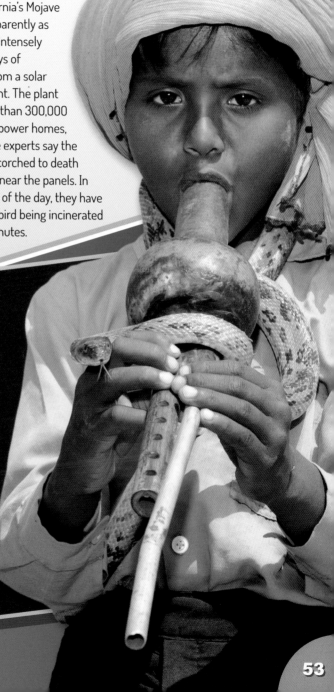

WORLD TOUR

By age 24, James Asquith of Hertfordshire, England, had visited every one of the world's 196 internationally recognized countries. Starting with Vietnam in 2008, he funded his £125,000 ($190,000) adventure by taking jobs in bars and hostels as he traveled. He spent five months in North America, getting to 27 states, including Hawaii and Alaska.

BULLET BLOCKER

A Modesto, California, store clerk was saved when armed robbers shot him—the wallet in his back pocket stopped the bullet from hitting his butt!

BURNING BIRDS

Thousands of birds have been bursting into flames over California's Mojave Desert, apparently as a result of intensely focused rays of sunlight from a solar energy plant. The plant uses more than 300,000 mirrors to power homes, but wildlife experts say the birds are scorched to death as they fly near the panels. In the middle of the day, they have counted a bird being incinerated every 2 minutes.

CHILD CHARMERS

Children among the 600-strong nomadic Vadi tribe in western India begin charming cobras from just a few feet away at the age of just two. It is the start of ten years of training—the boys charm the snakes with flutes while the girls handle and care for the reptiles. After capture, the normally deadly cobras are fed an herbal mixture that supposedly makes their venom ineffective. Snake charming has been banned by the Indian government since 1991, but there are still around 800,000 snake charmers in the country and the Vadi are determined to maintain the tradition.

LIQUID LUNCH

There is never any need to ask for water with your meal at this jungle restaurant in San Pablo City in the Philippines, because the dining tables are located right at the foot of the man-made Labasin Falls. While customers eat at the Waterfalls Restaurant at Villa Escudero, the clear spring water from the falls runs over their feet, and between courses they can cool down by standing directly under the cascade.

BURNING TONGUE!

Camphor—a highly flammable substance—burns brightly on the tongue of a devotee at the Ganga Dhaaraa Hindu festival in Trinidad.

The annual ceremony mirrors a much larger religious celebration, which is attended by hundreds of thousands of pilgrims, held on India's Ganges River.

SHARP PRACTICE

At the annual Phuket Vegetarian Festival in Thailand, devotees have needles pierced through their arms, legs, back, and even their face as a way of bringing good luck to the community. The ritualized mutilation is performed while the recipient is placed in a trancelike state at a local Buddhist shrine.

SHORTEST HIGHWAY

I-97 is the shortest 2-digit interstate highway in the contiguous U.S.A. It is only 17 mi (27 km) long and lies entirely in Anne Arundel County, Maryland.

BUSY CROSSING

Every day of the year, about one million people walk on the Shibuya pedestrian crossing outside Shibuya railway station in Tokyo, Japan. At its busiest, in half an hour enough people use the crossing to fill a 45,000-seat sports stadium.

SALTY SEA

California's largest lake is located in the middle of its biggest desert. The 362-sq-mi (940-sq-km) Salton Sea in the Colorado Desert was formed after the Colorado River flooded in 1905. Its surface is 220 ft (67 m) below sea level and its water is 30 percent saltier than the Pacific, meaning few species of fish can survive there.

ROOF BOOTH

There is a phone booth on the roof of the two-story Lincoln City Hall, Illinois. It was installed in the 1960s as a weather station so that watchers could use the phone to warn of bad weather, and it now attracts inquisitive tourists from all over the world.

CAVE HOTEL

Visitors to Farmington, New Mexico, can stay in a cave guesthouse within vertical sandstone cliffs located 300 ft (90 m) above the La Plata river valley.

With its entrance set in the cliff face, the 1,700-sq-ft (149 sq-m) Kokopelli's Cave was originally built for geologist and owner Bruce Black to use as an office, but is now a bed-and-breakfast hotel, complete with bedroom, kitchen, dining area, and bathroom with jacuzzi. The temperature inside stays at about 70°F (21°C) all year round.

LOCAL BIGWIG

Chichester Cathedral in West Sussex, England, boasts a modern gargoyle depicting former barrister and cathedral chapter clerk Clifford Hodgetts, complete with wig, glasses, and an appropriately placed spout to carry excess rainwater off the roof and away from the walls.

GARGOYLES

SMILING FACE

Nora Sly from Gloucestershire, England, has an image of her smiling face carved as a gargoyle into a stone tower on the roof of St. Mary's Church, Cowley. Local people voted unanimously for the honor to go to the retired secretary, who has been a church regular for over 60 years and has lived in the village all her life. "I was astounded," she said, "but I did not feel the carving was all that flattering!"

STONE TRIBUTE

David Rice, who worked as a stonemason at Wells Cathedral in Somerset, England, for half a century, is immortalized in the framework of the building in the form of a stone gargoyle.

EVIL VISION

When Washington National Cathedral held a decorative sculpture competition for children in the 1980s, a drawing of Darth Vader by Christopher Rader from Kearney, Nebraska, was so impressive that it was sculpted and carved as a gargoyle high up on the building's northwest tower.

ALIEN MONSTER

A gargoyle that was added to the 13th-century Paisley Abbey in Scotland in the 1990s looks just like the monster from the movie *Alien*.

ROYAL GARGOYLES

The church tower of St. John the Divine in Kennington, London, features stone gargoyles of Queen Elizabeth II, Prince Charles (seen here), as well as a young William, Duke of Cambridge.

VOLCANO HOAX

As an elaborate April Fool's Day hoax in 1974, prankster Oliver "Porky" Bickar hired a helicopter to drop hundreds of tires into the crater of Mount Edgecumbe, a dormant Alaskan volcano, and then set them on fire to try and trick local people into believing that the rising plume of black smoke meant the volcano was active again.

FAST FLOW

The men's room urinal at the Madonna Inn at San Luis Obispo, California, features an 8-ft (2.4-m) waterfall.

MOUNTAIN MISERY

The 2,600-ft-high (800-m) Mount Disappointment in Victoria, Australia, was named in 1824 by explorers Hamilton Hume and William Hovell, who were prevented from crossing it by dense undergrowth.

FLAG ERROR

The flag of the Turks and Caicos Islands, a British colony in the Caribbean, mistakenly featured an igloo for 100 years because a British flag maker mistook piles of salt in a sketch for an igloo.

COIN DROP

Every year tourists throw more than $1,000,000 in coins into the famous Trevi Fountain in Rome, Italy. All the money goes to a charity that helps the city's needy.

DEERLY DEPARTED

In February 2012, the Russian town of Naryan-Mar built a memorial to 6,000 reindeer and their herders who served in the Soviet Army, transporting ammunition, orders, and wounded soldiers, in World War II.

TOGETHER FOREVER

A husband and wife in Roermond, the Netherlands, have been holding hands for more than 120 years.

A Catholic noblewoman married a Protestant Colonel in 1842, causing a religious and social scandal, but their union lasted nearly 40 years, until the colonel died. When his widow passed away eight years later, religious segregation meant they couldn't be buried together. However, she had ordered a monument to be built on one side of the cemetery wall, where she was laid to rest, and another on the other side of the wall for her husband, and stone hands join the couple together forever.

POO SCULPTURE

American artist Paul McCarthy built this 51-ft-high (15-m) inflatable poop—the size of a house—as an art installation.

Complex Pile has been exhibited all over the world. In 2008, a sudden gust of wind cut it loose from its moorings outside a modern art museum in Bern, Switzerland, and sent it soaring through the air before it landed 600 ft (180 m) away on the grounds of an orphanage.

REPLICA COLON

A hotel located on an island near Antwerp, Belgium, is designed to resemble a giant human colon. Made of wood, foam, and fiberglass, the Hotel CasAnus follows the contours of the digestive system, starting with the tongue, continuing through the stomach, then the small and large intestines, and ending with the anus. It was originally created by Dutch designer Joep van Lieshout as an artwork, but has been converted into one-bedroom living quarters, allowing guests to curl up in a replica butthole.

BLOTTO GROTTO

Richard Pim of Herefordshire, England, created a garden shed out of 5,000 old wine bottles. He calls the glass dome, which measures 19 ft (5.8 m) wide and 11 ft (3.4 m) high, the Blotto Grotto.

TONGUE TWISTER

Muckanaghederdauhaulia is the name of a small village in County Galway, Ireland. It means "piggery between two brines."

STREET CATCH

Jake Sawyer, 16, used his bare hands to catch a huge 40 lb (18 kg) carp in a flooded street in North Royalton, Ohio. Heavy rain on May 12, 2014, had caused flash flooding, and the 3-ft-long (0.9-m) fish probably swam out of a nearby pond as the waters rose.

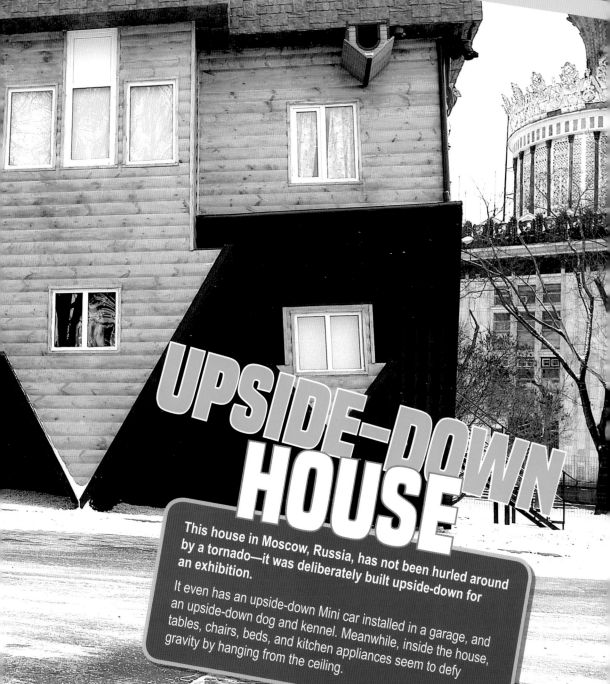

UPSIDE-DOWN HOUSE

This house in Moscow, Russia, has not been hurled around by a tornado—it was deliberately built upside-down for an exhibition.

It even has an upside-down Mini car installed in a garage, and an upside-down dog and kennel. Meanwhile, inside the house, tables, chairs, beds, and kitchen appliances seem to defy gravity by hanging from the ceiling.

MAYBE MONARCHY

When Jeremiah Heaton's daughter Emily asked in 2014 if she could be a real princess, he created a kingdom for her by laying claim to an unused 800-square-mile swath of desert in the African region of Bir Tawil, calling it the "Kingdom of North Sudan"—and naming her its princess! The Abingdon, VA, natives are currently seeking recognition of the claim from authorities.

SEE-SAW

The British Isles are slowly rising in the north and sinking in the south—by about 2 in (5 cm) a century—owing to the melting of northern ice since the last Ice Age 20,000 years ago.

TALL STORY

This giant sequoia tree called "The President" in California's Sequoia National Park is 3,200 years old, has two billion leaves, and stands 247 ft (74 m) tall. The tree is so big that to show it all, *National Geographic* magazine needed 126 individual photographs pieced together in a five-page foldout.

BEAR NECESSITY

Many people in Churchill, Manitoba, Canada, leave their cars and their houses unlocked in case pedestrians need to make a quick escape from polar bears.

RAIN DAY

The town of Waynesburg, Pennsylvania, holds an annual Rain Day festival—complete with a Miss Rain Day pageant—on July 29 to recognize the fact that it has rained there on that date 114 times in the past 141 years.

MISSOURI MOVE

During the American Civil War (1861–1865), Marshall, in the state of Texas, was the capital city of the state of Missouri. A major Confederate city, Marshall became the headquarters of Missouri's Confederate government-in-exile.

SHRINKING EARTH

The Earth loses weight by 50,000 tons every year as hydrogen and helium gases leave the atmosphere because they are too light for gravity to keep them around. Even so, it will take trillions of years to deplete Earth's supply of hydrogen.

DAINTY DOGGY

Xiaoniu the dog wears clothes and struts upright on the streets of Shanghai, China.

Abandoned as a puppy, the dog found a home—and a fashion designer—in her 62-year-old owner, Mr. Fang. This furry fashionista now brings a smile to all of her neighbors by wearing fabulous custom-made outfits Mr. Fang creates. These dog-tastic clothes are accessorized with everything from sunglasses and hair bows to Santa hats and backpacks.

69

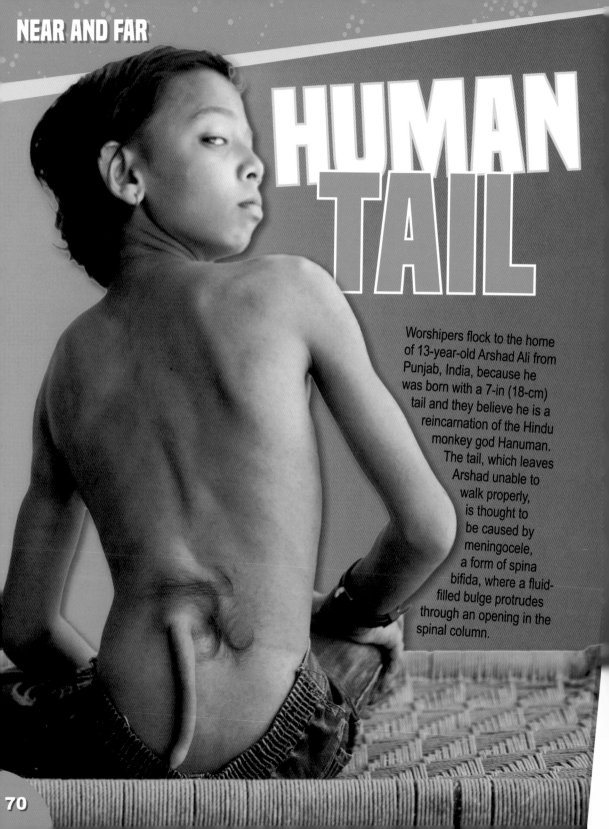

HUMAN TAIL

Worshipers flock to the home of 13-year-old Arshad Ali from Punjab, India, because he was born with a 7-in (18-cm) tail and they believe he is a reincarnation of the Hindu monkey god Hanuman. The tail, which leaves Arshad unable to walk properly, is thought to be caused by meningocele, a form of spina bifida, where a fluid-filled bulge protrudes through an opening in the spinal column.

TOUGH MAZE

A corn maze built for Halloween each year since 2007 by brothers Matt and Mark Cooley in Dixon, California, is so difficult to navigate that lost visitors have been forced to call 911 for help in getting out. The maze consists of up to 5 mi (8 km) of hand-cut twisting paths.

APRON MUSEUM

Carolyn Terry of Iuka, Mississippi, is the owner and curator of the world's only apron museum. She has collected more than 3,000 aprons, some dating from the 1860s.

TOO DIM

The Statue of Liberty became the U.S.A.'s first electric lighthouse in 1886. It was decommissioned in 1902 because it was not bright enough.

GLOBETROTTING BUNNY

Travel Bunny, a toy rabbit owned by Peter Franc of Melbourne, Australia, traveled with him to 24 countries, posing at such iconic locations as Italy's Leaning Tower of Pisa, the Petronas Twin Towers in Malaysia, and Stonehenge, England. He even went diving with Peter on Australia's Great Barrier Reef.

EARTH SLOWING

The rotation of planet Earth is slowing down by 0.002 seconds per century, meaning that in 180 million years' time, Earth days will be 25 hours long.

DOORLESS VILLAGE

None of the 300 houses in Shani Shingnapur, a village in Maharashtra, India, have doors. Villagers say that a local deity once told them they do not need doors because he will always protect them. Some households do erect loose door panels at night to keep out wild animals.

ROCKET**MAN**

Huang Yuzhan, a farmer from Guangdong Province, China, has built an enormous replica space shuttle and rocket, complete with boosters on either side, on the roof of his house. It took him over a year to fulfill a childhood dream by building the 23-ft-high (7-m) rocket and 12.4-ft-high (3.8-m) shuttle, which tower spectacularly over his neighbors' homes.

Your Uploads

TREE FACE

Janet Potter sent Ripley's this amazing picture of a maple tree near her home in Malone, New York, with a large burl that resembles either the face of one of the Seven Dwarfs or Edvard Munch's famous painting *The Scream*.

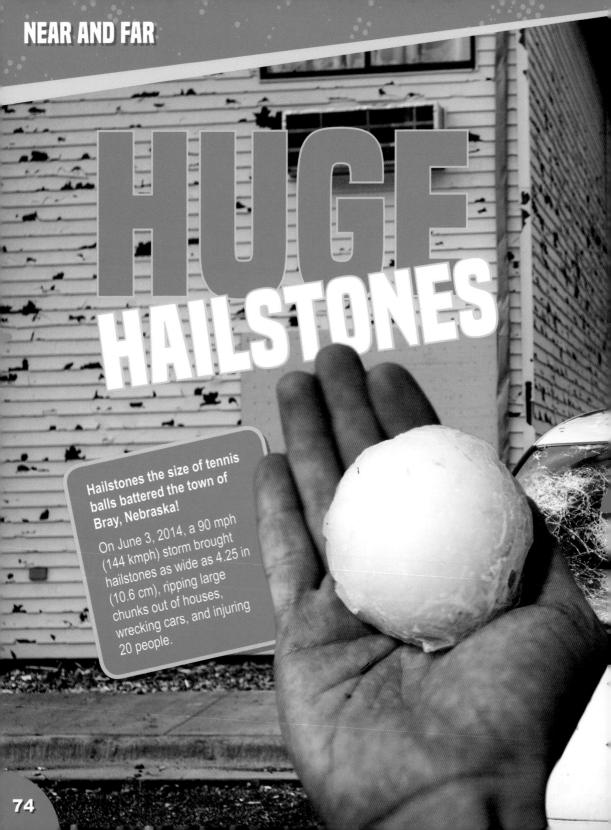

HUGE HAILSTONES

Hailstones the size of tennis balls battered the town of Bray, Nebraska!

On June 3, 2014, a 90 mph (144 kmph) storm brought hailstones as wide as 4.25 in (10.6 cm), ripping large chunks out of houses, wrecking cars, and injuring 20 people.

EXTREME WEATHER

A blistering temperature of 134°F (56.7°C) was recorded at Death Valley, California, on July 10, 1913.

At Vostok Station, Antarctica, the temperature plunged to -128.56°F (-89.2°C) on July 21, 1983.

A staggering 71.9 in (1.8 m) of rain fell in just 24 hours at Foc-Foc on the Indian Ocean island of La Réunion on January 7-8, 1966.

An impressive 93 ft 6 in (28.5 m) of snow fell in one year on Mount Rainier, Washington, between February 19, 1971, and February 18, 1972.

A snowflake 15 in (38 cm) in diameter landed at Fort Keogh, Montana, on January 28, 1887.

A hailstone 8 in (20 cm) in diameter fell at Vivian, South Dakota, on July 23, 2010.

A huge hailstone that fell during a storm in Gopalganj, Bangladesh, on April 14, 1986, weighed 2 lb 4 oz (1.02 kg), the heaviest ever recorded.

When a tornado hit the suburbs of Oklahoma City on May 3, 1999, the wind reached a speed of 302 mph (486 kmph).

There was not a single drop of rain in Arica, Chile, for more than 14 years between October 1903 and January 1918—a total of 173 months.

75

UNDERGROUND CITY
Seattle has a mysterious "underground city" in which many streets and storefronts, damaged in the Great Seattle Fire of 1889, exist below street level.

BIG FOOT
The Statue of Liberty has a 35-ft (10.6-m) waistline and wears size 879 shoes on her 25-ft-long (7.6-m) feet.

LOST FOREST
Buried underwater off the coast of Norfolk, England, is a 10,000-year-old prehistoric forest, including fallen oak trees with branches over 25 ft (7.6 m) long.

MALE MONOPOLY
The European country of Liechtenstein did not give women the right to vote or run for office until 1984.

CREMATION RIDE
A ghoulish ride at the Window of the World theme park in Shenzhen, China, aims to replicate the experience of being cremated! Passengers on the 4D Death Simulator lie down in a coffin before being pushed into a furnace where temperatures reach a sweltering 104°F (40°C). Although they are removed soon after, many say it feels like being burned alive.

SLEEPING BEAUTY
The mummified body of Rosalia Lombardo, an Italian girl who died of pneumonia in 1920 just short of her second birthday, has been so well preserved in the Capuchin catacombs of Palermo, Sicily, that it looks as if she is merely sleeping peacefully. Her grief-stricken father had asked for her body to be embalmed and the embalmer, Alfredo Salafia, did such a good job that all of Rosalia's organs remain intact almost a century later. He replaced her blood with a liquid mixture made up of formalin to kill bacteria, alcohol and glycerin to dry the body to the right level, salicylic acid to kill fungi, and zinc to keep the corpse rigid.

BRIDAL COFFIN

During a Valentine's Day wedding ceremony at a temple near Bangkok, Thailand, seven couples chose to lie down in a pink-lined coffin for good luck. During the ceremony, monks drape a white sheet over the newlyweds—symbolizing their death—and perform chants typically reserved for funerals. The monks finish with a blessing for the couple's new life together.

Swelling caused by carrying structure!

ROOM TO ROAM

The biggest piece of property in Australia, the Anna Creek cattle station in South Australia, covers 9,400 sq mi (24,000 sq km), which is larger than the entire country of Israel.

DIRT PYRAMID

The 1,000-year-old Dirt Pyramid of the ancient city of Cahokia, built by Native Americans in modern Illinois, covers 14 acres (5.7 ha) and was the largest building by volume in the U.S.A. at that time.

SWOLLEN SHOULDERS

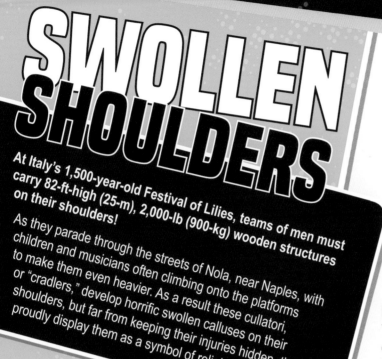

At Italy's 1,500-year-old Festival of Lilies, teams of men must carry 82-ft-high (25-m), 2,000-lb (900-kg) wooden structures on their shoulders!

As they parade through the streets of Nola, near Naples, with children and musicians often climbing onto the platforms to make them even heavier. As a result these cullatori, or "cradlers," develop horrific swollen calluses on their shoulders, but far from keeping their injuries hidden, they proudly display them as a symbol of religious devotion.

HOUSE MOVE

When Walter Thornton-Smith decided to move from Essex to Surrey, England, in 1912, he arranged for his home, a 400-year-old Tudor mansion, to be transported brick by brick more than 70 mi (112 km) to its new location. Every part of the 12-bedroom Cedar Court was numbered so that it could be reassembled as before.

BIG BUG

The giant blue termite sculpture on the roof of the Big Blue Bug Solutions building in Providence, Rhode Island, is 58 ft (18 m) long and 9 ft (2.7 m) tall—nearly 1,000 times the size of a real termite. Called Nibbles Woodaway, it is made of steel and fiberglass and weighs 4,000 lb (1,816 kg).

ACID RAIN

Scientists studying rocks in Italy have discovered that rain as acidic as vinegar fell on Earth 250 million years ago. The acid rain was caused by sulfur dioxide spewing from a series of deadly volcanic eruptions.

DELAYED SNOW

Weather patterns in the U.K. mean that statistically there is always a higher chance of a white Easter than a white Christmas.

TWIN TESTS

Twins Steve and Matt Rudram from Norfolk, England, took their driving tests at 11:11 a.m. on consecutive days and both passed with seven minor errors, two of which were identical.

GRAND BOWL

The Inazawa Grand Bowl in Japan is a bowling alley with 116 lanes. Opened in 1972, the bowl spans 91,500 sq ft (8,500 sq m) across the lanes with no supporting beams and can accommodate nearly 700 bowlers at any one time.

ONLY ONE

People in North Korea are banned from having the same name as the country's leader, Kim Jong-un. Anyone already born with that name was ordered to get a new name, and authorities were also told to reject all registrations of newborn babies called Kim Jong-un.

BUSY DAY

More than eight million people—equal to the entire population of Switzerland—visited the Great Wall of China in a single day in October 2014.

SALT PONDS

A salt mine in Maras, Peru, which has been in operation for more than 800 years, consists of 4,500 ponds on the side of a steep mountain. The salt water emerges from a nearby spring from where it is directed by a network of channels into the ponds. There, the water evaporates in the hot, dry air to form salt crystals, which the miners are then able to collect.

SKYPE RULER

Togbe Ngoryifia runs a car repair garage in Frankfurt, Germany, but is also an African king with 200,000 subjects whom he rules via Skype. He became King Banash of the Hohoe people in southeast Ghana in 1987, after being named as the successor to his grandfather. His father and older brother were not permitted to rule because they are left-handed, a sign of dishonesty among the Hohoe.

LAZY OLYMPICS

Montenegro, a country that prides itself on its slow pace of life, stages an annual Lazy Olympics where the only event involves lying in the shade of an oak tree near Breznik for as long as possible. Vladan Bajalica won the inaugural event in 2013 by lazing under the tree for 32 hours. Any competitor who appears to be putting too much effort into relaxing is disqualified.

SPELLING ERROR

The Colorado Rockies baseball team handed out 15,000 jerseys to fans with the name of their star player, Troy Tulowitzki, spelled incorrectly.

FINGER JEWELRY

The Angu people of Papua New Guinea wear the smoked fingers, hands, and breastbones of dead relatives as jewelry.

TORNADO FIRE

Janae Copelin photographed this spectacular "tornado fire" as a funnel of flame twisted into the sky while a farmer was burning his field in Chillicothe, Missouri.

Sometimes called a "fire devil," the natural phenomenon occurs when strong winds whip a fire upward, and funnels can reach nearly 100 ft (30 m) high. This funnel lasted only a couple of minutes, but Janae described it as the coolest/scariest thing she had ever seen.

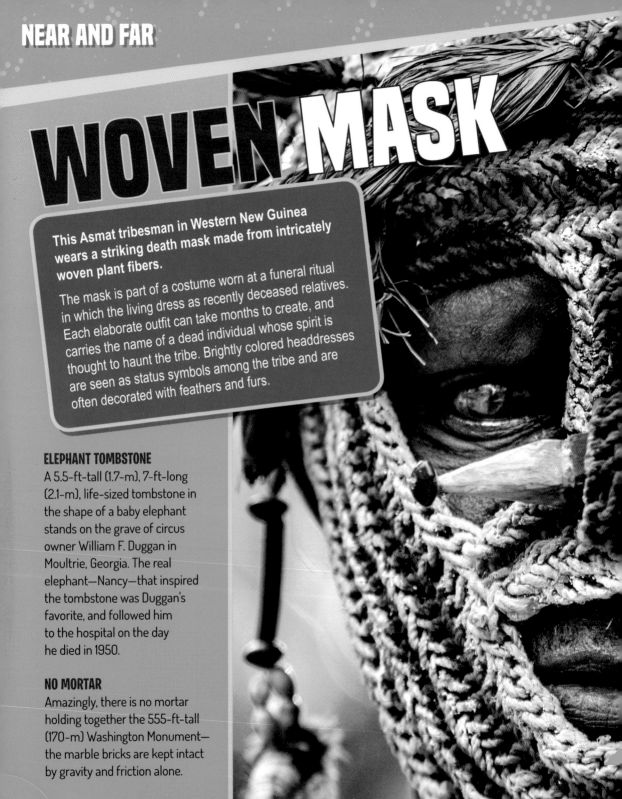

WOVEN MASK

This Asmat tribesman in Western New Guinea wears a striking death mask made from intricately woven plant fibers.

The mask is part of a costume worn at a funeral ritual in which the living dress as recently deceased relatives. Each elaborate outfit can take months to create, and carries the name of a dead individual whose spirit is thought to haunt the tribe. Brightly colored headdresses are seen as status symbols among the tribe and are often decorated with feathers and furs.

ELEPHANT TOMBSTONE
A 5.5-ft-tall (1.7-m), 7-ft-long (2.1-m), life-sized tombstone in the shape of a baby elephant stands on the grave of circus owner William F. Duggan in Moultrie, Georgia. The real elephant—Nancy—that inspired the tombstone was Duggan's favorite, and followed him to the hospital on the day he died in 1950.

NO MORTAR
Amazingly, there is no mortar holding together the 555-ft-tall (170-m) Washington Monument— the marble bricks are kept intact by gravity and friction alone.

LARGE LEAF

While walking with his family, four-year-old Tommy Lindsey of Mount Vernon, Washington, found a maple leaf that measured more than 2 ft (61 cm) from stem to tip and more than 21 in (53 cm) wide, making it almost as big as him.

NATURE LESSON

Gan Lin, the wife of a wealthy businessman from Chongqing, China, rented an entire mountain at a cost of more than $5,000 a month just so that her daughter Yin could learn about nature.

TUMBLING TOWER

The 47-story, 612-ft-tall (187-m) Singer Tower in New York City—the world's tallest building when it was constructed in 1908—was also the tallest to be demolished when it was pulled down by its owner in 1967.

HEMORRHOID FESTIVAL

The Kunigami Shrine in Japan's Tochigi prefecture is home to an annual festival dedicated to preventing and curing hemorrhoids. Visitors point their backsides at a large, egg-shaped washing stone at the center of the shrine in recognition of an ancient hemorrhoid cure, which required sufferers to wash their backsides in a nearby river and to eat eggs.

TREE TUNNEL

Overgrown trees have formed a beautiful 1.86-mi (3-km) green tunnel along a railway track in Klevan, Ukraine. Visitors regularly walk along the "Tunnel of Love," even though the track is still used by trains up to three times a day to transport wood to a nearby factory.

SPELLING MISTAKE

Workmen in Bristol, England, blundered by painting BUP STOP instead of BUS STOP in large yellow letters on the road during street repairs in August 2014!

MISSPELLED SIGNS

In 2010, workmen painted **SHCOOL** in big white letters on the road leading to Southern Guilford High School, North Carolina.

A sign erected in 2009 on Interstate 39 near Rothschild and Schofield, Wisconsin, spelled only one word correctly—"exit." It read: **"Exit 185 Buisness 51 Rothschield Schofeild."**

In 2002, California highway department employees painted the warning sign **CRUVE** near a bend in the road.

In 2003, highway workers in Richmond, California, painted a warning sign in 4-ft-high (1.2-m) letters on the road, which read **BMUP**. While doing this, they had erected a sign saying **SLOW MEN WORKING**.

CARS SWALLOWED

In February 2014, a gaping sinkhole 40 ft (12 m) wide and 30 ft (9 m) deep opened beneath the National Corvette Museum in Bowling Green, Kentucky, swallowing eight iconic American cars.

CLAY HOUSE

Architect Octavio Mendoza has spent 14 years building his house in Villa de Leyva, Colombia, entirely from clay. Named Casa Terracotta, it is also known locally as "Flintstone House," and even has furniture, beds, and kitchen utensils made from clay.

YARD SALE

An annual yard sale known as the "127 Corridor Sale" stretches from Addison, Michigan, to Gadsden, Alabama—a distance of 690 mi (1,110 km). Following the route of Highway 127, it travels through six states—Michigan, Ohio, Kentucky, Tennessee, Georgia, and Alabama— and boasts thousands of vendors along the way.

PLASTIC BRIDGE

Stretching nearly 25 ft (7.6 m), the Onion Ditch Bridge in West Liberty, Ohio, is made from 120,000 lb (54,431 kg) of recycled plastic, including old detergent bottles and car dashboards. Although it cost $250,000 to build, its projected 150-year life span is more than three times longer than conventional materials such as concrete or steel.

POND HOCKEY

Every January, 250 teams and nearly 2,000 skaters from across North America descend on Lake Nokomis in Minneapolis, Minnesota, for the U.S. Pond Hockey Championships. Staged on 25 man-made rinks on the frozen lake, the teams compete for the Golden Shovel, pond hockey's answer to the Stanley Cup. The games are four-a-side with no goalies, and the players call the penalties. The referees only keep track of the score.

UNDERSEA BEDROOM

A hotel in Zanzibar, Tanzania, has a suite that floats in the sea with an underwater bedroom so that guests can watch fish swimming by. The suite is anchored 820 ft (250 m) off the coast above a coral reef, and it costs $1,500 for two to stay there for one night.

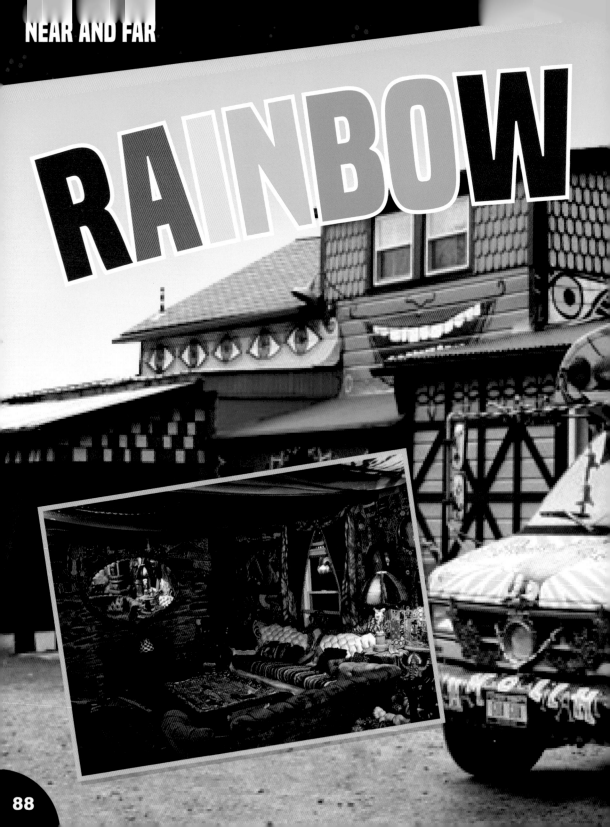

RAINBOW

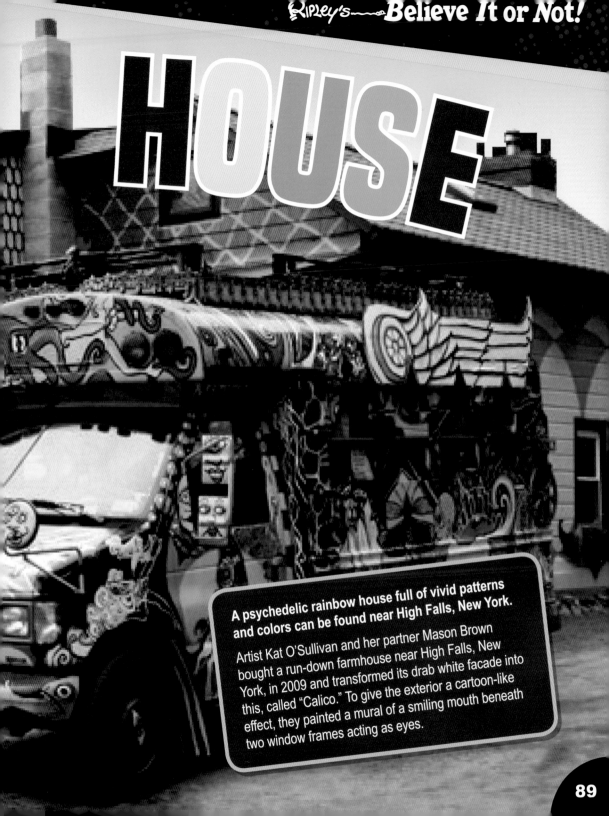

HOUSE

A psychedelic rainbow house full of vivid patterns and colors can be found near High Falls, New York.

Artist Kat O'Sullivan and her partner Mason Brown bought a run-down farmhouse near High Falls, New York, in 2009 and transformed its drab white facade into this, called "Calico." To give the exterior a cartoon-like effect, they painted a mural of a smiling mouth beneath two window frames acting as eyes.

DOG
WEDDING

An 18-year-old girl called Mangli Munda married a dog in Jharkhand, India, in 2014 after village elders told her that the union would ward off a curse.

More than 50 guests attended the elaborate Hindu wedding ceremony, and the canine groom, a stray named Sheru, arrived in a chauffeur-driven car. The dog wedding is not legally binding, leaving Munda free to marry a human in the future.

WACKY WEDDINGS

In Scotland, friends and relatives carry out a tradition called blackening, where they pour substances like tar, dead fish, eggs, mud, and curdled milk over the bride- or groom-to-be in a bid to ward off evil spirits.

Newlyweds from the Tidong people of Borneo are not allowed to go to the toilet after their wedding for 72 hours, as it will bring bad luck.

In Korea, the groom's friends beat his feet with a fish on his wedding night.

At a Maasai wedding in Kenya, the father of the bride blesses his daughter by spitting on her head and breasts. She then leaves the village with her husband and dare not look back for fear of being turned to stone.

After a Greek wedding, the bride throws a pomegranate at a door covered with honey. If the fruit seeds stick to the door, it is a sign that the couple will have many children.

Among the Tujia in China, the bride will cry and sing every day in the month leading up to the wedding. Gradually the other women join in for what is seen as an expression of joy.

GOLDEN GUMBOOT

Towering over the town of Tully in Queensland, Australia, is a 26-ft-high (7.9-m) golden gumboot. The dimensions of the fiberglass boot, which has an internal spiral staircase leading to a viewing platform at the top, represent the record 311 in (7,900 mm) of rain that fell on the town in 1950.

PRISON COMPETITION

The Prison World Cup for soccer-playing inmates of different nationalities is held every four years at the Klong Prem Prison in Thailand.

HUMONGOUS FUNGUS

A single 2,400-year-old honey mushroom in the Malheur National Forest, Oregon, is believed to be the world's largest living organism, covering 2,200 acres (890 ha). Most of it lies underground, but it is estimated to weigh up to 35,000 tons—350 times the weight of an adult blue whale.

POISON FLOWER

The Alutiiq people of Alaska once hunted using weapons tipped with poison made from larkspur-leaf and monkshood flowers, a dose of which is powerful enough to paralyze a 40-ton humpback whale.

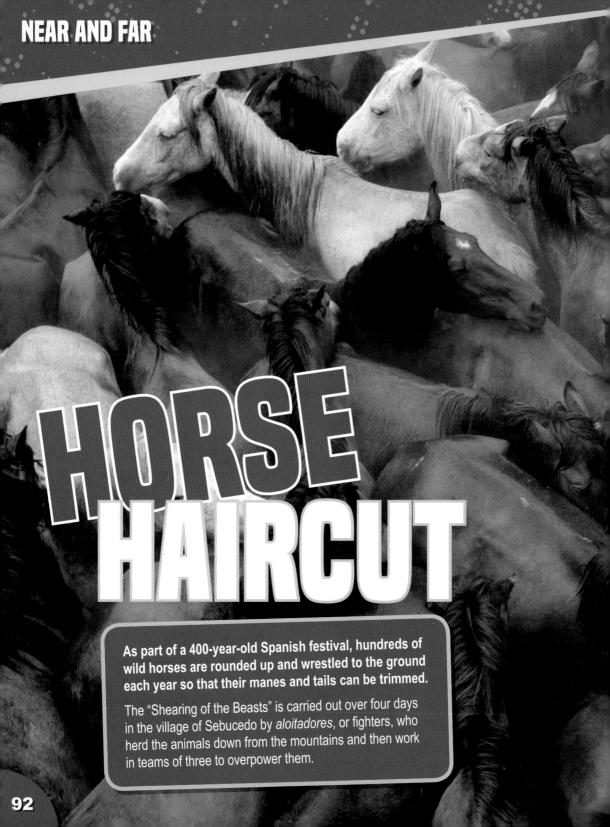

HORSE HAIRCUT

As part of a 400-year-old Spanish festival, hundreds of wild horses are rounded up and wrestled to the ground each year so that their manes and tails can be trimmed.

The "Shearing of the Beasts" is carried out over four days in the village of Sebucedo by *aloitadores*, or fighters, who herd the animals down from the mountains and then work in teams of three to overpower them.

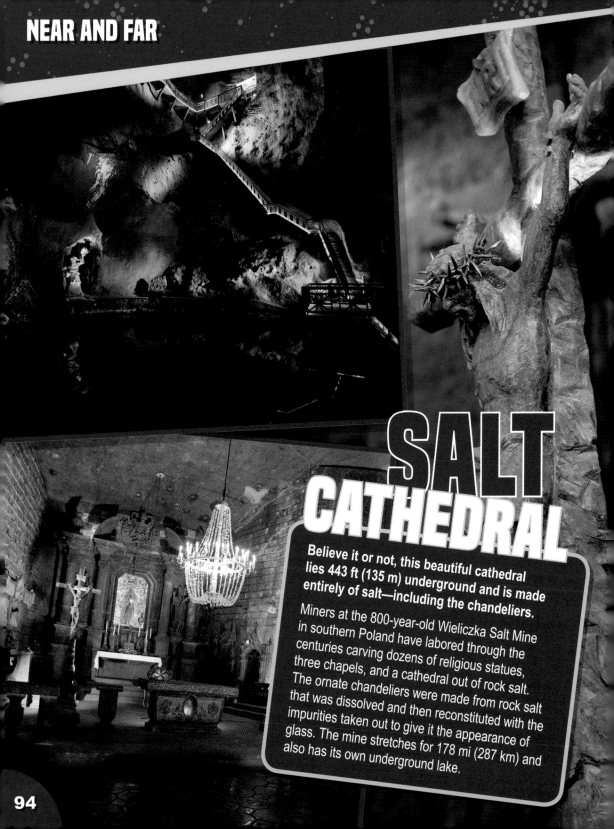

SALT CATHEDRAL

Believe it or not, this beautiful cathedral lies 443 ft (135 m) underground and is made entirely of salt—including the chandeliers.

Miners at the 800-year-old Wieliczka Salt Mine in southern Poland have labored through the centuries carving dozens of religious statues, three chapels, and a cathedral out of rock salt. The ornate chandeliers were made from rock salt that was dissolved and then reconstituted with the impurities taken out to give it the appearance of glass. The mine stretches for 178 mi (287 km) and also has its own underground lake.

FISHING FRENZY

At the sound of a gunshot, up to 35,000 fishermen, teamed in pairs, jump into Nigeria's muddy Matan Fada River for the annual Argungu Fishing Festival. One fisher carries gourds for flotation, while the other wields large nets, although some fishermen prefer to catch the fish with their bare hands. Fish weighing 145 lb (66 kg) have been caught within the 1-hour time limit, and the winning team receives a prize of $7,500 and a new bus.

EPIDERMIS EDITION

Harvard University's Houghton Library contains countless curiosities—including skin—among its stacks. A nineteenth century copy of Arsène Houssaye's Des destinées de l'ame is bound in the human skin of an unclaimed female mental patient who had died of a stroke.

SOLEMN VOW

After jubilant Austrian generals celebrated victory over Hungary in 1849 by clinking glasses and drinking beer, Hungarians vowed not to clink glasses for the next 150 years.

DRAGON BLOOD

The dragon blood tree of the Amazon gets its name from its blood-red sap, which is used by native tribes as a dye, and has been developed as a medicine to treat diarrhea and some skin conditions.

HOME MOVIES

Movie fan Paul Slim from the West Midlands, England, has spent £15,000 ($25,000) converting his garden shed into a 20-seat cinema, complete with 119-inch (3-m) screen, 3-D projector, surround sound system, and his collection of 3,000 DVDs.

RITUAL SCARRING

In a traditional ceremony designed to turn boys into men, teens in villages along the Sepik River in Papua New Guinea have their skin cut deep with razors until they are left with dozens of scars.

After the cuts have been made, the skin is infected using plant ashes and river mud so that the scars swell up to resemble the skin of the sacred crocodile.

RAT CATCHERS

The Canadian province of Alberta has been rat-free for over half a century thanks to a 5,822 sq mi (15,080 sq km) rat control buffer zone along the vulnerable eastern border—a zone that remains staffed by eight professional rat catchers.

CHILD BRIDES

As part of a lesson on family life, a kindergarten in Zhengzhou, China, "married" more than 100 toddlers. The brides and grooms— all aged between three and six years old and wearing wedding dresses and suits—had to choose their partner before exchanging rings and making vows in front of a registrar. Their parents were assured that the ceremony was not legally binding.

ROCK SLIDE

A landslide at a copper mine outside Salt Lake City, Utah, in April 2013 sent 165 million tons of rock, dirt, and debris crashing at speeds of 100 mph (160 kmph) into a nearly mile-deep pit with such force that it triggered 16 small earthquakes. The avalanche, which loosened enough material to bury New York's Central Park in 66 ft (20 m) of debris, is thought to be the largest non-volcanic slide in modern North American history.

BLOODY THEME

Haw Par Villa, a Chinese mythology theme park in Singapore, has more than 1,000 gruesome scenes, including the Ten Courts of Hell, which showcase blood-curdling punishments for minor misdemeanors. Exhibits depict the fleshy heart being torn out of a woman for being ungrateful, a young girl being flung by the Devil into a hill of knives, and an executioner pulling the intestines from a man tied to a pole because the victim had cheated during exams.

OVERNIGHT OASIS

A large 60-ft-deep (18-m) lake suddenly appeared in the Tunisian desert in July 2014. One minute the area was sand, the next it was a turquoise body of water dubbed Lac de Gafsa in honor of the nearest town. The lake is believed to have been caused by a rupture in the rock above the local water table.

FIRE FIGHT

At the annual Mesabatan Api fire fight in Gianyar, Bali, bare-chested young men pick up blazing coconut husks with their bare hands before swinging and hurling them at each other's bodies.

The centuries-old Hindu tradition symbolizes purification of the body, but often leaves participants battle-scarred with nasty burns that have to be treated with a mixture of turmeric and coconut oil.

TALL TAILS

RAY SCHOOL

Schools of Munk's devil rays can number tens of thousands of fish and cover an area of over 32,000 sq ft (3,000 sq m)—more than half the size of a football field.

This aerial view was taken over the Sea of Cortez, off Baja California, Mexico. Scientists are mystified as to why the fish, which often somersault out of the water, gather in such large numbers.

MEGA MIGRATIONS

40 billion African migratory locusts can form a swarm covering 11,000 sq ft (1,000 sq km) and eat 80,000 tons of vegetation per day—enough food to feed a million people.

120 million red crabs migrate to the seashore to mate every fall on Christmas Island in the Indian Ocean.

As many as 60 million monarch butterflies fly from Canada to the California coast and Mexico every November for the winter.

30 million sockeye salmon migrate to Canada's Fraser River in the annual salmon run.

8 million straw-colored fruit bats fly 2,000 mi (3,200 km) from the Republic of the Congo to Zambia from October to December to feed on their favorite delicacy, the musuku fruit.

1.5 million wildebeest stampede through Kenya's Mara River each year in search of greener pastures.

AGENT SWAN

An Egyptian man arrested a swan and took it to a police station because he thought the bird was a spy. He became suspicious when he noticed the swan was carrying an electronic device, but it turned out to be a wildlife-tracking instrument.

FIERY SHRIMP

Acanthephyra purpurea, the fire-breathing shrimp, blinds and distracts its would-be predators by spewing out a blue-glowing bacterial cloud.

HARMFUL ARMS

A mysterious plague has been causing starfish to tear themselves to pieces. An afflicted starfish's arms crawl in opposite directions until their bodies are pulled apart—and, unlike healthy starfish, diseased specimens are not able to regenerate.

HUNGRY HIPPOS

Although they are thought of as herbivores, hippos occasionally eat each other when food is scarce.

PATRIOTIC CAT

Margo, a cat owned by Oleg Bouboulin of Yekaterinburg, Russia, stands to attention like a soldier whenever the Russian national anthem is played. She stands on her back legs without moving a muscle and even seems to know when the anthem is about to end because she relaxes as the final notes are played.

SILK THREAD

The silk used to form a silkworm's cocoon is actually hardened saliva that has been secreted from its mouth, and it can unravel into a single thread up to 1 mi (1.6 km) long.

CUDDLE CLONE

Working from submitted photographs, Louisville, Kentucky, online retailer Cuddle Clones offers custom-made, exact stuffed replicas of pets for people who want to present their furry best friends with life-sized plush pet "clones." Founded in 2009, the company spends between eight to ten weeks creating the lifelike likenesses of dogs, cats, birds, lizards, and other pets—such as Stan, a schnauzer in Toronto, Canada (pictured right), and his carbon copy Cuddle Clone.

EXTRA LEGS

In the mid-1990s, hundreds of frogs in ponds across the U.S.A. and Canada developed extra legs.

Some frogs had as many as a dozen! The condition was caused by a parasitic flatworm, *Ribeiroia*, which can invade the bodies of tadpoles. The parasites bury themselves in the tiny buds that eventually grow into the hind legs, resulting in the developing leg either being missing or malformed.

PREGNANCY TEST

In the 1950s the African clawed frog was used as a pregnancy test on humans. A woman's urine was injected into a frog, and if the frog produced eggs, the woman was declared pregnant.

SHARK DIVER

Hawaiian freediver Ocean Ramsey swims and rides with great white sharks up to 17 ft long (5.2 m) in order to prove they are nothing like the terrifying maneater from the movie *Jaws*. She travels the globe in search of sharks and has swam with more than 30 species.

TALENTED FISH

Ilana Bram of Poughkeepsie, New York, spent two months training her pet cichlid fish Erasmus to play soccer in his tank with a miniature ball. The talented fish can also weave his way through a slalom course and perform a limbo dance.

ROAMING FISH

A 3-ft-long (1-m) sturgeon that escaped from an aquatic center in Hampshire, England, during floods in February 2014 was found alive and well in a puddle at a car wash one mile away.

STRETCH JELLY

Although its body is sometimes only about 6 ft (1.8 m) long, the lion's mane jelly has tentacles that can grow up to 120 ft (37 m), making it longer than the length of a blue whale.

FISH DRUGGED

The slow-moving geographic cone snail, which lives off the coast of Australia, drugs fish to catch and eat them. The snail releases a toxic cloud containing insulin, which causes the fish's blood-sugar levels to plummet and puts it in a coma.

LONG WHISKERS

CLEAN CAT

Natasha, a six-month-old Siberian forest cat owned by Daryl Humdy of Oakland, California, survived a 40-minute cycle inside a running washing machine after climbing in with a load of laundry.

BAT CAVE

A cave near San Antonio, Texas, is home to 10 million Mexican free-tailed bats, crammed together on the walls at 400 bats per sq ft (4,300 per sq m).

Whiskers, a two-year-old black and white cat at an animal center in Somerset, England, gets her name from her huge whiskers that stretch 12 in (30 cm) from tip to tip—and they're still growing.

Extended facial hair obviously runs in the family because when she gave birth to a litter of kittens they, too, had very long whiskers.

SNAKE'S HEAD

In order to deter predators, the moth caterpillar *Hemeroplanes triptolemus* can transform itself in seconds so that its body looks just like the head of a venomous green viper snake.

KILLER CROC

After a 20-ft-long (6-m) crocodile ate his pregnant wife, distraught fisherman Mubarak Batambuze, of Kibuye village, Uganda, spent his savings on a spear and killed the 2,200-lb (1,000-kg) reptile.

CLAM CALAMITY

By counting the number of rings on the inside of the shell, scientists have calculated that a deep-sea clam discovered alive off the coast of Iceland in 2006 was 507 years old, meaning that it was born seven years after Christopher Columbus landed in America. Sadly, in removing it from its ocean home and putting it in a freezer for further study, the scientists accidentally killed what could have been the world's oldest-living sea creature.

DRASTIC MEASURES

After mating, the male coin spider bites off its own genitals so that it is more agile and better able to keep rival males away from the female. As an extra precaution, it also uses the severed genitals to block the route to the female's reproductive organs.

BURPING MONKEYS

To get rid of the excess methane and carbon dioxide that is a by-product of digestion, leaf-eating African colobus monkeys often burp in each other's faces. The animals interpret the gesture as a sign of friendship.

HEDGEHOG HUNTERS

In Tudor England, people were encouraged to kill hedgehogs because it was believed that they suckled milk from cows at night.

JUMPING RAT

The giant legs of the kangaroo rat of North America help it leap ten times its own height and 30 times its own body length.

SNAKE MASSAGE

Cebu City Zoo in the Philippines offers visitors free massages from four giant Burmese pythons, weighing a combined 550 lb (250 kg).

The snakes are placed one at a time on top of the volunteers who lie down on a bamboo bed for the 15-minute massage. The pythons are each fed ten chickens beforehand to stop them from feeling hungry, therefore preventing them from squeezing anyone to death to make them their dinner.

SEE-THROUGH FISH

The head of the Pacific barreleye fish is covered with a transparent shield, like the glass canopy of a jet fighter plane, which helps it see better in the dark ocean depths where it lives. Researchers at the Monterey Bay Aquarium Research Institute discovered that it also has rotating eyes, allowing it to look up through the shield at potential prey, as well as to look forward. Believe it or not, the eyes are not the indentations above its mouth (these are the equivalent of nostrils), but the huge green tubular, barrel-shaped objects, which give the fish its name.

LOUD SQUEAKS

If the high-pitched echolocation squeaks of the fishing bat were in human hearing range, they would be as loud as gunshots.

SPOILED SHELLS

Fewer than 500 of Madagascar's ploughshare tortoises are living in the wild, prompting some conservationists to deface the animals' beautiful shells in order to reduce their value to poachers

FREE CAT

Russian bank Sherbank offers a free cat with every mortgage. Customers choose from one of ten breeds, but are not allowed to keep the animal for more than two hours—long enough for the cat to enter the property ahead of the owner, a good-luck tradition in Russia.

DOG POOL

The Spanish town of La Roca del Valles has a special swimming pool just for dogs. The Resort Canino Can Jane is designed to be the right depth for all shapes and sizes of dogs and includes a doggie slide as well as extra tough inflatables for the dogs to play on.

DOGGY DENIM

Matt and Mel Westwood, from Melbourne, Australia, design custom-made denim jackets for dogs—from Chihuahuas to greyhounds—which they sell all over the world.

BLOOD SUCKER

Before laying eggs, a female tick, in one feed, will drink up to 600 times her own body weight in blood.

DOLPHIN PLAYTIME

Bottlenose dolphins have been known to take rides on the heads of humpback whales—just for fun.

Years of neglect had left Matt, an abandoned Persian cat, with a thick, tangled coat, so veterinarians in London, England, shaved it all off and placed the fur (with a set of cartoon eyes) next to him as he awoke on the operating table.

There was enough fur to fill two carrier bags, and Matt was given a specially knitted jumper to wear until his own fur began to grow back.

CLOSE SHAVE

Matt the cat

Matt's fur!

WASP INVASION

A swarm of 5,000 wasps built its nest on a bed in the spare room of a house in Hampshire, England, after the window had been left open. The nest measured 3 ft (0.9 m) wide and more than 1 ft (0.3 m) deep, and when finally discovered, the wasps had started chewing through the pillows and into the mattress.

CHARCOAL CURE
The red colobus monkeys of Zanzibar steal man-made charcoal to eat as an anti-toxic medicine to help relieve stomachaches.

CANINE PILOT
When Graham Mountford of Bedfordshire, England, takes to the skies in his Cessna 210 Centurion light aircraft, his copilot is Callie, his chocolate Labrador dog. She has been flying since she was 12 weeks old and has clocked up more than 250 flying hours covering 50,000 mi (80,000 km).

BRAIN FOOD
A giant squid's food passes through its brain before it reaches its stomach. As a result, it has to eat small morsels because anything too large might get caught in the brain and cause brain damage.

GRIZZLY SAMARITAN
Vali, a grizzly bear at Budapest Zoo, Hungary, came to the rescue when it saw a crow drowning in the enclosure. The bear reached into the water, gently pulled out the bird with its mouth and left it poolside to recover.

SWINGING ASSASSIN
The white-handed gibbon of southern Asia is so agile it sometimes plucks birds from the air to eat as it swings from tree to tree.

SHARP HEARING
Blue whales can hear each other over distances of up to 100 mi (160 km), but zoologists believe the whales used to communicate over distances of up to 1,000 mi (1,600 km) prior to the increase of human noise pollution in recent decades.

HAIRY HEROES

New York City guide dogs Salty and Roselle were awarded a joint Dickin Medal, a British honor given by the People's Dispensary for Sick Animals, for loyally remaining at the side of their blind owners and courageously leading them down more than 70 floors of the World Trade Center and to a place of safety before the towers collapsed during the September 11, 2001, terrorist attack. Roselle, who had been sleeping under her owner's desk when one of the planes hit Tower 1, went on to be posthumously named American Hero Dog of the Year 2011 by the American Humane Society, and has a book written about her.

BOVINE GAS

A barn in Hesse, Germany, was badly damaged after a herd of 90 dairy cows passed so much gas that the resultant methane ignited and caused an explosion, which blew off the roof of the building.

VINTAGE VENOM

Poison from taipans, tiger snakes, and death adders that was collected by scientists and stored at the University of Melbourne's Australian Venom Research Unit is still deadly—even though some of it is more than 80 years old.

ALOHA, KITTY!

The feline of a family moving from Virginia to Hawaii in 2014 was supposed to stay with relatives—but had other plans. The land and sea journey for the Barth family's belongings took more than a month, but when they opened a box, their beloved cat Memeow was inside—somehow having survived without food or water!

EAGLE HAS LANDED

While Wendy Morrell was watching tennis on TV at her home in Dorset, England, a huge Russian steppe eagle with a 4-ft (1.2-m) wingspan suddenly flew in through the patio doors and perched on a cabinet. The escaped eagle, named Storm, was eventually coaxed down by a bird-of-prey expert who offered it a dead chick as a snack.

MONKEY WHISPER

Instead of making loud alarm calls when a distrusted stranger enters their territory, cotton-top tamarin monkeys of Colombia often communicate with each other in hushed whispers.

SUPER SUCKER

The northern clingfish, found off the Pacific coast of North America, possesses such strong suction power that it can support 300 times its own body weight.

JAWS VS CLAWS

An 18-ft-long (5.5-m) saltwater crocodile, one of the most fearsome predators on Earth, was seen wrestling with a highly aggressive bull shark, clamping it in its jaws in the Adelaide River, northern Australia.

Usually, the shark would expect to be eaten alive, but this one may have got lucky because the croc, Brutus, is 80 years old and missing a front leg and most of his teeth.

CHIMNEY ORDEAL

Chloe, a pet rabbit owned by nine-year-old Natasha Cameron, was sucked up the chimney of the family house in Cheshire, England, by a sudden gust of wind. The rabbit was trapped up the chimney for three days before being rescued by fire crews.

SHARK ATTACK

When a tiger shark took a bite out of his surfboard and knocked him into the ocean near Kilauea, Hawaii, 25-year-old Jeff Horton survived the attack by grabbing the shark's fin and repeatedly punching the fish in the eye until it finally spat out the surfboard and swam away.

DEEP BREATH

The nine-banded armadillo, found in North, Central, and South America, is able to cross rivers by holding its breath for up to six minutes while walking across the riverbed.

DUNG MOUNTAIN

A single elephant can produce 300 lb (136 kg) of dung—the weight of an average gorilla—in 24 hours.

SOCK SNACK

Veterinarians operating on a sick Great Dane in Portland, Oregon, were amazed to discover 43.5 socks in the dog's stomach!

The animal's owner knew he liked chewing socks, but had no idea he had actually been swallowing them. Once the socks were removed, the dog made a full recovery.

SNAKE BALLS

Each spring, more than 140,000 red-sided garter snakes emerge from hibernation and turn an area near Narcisse, Manitoba, into a writhing mass of bodies. They form wriggling mating balls on the ground and in bushes and trees, often with as many as 50 males wrapping themselves around a solitary female. The snakes come from miles away to hibernate at the Narcisse snake dens—a series of sinkholes where tens of thousands of snakes are crammed into a space the size of a living room.

HEAVY HEART

A blue whale's tongue can weigh as much as an adult elephant, while its heart can become as large as an automobile.

FOOT SUCKER

The thorny devil lizard, which lives in the harsh deserts of Australia, drinks water through its feet. By using a series of tiny capillaries located between its scales, it can cover its entire body in 30 seconds.

SPECIAL TALENT

According to Ripley fan Dan Paulun, a rescue dog named Maddie—who is owned by U.S. photographer Theron Humphrey—can keep her balance on top almost anything, from a horse to a tree branch. The amazing canine talent has earned Maddie more than 782,000 followers on the social media site Instagram.

This X-ray of the dog's stomach showed it was full of foreign objects—surgery revealed the socks in the picture to the right!

American naturalist Stephen Hopkins found this gigantic earthworm—5 ft (1.5 m) long and with a girth the size of a man's forearm—half-hidden under a rotten log in the foothills of the Sumaco Volcano in Ecuador.

MONSTER
EARTHWORM

CAT CANDIDATE

Morris, a black-and-white cat owned by Sergio Chamorro, ran for mayor in the Mexican city of Xalapa in 2014. Campaigning under the slogan "Tired of voting for rats? Vote for a cat," Morris received more than 130,000 likes on his Facebook page—far more than his human rivals—and received around 12,000 votes in the actual election, placing him fourth out of the 11 candidates.

DEADLY VENOM

Tim Friede has survived being bitten by more than 100 venomous snakes, including a lethal black mamba that can kill a person in under 20 minutes. He keeps dozens of the most poisonous snakes on Earth in the basement of his Milwaukee, Wisconsin, home, but says he has become immune to their bites after injecting himself with their diluted venom.

SURROGATE MOTHER

When Dina Alves adopted two orphaned baby armadillos in the Brazilian town of Guaporema, her pet dog Faisca became so attached to the new arrivals that she began producing her own milk to nurse them.

IN A SPIN

Chica, a guinea pig belonging to Marilyn Jones from New Plymouth, New Zealand, emerged unscathed after accidentally spending 30 minutes inside a running laundry dryer on an intense cycle at temperatures of 160°F (71°C).

SINISTER SKULL

The pink underwing moth caterpillar of Australasia has sinister face markings on its head that look uncannily like a human skull and which enable it to scare off predators.

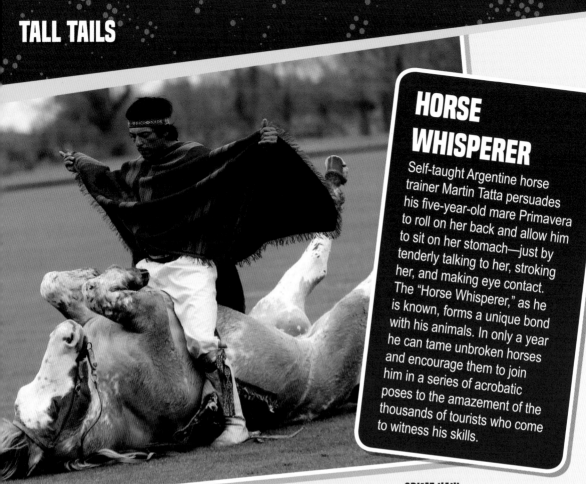

HORSE WHISPERER

Self-taught Argentine horse trainer Martin Tatta persuades his five-year-old mare Primavera to roll on her back and allow him to sit on her stomach—just by tenderly talking to her, stroking her, and making eye contact. The "Horse Whisperer," as he is known, forms a unique bond with his animals. In only a year he can tame unbroken horses and encourage them to join him in a series of acrobatic poses to the amazement of the thousands of tourists who come to witness his skills.

SALTY SNEEZE

Marine iguanas sneeze more than any other animal—as a way to expel excess salt and stop them becoming dehydrated. As their food is soaked in salt water from the sea, salt builds up in their bloodstream. Most of this salt collects in a special gland above the iguana's eyes, from which the animal can squeeze it out. The spray often falls back onto the iguana's head, where it quickly evaporates—leaving a crust that looks like a white wig.

FAMOUS FAN

Wilson, a 29-in-tall (74-cm) pony owned by Sarah Kessler, is the Seattle Seahawks' most famous fan—and even has his mane and tail painted in the NFL team's colors with nontoxic, washable paint.

FEARLESS RATS

Rats infected by the *Toxoplasma gondii* parasite lose their fear of cats, meaning that cats are more likely to catch and eat them, continuing the life cycle of the parasite—inside the cat.

CRIME HAUL

A dog that jumped into a pond in West Sussex, England, to fetch a stick came to the surface with a haul of stolen jewelry instead. Police divers discovered almost 1,000 stolen items, along with four handguns, a machete, and a bayonet in the pond.

BEE SWARM

A swarm of bees found in the ceiling of Frieda Turkmenilli's apartment in Queens, New York, consisted of a staggering 50,000 bees that had built 17 honeycombs.

HONEY THIEF

When raiding hives for honey, the death's-head hawkmoth of Europe disguises itself by chemically mimicking the scent of bees. This calms the bees and allows the moth to enter the hive and steal honey without being stung.

COMMUNAL NESTS

Huge haystack-like structures built on telephone poles in Southern Africa's Kalahari Desert are the nests of sociable weaver birds, and each can accommodate as many as 400 birds at a time, including several different species!

Lovebirds, finches, and pygmy falcons all nest alongside the weavers in up to 100 individual chambers. Meanwhile, vultures, owls, and eagles often roost on the nests' broad roofs. Built of sticks, grass, and cotton, such nests can be 20 ft (6 m) high, 13 ft (4 m) wide, 7 ft (2 m) thick, and weigh 2,000 lb (900 kg)—heavy enough to cause entire trees to collapse. The nests are so well constructed that some have remained occupied for 100 years.

INSIDE OUT

To illustrate the inner workings of animals, the Natural History Museum in London, England, staged an exhibition of almost 100 creatures inside out, including this dramatic shark showing the capillary blood vessel structures under its skin.

The exhibits were created by an anatomical process called plastination where resins preserve the organs and blood capillaries, and the surrounding tissue is dissolved with acid.

TOXIC FLESH

African spur-winged geese become so toxic after feeding on blister beetles that if a human were to consume the feasted bird's flesh, the result would be certain death.

TWO TONGUES

Bush babies have a second tongue under their main tongue, which they use to clean their teeth. Called a "grooming tongue," it is also used in conjunction with their front teeth to preen their fur.

PAIN RELIEF

Bino, an albino alligator at the São Paulo Aquarium, Brazil, had weekly 30-minute acupuncture sessions after he had lived for eight years with scoliosis, a condition that gave him a hunched back and left him unable to move two of his legs or to swish his tail. Before inserting up to a dozen needles into his back, veterinarian Daniela Cervaletti always made sure that Bino's jaws were taped shut.

SPERM SAVERS

Female guppy fish can become fertilized up to ten months after their male partner has died. Female guppies live eight times longer than males, and as they can store sperm inside their bodies, they are able to save it until the right time for fertilization. Older, larger females can carry the sperm of several dead males.

FLESH EATER

The screwworm fly of South America breeds by laying flesh-eating maggot larvae in the open wounds, ears, and eyes of mammals—including humans.

TROPHY COLLECTION

Waffle, a five-year-old Lakeland terrier, has sniffed out and collected almost 1,000 balls of all sizes from country walks near her home in Devon, England. She once brought home eight balls from a single walk and howls if her owner, Sarah Bennett, tries to throw any of them away.

STORY TIME

While rescue animals at the Battersea Dogs and Cats Home in London, U.K., were waiting for new homes, a group of schoolchildren cheered them up by reading them stories. The staff at the rescue home say that the rhythmic sound of reading can help calm stressed animals.

TRASH DIET

A puppy survived nearly a month trapped in a locked car that had been impounded in a Kansas City, Missouri, lot. Despite having no water, the 12-week-old terrier and schnauzer mix, named Kia, survived by eating trash left in the car.

PEE TALK

Crawfish communicate with each other by shooting streams of urine out of pores on the sides of their heads. Clusters of fan-like appendages direct the spout straight into the face of the other crawfish during a fight or during courtship. The urine contains hormone derivatives that give clues to the sprayer's current level of fitness and indicate whether or not that particular crawfish would make a fearsome adversary or a healthy mate.

BIG EYES

Each eye of the tarsier—a shy, nocturnal animal from Southeast Asia—is bigger than its brain. Its eyes are so large that they are unable to move in their sockets, but it has a flexible neck that allows it to swivel its head 180 degrees.

VOLCANIC NEST

The endangered maleo bird, which lives on the Indonesian island of Sulawesi, uses the heat from volcanoes to help hatch its eggs. The adult does not sit on the eggs, but buries them in the soil or sand near volcanoes and relies on the heat from geothermal activity for incubation. When the chicks hatch they claw their way up to the surface and are immediately able to fly.

DETERMINED DOGGIE

After being tossed a meatball, a stray dog refused to be left behind as a Swedish team trekked and kayaked through the grueling 430-mile (692-km) 2014 Adventure Racing World Championship in the Amazon jungle. Dubbed "Arthur," the intrepid canine accompanied the team to twelfth place—and a new home with Team Peak Performance leader Mikael Lindnord, who adopted him.

PRIZED PLUMAGE

The ancient Aztecs and Mayans valued the feathers of the colorful quetzal bird more than gold. The birds were considered sacred in both cultures, and the penalty for killing one was death.

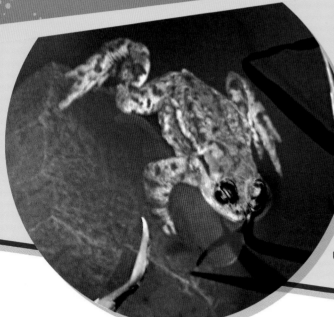

LAZY FROG

You've heard of Crazy Frog, well meet Lazy Frog! This frog could not be bothered to swim across a garden pond in Dorset, England, so it hitched a ride on a goldfish, clinging on with its webbed feet to make sure that it did not fall off. The goldfish repeatedly wriggled from side to side in an attempt to dislodge its amphibian jockey, but the frog refused to loosen its grip until it had reached its destination.

BUG'S LIFE

Yuan Meixia of Fujian, China, keeps 100,000 cockroaches in her home. She breeds them, feeds them daily with fruit or sugary treats, and keeps them warm in winter with a gas stove. Every two months, when they are ready to harvest, she drowns them, dries them in the sun, and sells them to pharmaceutical companies who pay $130 per kilo for the bugs to use in medicines.

BIRTHDAY GUEST

A 180-lb (82-kg) black bear crashed through the skylight of Alicia Bishop and Glenn Merrill's home in Juneau, Alaska, while they were preparing to celebrate their son Jackson's first birthday, and when the couple fled, the bear ate the party cupcakes!

MIGHTY MITE

The tiny moss mite *Archegozetes longisetosus* can resist 1,180 times its own weight—that's like a human holding back an airliner.

CLOTHES HORSE

Jessica Clarke and Annie Brown from Pontypool, Wales, make $255 (£170) one-piece suits for horses—in a range of designs including polka dot, stars, and leopard print! The equine onesies, which cover the entire body apart from nose, eyes, hooves, and tail, were originally designed to protect the horse from allergies and skin conditions, but have also been snapped up by customers in the U.S. and Australia, who are keen to keep the animals' coats clean before a show.

FANCY FROG

In an Indonesian rain forest, scientists have identified the first known frog out of the world's 6,455 species that gives birth to tadpoles instead of laying spawn. Herpetologist Jim McGuire grabbed a frog and discovered that it was a female with a dozen newborn tadpoles with her.

KOALA PASSENGER

A koala bear tenaciously clung to a car grille for 55 mi (88 km) after being hit by the vehicle in Queensland, Australia. The family in the car realized they had acquired an extra passenger when they stopped at a service station—and, astonishingly, the four-year-old marsupial's only injury was a torn nail.

IT'S A GEEP!

A baby animal named Butterfly, born at a petting zoo in Scottsdale, Arizona, in 2014, was half goat, half sheep—a geep. Butterfly's mother was a sheep, but the father was a pygmy goat, with the result that the newborn had a goat's head and the woolly body of a lamb.

CHIMP CHEF

Kanzi, a 34-year-old male bonobo chimpanzee who lives at the Great Ape Trust in Des Moines, Iowa, can break twigs to build a fire, light them with matches, and then toast marshmallows over the fire on a stick.

SALIVA PRODUCE

Dairy cows produce at least 26 gal (98 l) of saliva every day to help them chew their rough food.

After reading in *Ripley's Believe It or Not! Dare to Look!* about how Dutch artist Bart Jansen turned his cat into a radio-controlled model helicopter, 13-year-old Arnhem schoolboy Pepeijn Bruins asked Jansen and his inventor partner Arjen Beltman if they could do the same for his deceased pet rat, Ratjetoe. They stuffed the animal, attached three radio-controlled propellers and a computer to its body, and gave it a new lease of life as a "rat copter"—the world's first flying rat.

RAT COPTER

POND DIP

Rosie, a 12-week-old German shepherd puppy, landed in big trouble after driving both her owner and his car into a pond. John Costello of Canton, Massachusetts, had just got into his car and started the engine when Rosie excitedly jumped in, hit the gear shift, and fell on top of the gas pedal, sending the car and its passengers careening into a nearby pond.

ONE-EYED CHAMPION

In 2014, Adventure de Kannan became the first one-eyed horse to win the Hickstead Derby, the most prestigious prize available in British showjumping and where horses are required to jump fences that are more than 5 ft (1.5 m) high. The 14-year-old horse had his right eye removed the previous year following an infection.

PENGUIN JUMPERS

Volunteers with Knits for Nature, a program run by an Australian conservation group, knit sweaters for sick penguins that have been harmed by oil spills. The sweaters keep the birds warm, but they also prevent them trying to clean away the toxic oil with their beaks. Over the years, the group has come up with more than 300 different penguin sweater designs.

TALL COW

Blosom, a 13-year-old Holstein Friesian cow living on a farm in Orangeville, Illinois, stands an incredible 6 ft 4 in (1.93 m) tall, making her taller than Chicago Bulls basketball star Derrick Rose! Owned by Patty Hanson, Blosom weighs 2,000 lb (908 kg) and has her own Facebook page.

STREAKING BACON

Piglet Chris P. Bacon was born without the use of his hind legs, so his owner, Dr. Len Lucero of Sumterville, Florida, built him a two-wheeled harness using his son's K'Nex building set.

The wheelchair attaches to the pig's body with a harness around his neck and rear and has wheels in place of his back legs. The device has turned the little pig into an online celebrity with his own Facebook and Twitter pages.

AWESOME AMPHIBIAN

This little glass frog in Costa Rica certainly lives up to its name, and is using its transparent body to camouflage itself against a leaf to protect its precious eggs. Glass frogs lay their eggs out of water in order to steer clear of lurking predators and often choose leaves overhanging a stream so that when the tadpoles hatch, they drop directly into the water.

CANINE JOCKEY

Horse trainer Steve Jefferys has an unusual assistant at his equestrian center in Melbourne, Australia—his collie dog Hekan (short for "He can do anything"). The dog holds the horses as they are being saddled, takes them for walks on a leash, and most incredible of all, even sits on their backs and rides them.

HEROIC PARROT

When Rachel Mancino was attacked in a park in North London, England, she was saved by Wunsy, her African gray parrot who squawked and flapped her wings so loudly that the assailant fled. Wunsy always sits on Rachel's shoulder for their daily walk.

MONKEY SELFIE

The U.S. Copyright Office has explicitly stated "a photograph taken by a monkey" cannot be copyrighted after ruling against photographer David Slater's application to copyright a photograph taken by an Indonesian macaque on his camera. In addition, animals cannot own copyrights of self-portraits, including "a mural painted by an elephant."

DOG CONSOLE

San Diego, California, entrepreneurs Dan Knudsen and Leo Trottier have designed a game console for dogs. CleverPet has three sensitive touch pads, which light up when touched and release food for the pet when hit in the correct order.

MUMMIFIED CAT

While Andrew Hartley renovated the ceiling of an 18th-century house in North Yorkshire, England, a mummified cat fell on him. The cat was believed to be at least 100 years old and had probably been part of an old tradition where dead cats were put in the eaves and walls of properties to ward off evil spirits.

PET TRAILERS

Inspired by vintage trailers of the 1940s, Judson Beaumont of Vancouver, British Columbia, has designed a range of miniature camper vans on wheels for pets, especially small dogs. The $800 mobile homes have a battery-operated LED light and wireless speakers inside and can even be fitted with personalized license plates.

FARM DOG

Lemon, a Giant Schnauzer, stands on his hind legs to plow potato fields on the farm of his owner, Aleksandr Matytsin, in Omsk, Russia. In addition to learning how to push the plow, Lemon has been trained to plant potatoes, collect the harvested crops, carry buckets of water, and pump water from a tap.

BALANCING BUNNIES

In November 1946, *LIFE* magazine reported on these two acrobatic rabbits that walked on only their front paws. Mr. Walker and Junior were kept as pets by Reginald Freeman, a butcher from London, England. After Mr. Walker, the older rabbit, started getting around on just his front feet, Junior, who had been walking conventionally on all fours, copied him. The rabbits' spinal muscles were underdeveloped and so they found it easier to walk on two legs.

SLIPPERY CUSTOMER

Julius, a 16-ft-long (5-m) albino Burmese python belonging to American-born Jenner Miemietz, learned to open doors in her owner's German apartment by using her body weight to press down on the handles. She could also open the fridge door and drain the bathtub.

HAIR FLOSS

Macaque monkeys living near a Buddhist temple in Lopburi, Thailand, pull out hair from the heads of human visitors and use it between their teeth as dental floss.

WINTER WARMTH

Shortly after a group of ring-tailed lemurs arrived at Tropiquaria Zoo in Somerset, England, staff noticed that the wall heater in the lemur enclosure was repeatedly turned up to maximum during winter. They found that on particularly cold nights the lemurs—named Devine, William, Katrina, Barry, and Julien—were reaching into the heater cage and turning up the thermostat. When the weather warmed up, the lemurs left the thermostat alone.

POTTY PET

Luke Evans from Solihull, England, became so fed up with his nine-month-old cat Salem using a smelly litter tray that he trained the pet to use a human toilet instead. By offering cheese-flavored treats as a reward, it took Luke just a couple of months to train Salem to jump up on the toilet seat. "He can't use the flush yet," said Luke. "He needs more training for that!"

CAT ISLAND

Tonawanda Island, a small 85-acre (35-ha) patch of land in the middle of the Niagara River in New York, has been overrun by hundreds of feral cats. The feline population boom has been caused by people dumping their unwanted cats and kittens on the island.

TREE DISGUISE

The nocturnal common potoo bird of South and Central America pretends to be a tree branch during the day. Perfectly camouflaged, it likes to sit completely still on a broken stump for its daytime rest. To prevent its bright yellow eyes alerting potential predators, it has thin notches in its eyelids that allow it to see even when its eyes are apparently closed.

LETHAL WEAPONS

The great horned owl of North and South America has such powerful talons that it can kill and carry prey more than three times its own body weight—including cats and dogs.

 Your Uploads

FIVE LEGS

Monica Beckner from Saint Joseph, Missouri, sent Ripley's this picture of her two-month-old pet rat Timmy, who was born with five legs. Monica reports that Timmy has no issues with his extra leg and walks around and plays with his brothers and sisters just like a regular rat.

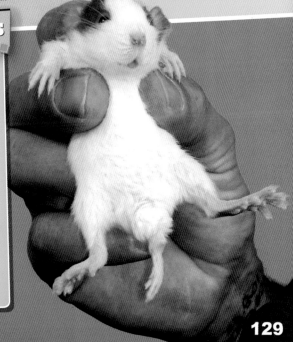

KILLER MANTIS

This amazing photograph captures the moment that a praying mantis killed and ate a hummingbird!

Although it was not much bigger than its prey, the deadly insect—a master of camouflage—used its spiny left foreleg to impale the unsuspecting bird through the chest. After feasting on the bird, the mantis released its lifeless body. The whole scene was captured on camera in the yard of Richard L. Walkup in West Chester, Pennsylvania.

SHELL SHOCK

A tortoise that vanished for ten months was found alive after being dug up by a mechanical digger laying foundations for an extension to his owners' house in Cambridgeshire, England. Paul and Yvette White think Sydney burrowed down into their garden to hibernate in June 2012 after mistaking the unusually cool summer for winter.

FREE RIDE

Randy, a seven-year-old African Gray parrot, escaped from owner Jean Hall's home in Cambridgeshire, England, and was found eight days later, 8 mi (12.87 km) away... perched on the back of a pony!

NOISY BIRD

During courtship the male nightjar, or nighthawk, attracts a mate with a distinctive chirping call that contains 1,900 notes per minute— that's more than 30 notes per second.

BIRDS BEWARE

Crocodiles and alligators use sticks as lures to hunt birds. They gather sticks on their snouts and lie motionless in the water, and when a bird seeks a perch or tries to grab one of the sticks to make a nest, the reptile pounces.

HUMAN SHIELDS

When under close observation by scientists, South African samango monkeys use the scientists as "human shields" to guard against predators such as leopards. Tests showed that the monkeys feel much safer eating on the ground if people are present.

GOLDEN BEETLE

The golden tortoise beetle (*Charidotella sexpunctata*), which is native to the Americas, can quickly change color from metallic gold to a ladybug-like orange with black spots, and back again. The color switch, which occurs during mating or when the beetle is disturbed, is an optical illusion. Tiny valves that control the moisture levels under the beetle's transparent shell cause a change in reflectivity to make the creature appear a different shade.

TIGHTROPE TERRIER

Melissa Millett from London, Ontario, Canada, sent Ripley's this picture of her five-year-old Boston terrier, Bella, who can walk 6 ft (1.8 m) along a narrow tightrope.

She is so adept at tightrope walking that the family plans to construct a 30-ft-long (9-m) tightrope for her. Bella can also scooter and skateboard down ramps, ride a rocking horse, skip, and play basketball and the piano.

MILITARY MONKEYS

The Chinese military has trained macaque monkeys to keep its air force safe by stopping birds from nesting near a major air base. As birds pose a hazard to planes, monkeys are taught to remove nests from treetops. They then leave a scent on the branches that discourages the birds from returning.

SHARK TRANCE

Divers Cameron Nimmo and Mickey Smith remove fish hooks from the jaws of 10-ft-long (3-m) silky sharks off the coast of Jupiter, Florida, by hypnotizing them. The pair can put the sharks into a trance for up to 15 minutes by holding them by the tail and twisting them upside down, paralyzing them in a state called *tonic immobility*.

HIDING PLACE

Oliver, a cat owned by the Waterfield family from Devon, England, hid undetected in the engine of the family's camper van for four days while the vehicle was at a garage for maintenance. The mechanics had thoroughly examined the engine and changed the oil, but had not seen the cat.

GOLDFISH OP

George, a ten-year-old goldfish owned by Pip Joyce from Melbourne, Australia, underwent emergency surgery to remove a tumor from his head—and is now expected to live for another 20 years.

Veterinarian Tristan Rich sedated George in a bucket of water with anesthetic, performed a 45-minute operation, and then gave him injections of antibiotics and painkillers.

CATCH SNATCH

This cheeky whale shark was spotted off the coast of Indonesia taking a bite out of a fisherman's net that was bulging with a fresh catch of fish. Whale sharks in the area regularly follow fishing boats as they work, tearing through nets and swallowing vast quantities of fish in their gaping mouths, which can open up to 5 ft (1.5 m) wide.

TWO-HEADED DOLPHIN

The corpse of a two-headed dolphin was washed up on a beach in Izmir, Turkey, in August 2014. The conjoined dolphin, which had a single tail, was about one year old, 3 ft 3 in (1 m) long, and one pair of its eyes was not fully formed.

STRONG SENSE

African elephants have 2,000 genes related to smell, the most found in any animal—more than twice that of dogs and five times more than in humans.

LONG MEMORIES

Bottlenose dolphins can remember their former friends by their unique whistles even after being separated for as long as 20 years.

JELLYFISH SWARM

Thousands of blue blubber jellyfish washed up on a beach near Brisbane, Australia, in January 2015. When at sea, the swarm stretched for over 160 ft (50 m), covering an area equal to nearly 10 tennis courts.

SPACE PETS

In a unique memorial, Celestis Inc., a company based in Houston, Texas, allows owners to launch their dead pets into space and even "set paw" on the moon. A rocket can carry part of the pet's cremated remains into space and back to Earth (cost $995); or the ashes can orbit Earth before re-entering the atmosphere and vaporizing like a shooting star ($4,995); or they can be taken all the way to the moon ($12,500).

TRUNK CALLS

Elephants use over 70 kinds of vocal sounds and can identify more than 100 other elephants from their calls at a distance of several miles.

OSTRICH CHAOS

An escaped ostrich caused rush-hour traffic chaos on roads in Kent, England, in January 2014 as it ran along a busy highway at speeds of 40 mph (64 kmph), running past at least 20 cars.

BEER CARRIER

Jana Salzman of Reykjavik, Iceland, has trained her collie Atlas to fetch cans of beer. The dog pulls a towel attached to the refrigerator door handle to open it and retrieve an ice-cold beer.

PURR-FECT PAIR

Abdullah Sholeh's friendship with this 10-ft (3-m) long Bengal tiger is an astonishing demonstration of love and trust.

Abdullah, 33, grew close to Mulan Jamilah—a full-grown, six-year-old female tiger—when he became her full-time caregiver at an Islamic school in Malang, Indonesia.

He has cared for the 382-lb (149-kg) tiger since she was a three-month-old cub, and even sleeps beside her with only metal bars separating them. Unafraid to show his love, Abdullah is often seen taking her in his arms, and even allows Mulan to "kiss" him!

WALKING FISH

Scientists at McGill University in Canada discovered that some species of fish that are capable of walking can change their anatomy and learn to walk more efficiently if left out of water for long periods. After being kept permanently on land for less than a year, *polypterus*, an African fish with air-breathing lungs that allow it to walk on land to reach water, mastered the art of walking with its head up and its fins closer to its body. It also developed stronger and more elongated shoulders to support its body while walking.

POWER NAPS

Swainson's thrushes, found in the Americas, sleep for just 10 seconds at a time. When they leave their wintering grounds in Mexico or South America, they travel at night and take hundreds of power naps en route. They are also able to sleep with one eye closed and rest half their brain, while the other eye remains open and the other half of the brain is alert to deal with threats from predators.

SAFE BIRTH

Sawfish, relatives to the shark, give birth to live babies that have sheaths on their saws to protect their mother. Shortly after birth, the fibrous sheath wears away.

FAKE ANTS

Believe it or not, these are not ants on the wings of this fly, but the fly's own extravagant wing markings. *Goniurellia tridens*, a species of fruit fly found in the Middle East and Asia, bears what looks like an ant image on each wing, complete with six legs, two antennae, a head, thorax, and abdomen. It is thought that the insect markings serve to confuse the fly's chief predator, a jumping spider.

SEX FACTOR

The sex of the painted turtle, native to North America, is determined not by its genes, but by the weather outside when it is an embryo. Cold temperatures produce male painted turtles and hot temperatures produce females.

DRUNK DOG

Veterinarians in Melbourne, Australia, saved Charlie the Maltese terrier from certain death by getting him drunk in a 48-hour vodka binge. The dog was suffering from a serious case of ethylene glycol poisoning—a chemical commonly found in brake fluids—the only known antidote for which is alcohol. Via a tube placed through his nose to his stomach, Charlie was given successive doses of vodka over a two-day period. As he began to recover, his owner, Jacinta Rosewarne, reported that he was stumbling around like a drunk.

COVER BLOWN

Less than 0.39 in (10 mm) long, this tiny, pink pygmy seahorse (*Hippocampus bargibanti*) looks startled to have been spotted by British wildlife photographer Alex Mustard while it thought it was camouflaged against its coral home off the coast of Indonesia.

TALENTED PUP

Jiff, a tiny Pomeranian dog from Los Angeles, California, has become an online star thanks to his trick of being able to walk on just his front two paws. He can also walk on his hind legs, on three legs, and even backward in a semi-moonwalk. The skateboard-riding pup has his own Facebook, Twitter, and Instagram profiles and has made several TV and movie appearances, in addition to being in musician Katy Perry's "Dark Horse" video.

WRESTLED GATOR

Nine-year-old James Barney Jr. fought off an attack by a 9-ft-long (2.7-m), 400-lb (182-kg) alligator in Lake Tohopekaliga, Florida, with his bare hands. The alligator bit him three times on the backside and also left 30 tooth and claw marks on his back, stomach, and legs, but he managed to pry its jaws open and force it to let go. Doctors found a tooth in one of the wounds, and James now wears it as a necklace to remind him of his bravery.

SHARK DANCE

California-based, English-born model Hannah Fraser performed a death-defying underwater dance with a school of wild, 16-ft-long (5-m) tiger sharks. Holding her breath for two minutes, she dived 50 ft (15 m) into the Atlantic Ocean in the Bahamas to encounter the sharks, moving the whole time to stop them from attacking. Before the dive, she had said good-bye to her family in case she did not resurface.

EGG-STRAORDINARY

This is not a trick photo—this jelly really does look like a fried egg.

Cotylorhiza tuberculata (or the fried egg jelly) lives in the Mediterranean Sea and gets its common name from its smooth, raised dome surrounded by a gutter-like ring. It can reach 14 in (35 cm) in diameter, but despite this large size, its sting is harmless to humans.

STUFFY NOSE

A 3-in-long (7.5-cm), blood-sucking leech lived in the nose of 24-year-old Daniela Liverani, from Edinburgh, Scotland, for more than a month.

She had started suffering frequent nosebleeds while traveling around southeast Asia, so when she got home and saw something dark poking out of her nose, she dismissed it as congealed blood. However, when she realized it was alive—sometimes protruding as far as her bottom lip—she rushed to the doctor who removed the leech with tweezers. The leech had been nesting in her nostril, feeding on her blood, and if it had not been removed it would probably have worked its way into her brain.

Yuck! 3-in (7.5-cm) leech!

ACTUAL SIZE

CHUTE FALL
An eight-year-old boy survived a six-story fall down a trash chute in Honolulu, Hawaii. The boy had been taking out the trash when he slipped and plunged 60 ft (18 m) down the chute. He was rescued by a neighbor who lowered him a fire hose.

FAT REMEDY
European executioners in the Middle Ages sold human fat from the corpses of those they had just killed as a health remedy for many ailments, from toothaches to arthritis, available at pharmacies as late as the 17th century.

HAPPY ENDING
In 1936, 30-year-old Samuel Ledward from North Wales was pronounced dead by doctors following a motorcycle accident, but on the way to the mortuary, his hand twitched and he went on to make a full recovery. In 2014, he celebrated his 108th birthday.

STABBING PAIN
A 42-year-old man from Trenton, New Jersey, awoke with a strange pain—and was told that he had been sound asleep with a knife in his back for ten hours.

Your Uploads

STRETCHY FLESH

This jaw-dropping picture was sent to Ripley's by Sam Ireland, from Grand Junction, Colorado, who can stretch his uvula (the small dangly piece of flesh in the back of the throat) out to nearly 3.4 in (8.5 cm) long. As you can see, when fully stretched, it reaches just under his chin!

HANDLESS JUGGLER

Jamie Andrew of Glasgow, Scotland, had all of his hands and feet amputated following a French mountaineering accident in 1999. However, despite his loss, he has continued climbing 19,000-ft-high (5,800-m) mountains and has taught himself to juggle.

DRASTIC CURE

The bushmen tribes of South Africa believed until recently that amputating the tips of the fingers could cure sickness.

FOREST FOOD

Lost for 18 days in California's Mendocino National Forest, 72-year-old hiker Gene Penaflor of San Francisco survived by eating squirrels, snakes, and lizards.

A-Z OF BEARDS

New York graphic designer Mike Allen created a new typeface—Alphabeard—out of his own facial hair. Over a period of two years, he sculpted his beard into the shapes of every letter from A to Z. He photographed each letter, shaved, and had to wait two weeks before sculpting the next.

MATH GENIUS

After being punched in the head in a bar near his home in Tacoma, Washington, 31-year-old furniture salesman Jason Padgett came round to find that he had become a math and physics genius. He had shown little academic interest before, but the brain injury he had suffered in the attack unlocked part of his brain that makes everything in his world appear to have a mathematical structure. He has been diagnosed with acquired savant syndrome, where once-ordinary people become skilled in math, art, or music following a brain injury.

WORLD CIRCUS SIDE SHOW
with
CONEY ISLAND

PIP and FLIP
TWINS from YUCATAN

Pip and Flip, real names Elvira and Jenny Lee Snow, were sisters and sideshow performers in the 1920s and 30s.

They suffered from microcephaly, a condition characterized by a small skull, relatively large face, short stature, and limited mental capabilities. Sufferers were often referred to as "pinheads" on the sideshow circuit, and Elvira and Jenny performed as "twins" Pip and Flip, Pipo and Zipo, or Zippo and Flippo in various circuses. It was often claimed they were found in Mexico's Yucatan peninsula, or were wild children from Australia, making them seem even more exotic. In reality, they were born in Georgia— Elvira in 1900, and Jenny Lee 12 years later. In the 1930s, they became the biggest draw at Sam Wagner's World Circus Sideshow at Coney Island, New York. They were paid $75 a week, three times the average American wage at the time, and returned home to Georgia in the off-season. In 1932, Pip and Flip were immortalized in the movie *Freaks*, featuring other famous sideshow characters such as Johnny Eck the half-man and the Earle family of midgets.

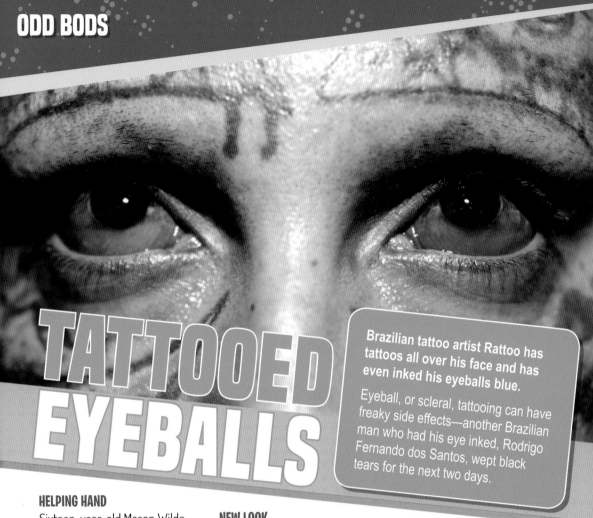

TATTOOED EYEBALLS

Brazilian tattoo artist Rattoo has tattoos all over his face and has even inked his eyeballs blue.

Eyeball, or scleral, tattooing can have freaky side effects—another Brazilian man who had his eye inked, Rodrigo Fernando dos Santos, wept black tears for the next two days.

HELPING HAND

Sixteen-year-old Mason Wilde of Louisburg, Kansas, used a public library's 3-D printer to craft a prosthetic hand for a family friend, nine-year-old Matthew Shields, who was born without fingers on his right hand. Mason spent eight hours printing 20 pieces on the printer, putting them together using screws, nylon string, a drill, and pliers. Matthew's new mechanical hand opens and closes, enabling him to pick up a pen and play catch, and to high-five his brothers.

NEW LOOK

Rene Koiter, a 29-year-old graphic designer from Lake Forest, California, spent 10 months transforming himself into the terrifying Khal Drogo from the TV series *Game of Thrones*. He underwent vigorous workouts—pumping iron to build up his body muscles—grew his hair, and learned to mimic his character's speech and mannerisms. Rene was already fluent in five languages before he added Khal Drogo's fictional tribal dialect.

MOUTH TATTOOS

Until the early 20th century, women of the Ainu people of Japan had mustache-like tattoos inked around their mouths.

BODY HEAT

Tibetan Buddhist monks can raise their body temperature by the power of thought alone, producing enough heat in around an hour to dry cold, wet sheets draped over their shoulders in a frigid room.

HIDDEN SPIDER

Georgian-born singer Katie Melua lived with a small spider inside her ear for a week. She felt a rustling sensation in her ear until a doctor using a micro-vacuum removed the live creepy crawly. She believes the spider had been living in a pair of earbud headphones that she had worn on a flight.

TONGUE SHOOTER

Paralyzed from the neck down by a rugby injury, Victor Morris of West Wales still pursues his hobby of rifle shooting by firing the weapon with his tongue—and regularly beats able-bodied shooters in competitions. He uses a rig made from old car parts that allows him to control the rifle with his chin and pull a special trigger with his tongue.

HAIR COAT

Xiang Renxian, a retired teacher from Chongqing, China, spent 11 years knitting her husband a coat and hat out of her own hair. When her long hair started to fall out as she got older, she began using the hair that she was shedding, weaving it into clothing. She used 116,058 hairs to make the lightweight coat, which weighs just 13.47 oz (382 g).

EYEBALL INSERT

Lucy Luckayanko from New York City paid $3,000 for a one-minute procedure to have a heart-shaped piece of platinum inserted into the white of her right eyeball. The 0.14-in (3.5-mm) stud was placed in a drop of water on her eye membrane and then floated into position.

CRAZY HAIRCUTS

Customers can get more than just a haircut when they go to see Rob "The Original" Ferrel, a hair artist based in San Antonio, Texas—they can have a lifelike portrait of their favorite actor, singer, or sports hero etched onto the back of their head. Using the hair and scalp as his canvas, Rob says he can replicate any design or image in a client's hair—just with standard barber clippers and razors, plus colored eyeliner for the finishing touches.

CHEEK HOLES

Body modification enthusiast Joel Miggler from Küssaberg, Germany, has created giant cheek holes in his face, which give an alarming side view of his teeth.

He has 1.4-in wide (3.6-cm) flesh tunnels in both cheeks, through which he can blow out cigarette smoke, but he has to plug them while eating soup or drinking. He also has to take smaller bites of food than before the tunnels were put in. Joel's first modification was at the age of 13, when he had his earlobes stretched. Now 23, he has 27 piercings, as well as several tattoos and implants, and has even had his buttock branded.

149

WEREWOLF FAME

Moung-Phoset (left), his mother Mah-Phoon, and his sister Mah-Me.

THE SACRED HAIRY FAMILY OF BURMA

"The Sacred Hairy Family from Burma," as they were known, suffered from hypertrichosis, meaning their faces were entirely covered in thick hair. Several generations of the family, headed by Shwe-Maong, lived and performed at the court of the King of Burma in the 19th century, until a revolution drove them from the palace.

They were discovered by an Italian soldier, who suggested they travel to Europe to make their fortune as living exhibits. In 1886, Shwe-Maong's daughter Mah-Phoon, and her son and grandson, all covered in hair, appeared in London to great interest from the public. They later traveled to France, and in the 1890s found fame in the U.S. sideshow of legendary showman P.T. Barnum, where they performed for one year as "unearthly beings," including an

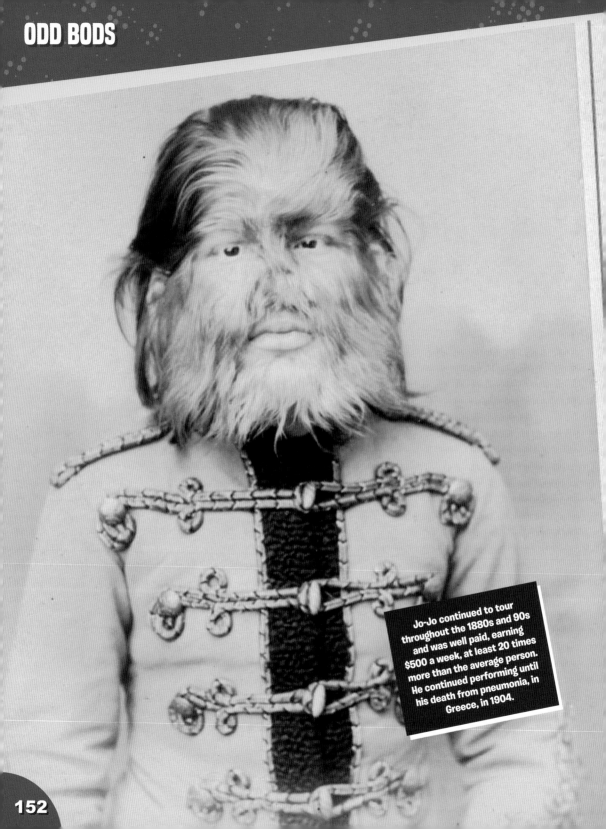

Jo-Jo continued to tour throughout the 1880s and 90s and was well paid, earning $500 a week, at least 20 times more than the average person. He continued performing until his death from pneumonia, in Greece, in 1904.

JO-JO
THE DOG-FACED
BOY

Fedor Jeftichew was born in Russia in 1868. The genetic condition passed on by his father caused thick hair up to 8 in (20 cm) long to grow all over his face.

As a child he was exhibited with his equally hairy father, Adrian, in European sideshows as a cross between a human and a bear.

In Paris and London, Fedor and Adrian were examined by scientists who thought they might be a long-lost race of men. They returned to Russia in the 1870s and, after Adrian died, the orphaned Fedor was thrust back into the spotlight as a solo act. He was then exhibited in St. Petersburg (Russia), Berlin (Germany), and eventually London (England).

In England he came to the attention of the famous American circus impresario P. T. Barnum, who invited then 16-year-old Fedor, nicknamed Jo-Jo, to the U.S.A. in 1884. He was soon performing in the Barnum & Bailey Circus at New York's Madison Square Garden as "Jo-Jo the Dog-faced Boy." Barnum described Fedor as "the human Skye terrier," and claimed that the boy had been captured by a hunter who found him living in the wild in a Russian forest cave, a tall tale designed to make him sound more frightening. Jo-Jo was happy to play along with the story, snarling and growling like a wolf on stage. In reality, he could speak perfectly well in English, Russian, French, and German.

P. T. BARNUM'S
Greatest Show on Earth Perpetually United to the ever Popular and Favorite
GREAT LONDON CIRCUS
Sanger's Royal British Double Menageries and Great International Allied Shows.
P. T. BARNUM, JAMES A. BAILEY & JAS. L. HUTCHINSON, Sole and only Owners.

DOG FACE BOY BEFORE THE CZAR

This advertisement for P.T. Barnum's circus featured a cartoon of Jo-Jo before the Russian Czar, with one of Barnum's agents at the door. In order to boost audiences, Jo-Jo's promoters pretended that he was the property of the Czar of Russia, and claimed that he was soon required to return to him.

153

BEARDED LADY

Harnaam Kaur from Slough, England, has polycystic ovary syndrome, which caused dark hair to appear on her face when she was 11, before spreading to her arms and chest. During her early teens, she waxed twice a week in an attempt to remove her beard and also tried bleaching and shaving. However, she decided to stop cutting her facial hair at 16 after being baptized as a Sikh—a religion that forbids the cutting of body hair. Now 23, she feels proud of her bushy beard, which she says makes her feel more empowered and feminine, and she has received many kind messages of support.

POT (HOLE) LUCK

Ray Lee of Wiltshire, England, was being rushed to a hospital with crippling chest pains and a potentially fatal heart rhythm of 186 beats per minute when the ambulance hit a large pothole in the road—and the resultant jolt caused his heart rate to plummet immediately to a safe 60 beats per minute.

POOP REWARD

A laboratory in Medford, Massachusetts, offered people $40 a day for their poop! The stools were used for fecal transplants to fight the superbug *C. difficile*, which kills 14,000 Americans every year.

IN DENIAL

Blind people with Anton-Babinski syndrome refuse to believe that they cannot see. The condition is believed to be caused by a rare form of brain damage and most often occurs following a stroke or head injury.

HEAVY SLEEPER

Morag Fisher of Lincolnshire, England, broke eight bones, including her neck, spine, nose, and jaw, when she fell down a flight of stairs while sleepwalking—but still did not wake up. She was found fast asleep lying in a pool of blood with life-threatening injuries. She regained consciousness only when paramedics woke her in the ambulance on the way to the hospital.

FALL GUY

Tom Stilwell, a 20-year-old Englishman, fell from the 15th floor of an apartment block in Auckland, New Zealand and, despite breaking several bones, survived to tell the tale. He plummeted 13 floors before landing on the roof of an adjacent building, which probably saved his life.

TOWERING NOSES

Students in China have been paying up to $10,000 to have their noses reconstructed to resemble the shape of the Eiffel Tower. The iconic Paris landmark's elegant curves are viewed as the ideal profile for ambitious young Chinese people.

232 TEETH

A normal adult mouth contains 32 teeth—but 17-year-old Ashik Gavai from a village in Mumbai, India, underwent a seven-hour operation to remove an unbelievable 232 teeth from his mouth. He had been complaining about a painful swelling, and when doctors operated they found a complex composite odontoma—a benign tumor deep in his lower jaw that contained hundreds of small pearl-like white teeth. After chiseling out the tumor and the tiny teeth, they still left him with 28 ordinary teeth.

KEN LOOKALIKE

Rodrigo Alves, a Brazilian air steward living in the U.K., has spent $150,000 in the past ten years on cosmetic surgery to transform himself into a real-life Ken doll. He has had over 20 procedures, including nose jobs, abdominal and pectoral implants, calf shaping, and laser comb hair treatment.

ANCIENT ANATOMY

FEMALE

Housed in two glass cases in the crypt of the Museo Cappella Sansevero in Naples, Italy, are the real skeletons of a man and a pregnant woman, showing their artery and vein systems in perfect detail.

These "Anatomical Machines" were made in 1763–64 by Palermo doctor Giuseppe Salerno, whose process of applying materials such as beeswax, iron wire, and silk to the bodies preserved their circulatory systems for 250 years. The skeletons were built on the orders of the Prince of Sansevero, who may have had two of his servants killed to provide the bodies for the models.

SURPRISE ADDITION

Expecting triplets, Kimberly Fugate instead gave birth to identical quadruplets in Jackson, Mississippi, beating odds of 13 million to one. The fourth girl had gone undetected by ultrasound imaging throughout the pregnancy.

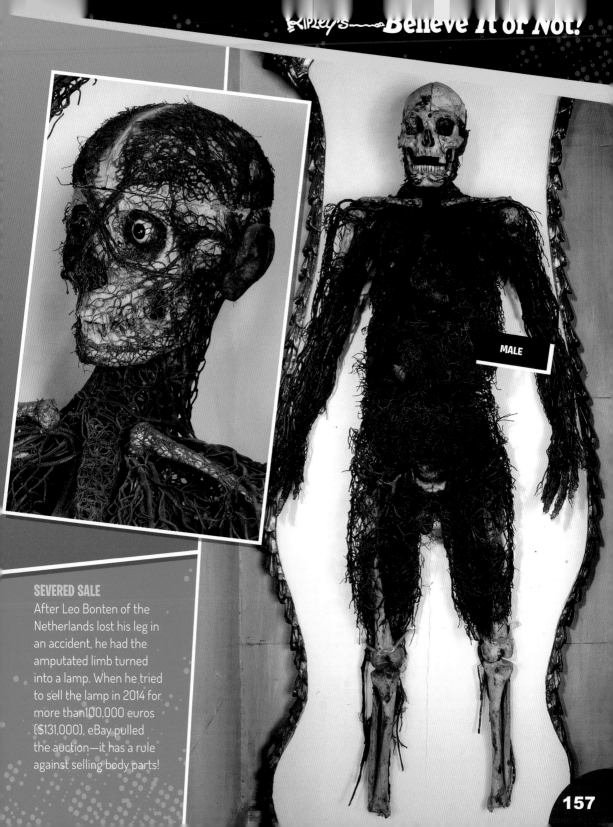

MALE

SEVERED SALE

After Leo Bonten of the Netherlands lost his leg in an accident, he had the amputated limb turned into a lamp. When he tried to sell the lamp in 2014 for more than 100,000 euros ($131,000), eBay pulled the auction—it has a rule against selling body parts!

LITTLE STAR

One of Australia's greatest contortionists, Little Verlie first performed onstage in 1911 at the age of six and went on to amaze audiences by twisting her body into a series of complex poses.

Her speciality was a one-legged skipping rope dance, which she performed while the other leg was twisted around her neck. She was adopted by Brisbane vaudeville trainer Lilian Ross, who later also adopted a young boy, Wee Darrell, to form a child contortionist double act. Verlie eventually tired of the arrangement and ran away in 1922, never to perform again. She never lost her flexibility and could still walk on her hands when she was in her fifties.

SAMURAI BARBER

Nguyen Hoang Hung, a barber in Da Nang City, Vietnam, cuts customers' hair with a razor-sharp Samurai sword traditionally used by Japanese warriors to behead an enemy. After practicing with the sword on wigs for four years, he can now cut beautiful hairstyles in minutes. He says the sword is especially good for creating a light, feathered look.

PERSONALITY CHANGE

After suffering a stroke in 1989, chiropractor Jon Sarkin of Gloucester, Massachusetts, woke up to find that he had suddenly acquired a talent for painting. He previously had no flair for art at all but has gone on to become a prolific painter whose works sell for more than $10,000 each.

MELODIC MANIA

Suffering from the medical condition tinnitus, Susan Root of Essex, England, endured an earworm of Patti Page's rendition of the song "How Much Is That Doggie in the Window?" non-stop for four years—when, just as mysteriously, she switched to hearing Judy Garland's "Somewhere Over the Rainbow."

MILITARY MUSTACHES

Mustaches were compulsory for British Army soldiers until 1916—and shaving the upper lip could result in a court martial.

NO BLOOD

Maisy Vignes from County Waterford, Ireland, miraculously made a full recovery despite being born without any blood. When she was born six weeks premature in 2009, instead of blood she had just a thin, plasma substance in her veins because her mother Emma had absorbed all the blood during pregnancy. Maisy was not expected to survive but, against all the odds, four years later she was able to start school.

TALL TEEN

Rumeysa Gelgi of Safranbolu, Turkey, at age 17 stands over 7 ft (2.1 m) tall. She also has 10-in (24.5-cm) hands and 12-in (30-cm) feet, meaning that she has to get her shoes custom-made in the U.S.A. She must use a walker to get around because she is so tall she finds it difficult to keep her balance. Doctors believe her height is due to a rare genetic disorder called Weaver syndrome, which causes rapid growth, but she is now not expected to get any taller.

YOUNG HERO

When Coy Jumper suffered a stroke and fell into deep water near Swansea, South Carolina, his ten-year-old granddaughter Cara leaped in and saved him from drowning. She then dragged her 230-lb (104-kg) grandfather ¼ mi (0.4 km) through the woods, got into his car, and drove him 3 mi (4.8 km) back home to safety.

SONIC GENE

There is a gene in the human body called sonic hedgehog. It plays a vital role in ensuring that all our limbs and organs are in the correct place.

Your Uploads

FLYING TOOTH

Meredith Cahill from Cherry Hill, New Jersey, sent Ripley's this picture of a tooth that flew out of her nose when she blew it! Her dentist had noticed the canine tooth in her upper gum five years earlier, and it must have worked its way from the gum into her nasal passage.

Since giving up his job as a heavy equipment mechanic in the late 1990s, former Marine Mick Dodge has lived like a wild man in the Hoh Rain Forest near Forks, Washington, bartering for essentials and sleeping in tree stumps.

He often climbs the region's mountains barefoot, and to illustrate his love of the environment, he had images of tree roots tattooed on his feet. He eats whatever he finds on his travels, including maggots, an elk killed by a cougar, and a sea lion he found washed up on a beach.

WILD LIFE

Hodge's tree root tattoos show he is one with the forest.

3-D HEART

When 14-month-old Roland Lian Cung Bawi of Owensboro, Kentucky, needed urgent heart surgery, his life was saved thanks to a super-sized 3-D printout of his heart. Engineers at the University of Louisville teamed up with Kosair Children's Hospital to create a three-piece reproduction of the boy's heart 1 ½ times its actual size, which enabled surgeons to develop a detailed plan and complete the repair in a single operation.

DEAD BODIES

The Monroe Moosnick Medical and Science Museum in Lexington, Kentucky, has a dissectible life-sized wax figure of a woman that was created by casting organs and tissues from 200 human corpses.

SKELETON REPLACEMENT

The average 70-year-old human has grown and replaced seven whole skeletons during their lifetime.

AXE HORROR

Sheldon Mpofu from West Yorkshire, England, cheated death by millimeters after the sharp head of a pickaxe entered his skull. He was working in his garden when he swung the pickaxe, but on the way down it hit a washing line and the pointed end of the axe flew into his forehead. Luckily the axe head narrowly missed his brain and lodged in a sinus—an empty space in the skull.

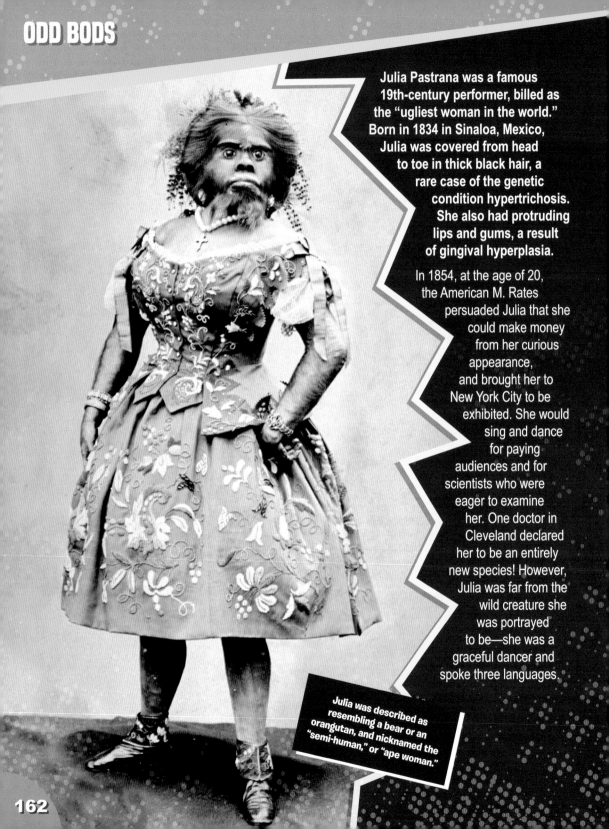

Julia Pastrana was a famous 19th-century performer, billed as the "ugliest woman in the world." Born in 1834 in Sinaloa, Mexico, Julia was covered from head to toe in thick black hair, a rare case of the genetic condition hypertrichosis. She also had protruding lips and gums, a result of gingival hyperplasia.

In 1854, at the age of 20, the American M. Rates persuaded Julia that she could make money from her curious appearance, and brought her to New York City to be exhibited. She would sing and dance for paying audiences and for scientists who were eager to examine her. One doctor in Cleveland declared her to be an entirely new species! However, Julia was far from the wild creature she was portrayed to be—she was a graceful dancer and spoke three languages.

Julia was described as resembling a bear or an orangutan, and nicknamed the "semi-human," or "ape woman."

BILLED AS:

THE UGLIEST WOMAN IN THE WORLD

In New York, Julia met the showman Theodore Lent, who became both her new manager and her husband. Lent took Julia on a European tour, performing shows from London to Moscow, promoting her as a mysterious "nondescript."

In 1859, Julia became pregnant and, while in Moscow, gave birth to a boy, Theodore, who was also covered in hair. Tragically, he did not survive, and Julia passed away soon afterward. This should have put an end to Julia's remarkable journey, but after Lent had sold her body to St. Petersburg University to be mummified, along with young Theodore, he decided that the show must go on, and took the preserved corpses back on the road.

Mother and son spent the next few decades being exhibited at sideshows around Europe, finding their way to Norway in the 1920s, where they were displayed until the 1970s, before being looted by fairground vandals. Sadly, Theodore was lost, but Julia was rescued by the Oslo University Hospital, where she was placed in storage until 2013, when her story took one more incredible twist. Following a longstanding campaign from a Mexican artist, Julia's body was repatriated to her hometown in Sinaloa, where she was finally laid to rest in a Catholic funeral, more than 150 years after her death.

The bodies of Julia and her son were preserved and toured across Europe.

6 FINGERS

Spanning four generations, all 14 members of the Silva family from Brasilia, Brazil, were born with six fingers on each hand as a result of a genetic condition known as polydactyly.

Far from being downhearted, they have learned to use their condition to their advantage. For example, 14-year-old Joao de Assis da Silva has become a talented guitarist with the help of his extra fingers.

STRETCHY SKIN!

Jorge Iván Latorre Robles has some very unusual talents—he can stretch his skin, pop out his eyes, and dislocate his joints.

The 24-year-old from Puerto Rico, known by his friends as "Chicle" (meaning "chewing gum" in Spanish), didn't discover his talents until he was 18, when he was breakdancing and found that his flexibility meant that he could perform tricks unlike the other dancers.

Jorge was diagnosed with Ehlers-Danlos syndrome, a condition that affects his body's production of collagen (which provides strength and structure to the skin), causing the skin to loosen.

Jorge embraces his stretchy skin and impressive flexibility, frequently performing for children and adults alike.

Jorge mostly uses his talents to entertain people, performing at theaters, working as a street performer and volunteering at the hospital entertaining sick children, who often think he is a superhero with stretchy skin powers.

Jorge has been a fan of Ripley's since he was young, when he was into "weird" stuff, and felt he finally became a part of the Ripley family when he discovered his skills. He loves Ripley's so much he said he could happily live in a Ripley's Believe It or Not! Odditorium!

Don't try this at home! Jorge's bendy joints make it easy for him to cram himself into a suitcase.

How stretchy is your skin? Gently pinch and pull the skin on the back of your hand. Squish your face together while looking in the mirror! How do you compare to Jorge?

169

SEVERED HAND

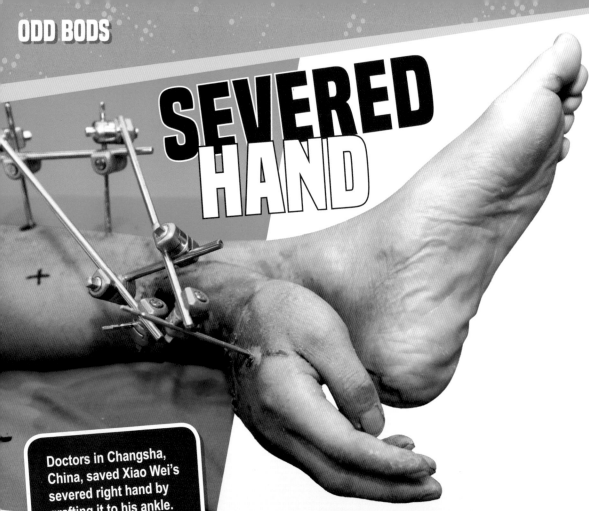

Doctors in Changsha, China, saved Xiao Wei's severed right hand by grafting it to his ankle.

He lost the hand in a work accident, but could not have it reattached to his arm immediately. Instead, surgeons grafted it to his left ankle and used the blood supply from the arteries in his leg to keep the hand alive. A month later, the doctors were able to replant the hand back in its rightful place on the end of his arm.

EYEBALL TATTOO

Fifty years after suffering a serious eye injury as a child, which left his iris looking permanently white and cloudy, New Yorker William Watson had the damage repaired with an eyeball tattoo. The hour-long procedure, which involved injecting colored ink into his left eye, was performed by a doctor—and a tattoo artist who practiced beforehand on a grape.

DISTINCTIVE SMELL

No two people's body odor smells exactly the same—apart from identical twins whose smell is too similar to differentiate.

LINCOLN HAIR

A lock of hair that was removed from Abraham Lincoln's head by Surgeon General Joseph K. Barnes shortly after the President was fatally shot on April 14, 1865, sold at auction for $25,000 in Dallas, Texas, in 2015.

ARM DOODLES

Keith Anderson from Peterborough, Ontario, Canada, has covered his arms in tattoos of his son Kai's doodles and drawings. He started inking the images onto his skin in 2008 when Kai was just four years old, and has added a new image every year since. To make sure there's enough room on his body to keep going, Keith has asked his son to draw smaller pictures!

STRANGER DELUSION

People with Capgras syndrome are convinced that all friends and family are imposters, but anyone with Fregoli syndrome believes just the opposite—that all strangers are really friends and family members in disguise. A woman in Pittsburgh, Pennsylvania, who had Fregoli syndrome following head trauma from a car accident told hospital staff that a fellow patient was her boyfriend, that a visiting social worker was her sister, and that her mother was posing as one of the nurses.

THIRD SET

Kristian Vollick of Arizona tells Ripley's that his great-grandmother Edith West grew her third set of teeth at the age of 102. Whereas most people only get two sets of teeth in a lifetime, Edith, who was born in 1911, started losing her second set when she was 98, only to grow more teeth four years later.

IMAGINARY STARDOM

People suffering from the medical condition Truman Show delusion—named after the 1998 Jim Carrey movie—believe that they are the stars of an imaginary TV show and are being filmed at all times. There have been more than 40 recorded cases in the world.

DANCING PLAGUE

In July 1518, more than 400 people in Strasbourg, France, mysteriously began dancing for days without rest until many died from heart attacks, strokes, or exhaustion. No explanation has ever been given for "The Dancing Plague." After about a month, it stopped as suddenly as it had started.

PUSH-UPS

Georgian Corporal Temur Dadiani lost both his legs in an explosion in Afghanistan in 2011, but, by balancing on his arms only, the double amputee can perform 36 push-ups in just 38 seconds.

TAPEWORM TORMENT

When Tain Liao, from Guangzhou, China, complained of stomach ache and itchy skin, an X-ray revealed that almost his entire body was infected with hundreds of tapeworms. He is thought to have eaten sashimi that was contaminated with the parasites' eggs.

CLOWN FACE

Richie the Barber from West Hollywood, California, has the face of a clown tattooed over his own face.

Tattoos of big red eyebrows arch above the real ones he shaves daily, and he has a clown's red-nose tattoo, plus oversized red lips that protrude beneath his own mustache. The rest of his face is inked blue, including his ears and eyelids. On the sides of his head he is growing Bozo the Clown hair, which he has dyed bright red, and he has a tattoo of Bozo on the back of his head. He also has a third eye tattooed on his face, and the words "Good" and "Luck" inked on his eyelids.

BROKEN BONES

Darryle See, 22, survived with just a few broken bones after being hit full-on by a Chicago-bound Amtrak train travelling at 110 mph (177 kmph). The impact, near Michigan City, Indiana, was so powerful it hurled him 20 ft (6 m) from the tracks.

BRAIN WORM

Doctors in Chengdu, China, removed a 6-in (15-cm) parasitic worm from the brain of a 60-year-old man suffering from headaches. They blamed the man's condition on eating uncooked frogs and eels, which contain parasites that can enter the human body.

HORNED MAN

Li Zhibing, 62, from Shiyan, China, has had a cutaneous horn growing out of his neck for more than 30 years. The horn first appeared in 1980 and grows so quickly that his friends have to saw it off twice a year. He once let it grow to 6 in (15 cm), but found that it made his neck swollen and gave him a fever.

EARLY BIRTH

While being driven to a hospital in Plymouth, Devon, England, by her husband, Vicki McAteer gave birth to baby daughter Niamh in the leg of her jogging pants.

SKIN LARVAE

After being bitten three times by mosquitoes on a trip to Belize, Harvard entomologist Piotr Naskrecki found that the bites contained botfly larvae. He removed one of the larvae with a suction device, but then deliberately allowed the other two maggots to grow under his skin for two months and then filmed the moment they finally crawled out of his body.

SELF-SURGERY

Attacked by a shark that clamped its jaws around his leg while he was standing in water fishing near Invercargill, New Zealand, doctor James Grant fought off the fish, sewed up the wounds with a first-aid kit, and then went to the pub for a beer.

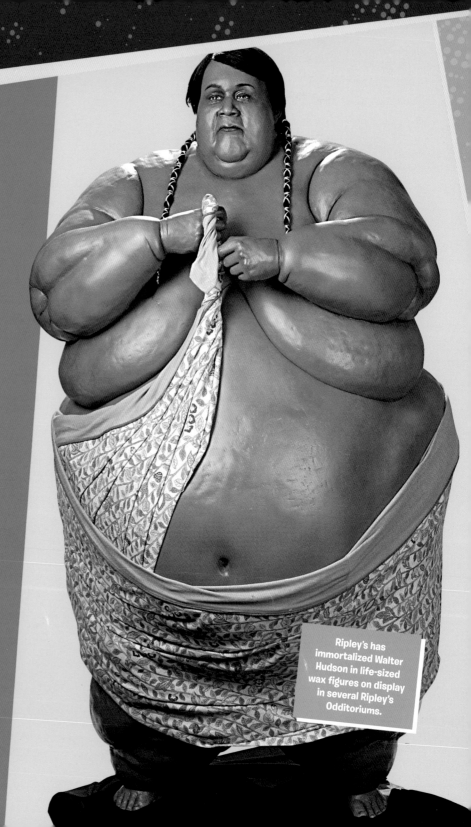

WALTER HUDSON

Ripley's has immortalized Walter Hudson in life-sized wax figures on display in several Ripley's Odditoriums.

Walter helps decorate the tree in his home on Christmas 1987. It was the first time he had been in his living room for 16 years.

Walter Hudson of Hempstead, New York, was one of the largest men ever to have lived. In 1987, at the age of 42, his weight was at least 1,200 lb (544 kg), heavier than an average horse, and he was easily the biggest man on Earth at the time.

Walter's insatiable appetite led to his ballooning to 125 lb (57 kg) by the age of six. At age 15 he weighed as much as two grown men and rarely left his house. By the 1980s, his waist was 103 in (261 cm) in circumference and, at 55 in (140 cm), his legs were wider than most people's waists.

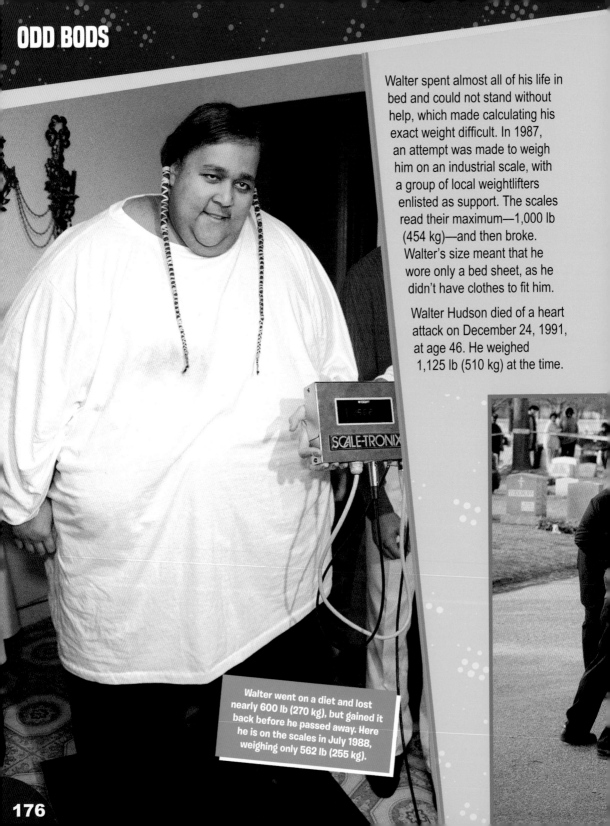

Walter spent almost all of his life in bed and could not stand without help, which made calculating his exact weight difficult. In 1987, an attempt was made to weigh him on an industrial scale, with a group of local weightlifters enlisted as support. The scales read their maximum—1,000 lb (454 kg)—and then broke. Walter's size meant that he wore only a bed sheet, as he didn't have clothes to fit him.

Walter Hudson died of a heart attack on December 24, 1991, at age 46. He weighed 1,125 lb (510 kg) at the time.

Walter went on a diet and lost nearly 600 lb (270 kg), but gained it back before he passed away. Here he is on the scales in July 1988, weighing only 562 lb (255 kg).

WALTER'S DAILY DIET

Walter generally consumed up to 20,000 calories a day—that's more than the suggested WEEKLY intake for a normal person. This would typically consist of:

Two boxes of sausages
12 eggs
Eight hamburgers
Eight portions of fries
18 cupcakes
Eight baked potatoes

One loaf of bread
Two chickens
1 lb (454 g) of bacon
Three ham steaks
6 quarts (6 l) of soda

Walter was buried in a 4-ft-6-in-wide (1.4-m) casket made from 800 lb (363 kg) of reinforced steel. It required a crane to maneuver.

FAN FAVES

CARDBOARD BOX OFFICE

A couple in Australia have recreated dozens of their favorite movie scenes using cardboard boxes and everyday junk.

When Leon Mackie, Lilly Lang, and their baby son Orson moved from New Zealand to Sydney, they were left with a lot of boxes. So the movie buffs started Cardboard Box Office, where each week they would build a film set from old household materials and a few toys, and reenact iconic scenes, usually with Orson taking center stage. When they posted the results online, the response was overwhelming.

Bubbalien

Wah Wars

Kid Kong

The Dark
Knighty-Knight

The Little Lebowski

181

Raiding their own wardrobes for costumes and building cheap props and sets, they tackled everything from *The Lion King* to *Pulp Fiction*. They built a cardboard rocket to represent *Apollo 13* and a great white shark for *Jaws*; the creature in *Alien* is a sock puppet with plastic teeth and the blood is made from red yarn.

As Orson is the star of the show, all of their works have baby-related titles, like *Kid Kong*, *Parents of the Caribbean*, *Fleece Willy*, *The Lord of the Teething Rings*, and *The Good, The Bad and The Dribbly*.

The Lion Kid

Lord of the Teething Rings

The Birdies

Castababy

E.TED

183

"Houston, We have a poopy..."

"You're Gonna Need a Bigger Baby..."

Ripley's ASK

How do you choose the scenes you want to show? We just think of movies and, if they fit the requirements, we make them. Generally, the films need to be well known. They also need to have an iconic set, creature, or vehicle.

Where do you create the scenes? In our house, but house lighting is terrible for photos because it nearly always comes from above and doesn't spread very far. We use lamps to highlight faces and shadowed parts of the sets. We now have a lot of lamps.

Is baby Orson easy to work with? Yeah, he's great. He never really makes a fuss. *Star Wars* was probably the most challenging. We needed Orson to look serious, but he kept laughing.

How long does each scene take to set up? It ranges from one to five hours, depending on how many props need to be made and the complexity of the set. The one that's taken the longest to set up to date has probably been *The Dark Knight*, as we had to make each of the buildings in "Gotham City" by hand. It took hours.

Which is your favorite scene? Probably *Lord of the Rings*. The set, costumes, and props all came together really well. I also especially like the lighting in that scene.

Parents of the Caribbean

Walk, Forrest, Walk!

Goonies Never Say Cry!

FAMOUS FINGERS

Comedian Mel Brooks left his mark at the TCL Chinese Theater in Hollywood on September 2014, where the hand and footprints of legendary celebrities are immortalized in concrete on the sidewalk.

The director of *Blazing Saddles* made sure his own prints would stand out by arriving with a fake sixth finger attached to his left hand, a trick that went unnoticed until he left a six-fingered imprint in the wet concrete.

Mel Brooks

SEPT. 8 2014

VADER BURNER

Star Wars fan Alex Dodson from Barnsley, England, turns scrap metal into movie-themed fireplaces. His first creation was Darth Vader, and after getting a positive reaction on the Internet, the technology teacher is now making the fireplaces to order, using 42-lb (19-kg) metal gas bottles. In addition to recreating Darth Vader's iconic mask, the self-taught welder turns scrap metal into the "minions" from *Despicable Me* and *Star Wars* stormtroopers.

FACEBOOK RESCUE

When 44-year-old John All, a professor of geography and environmental studies at Western Kentucky University, fell through an icy crevasse on a Himalayan glacier at 19,600 ft (6,000 m), his life was saved because he alerted friends on Facebook. Professor All dislocated a shoulder and broke five ribs, a knee, and an elbow in the fall, but still managed to post on the online page of the American Climber Science Program: "Please call Global Rescue. John broken arm, ribs, internal bleeding. Fell 70 ft crevasse. Climbed out. Himlung camp 2. Please hurry." Shocked members of the group alerted rescuers and 19 hours later, having posted two further messages and crawled back to his tent, John was taken to a hospital in Kathmandu, Nepal.

MINI ME

To attract the attention of potential employers, freelance photographer Jens Lennartsson from Malmo, Sweden, enhanced his résumé by mailing out 400 10-in-high (25-cm) plastic models of himself.

HIGH HEELS

High-heeled shoes known as chopines, some 18 in (45 cm) high, were worn in 16th-century Venice by women as a sign of status—and also to help keep their feet dry when the Venetian canals flooded.

SMURF LOVER

Karen Bell from Ayrshire, Scotland, has been collecting Smurf figurines and stickers for more than 30 years—and now has about 5,000 pieces of Smurf memorabilia.

CONGRESS LIBRARY

The U.S. Library of Congress has approximately 838 mi (1,348.63 km) of shelf space, holding more than 151 million items.

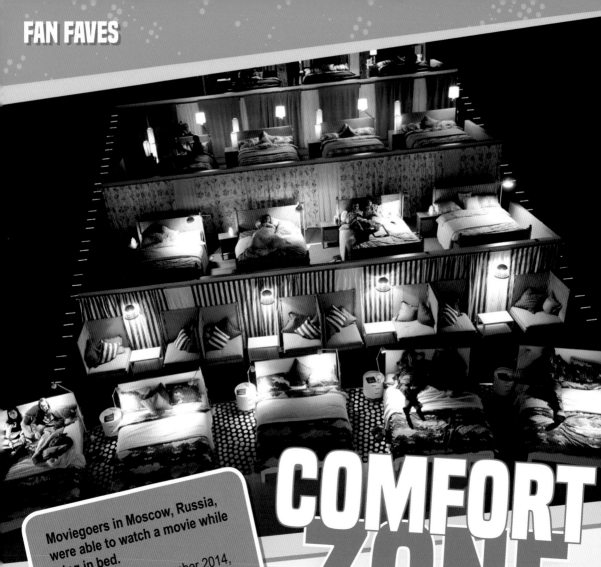

COMFORT ZONE

Moviegoers in Moscow, Russia, were able to watch a movie while lying in bed.

For two weeks in December 2014, furniture retailer IKEA ripped out all the traditional seats in one of the theaters at the Kinostar De Lux Multiplex in the suburb of Khimki and replaced them with its own furniture, including 17 double beds. The bed sheets were changed by the staff after each screening.

SELFIE SPREE

Mark E. Miller and Ethan Hethcote took 355 selfies in an hour at South Beach, Miami, Florida—with a different person in each picture.

DANCING BANANA

When she was 15, future Hollywood star Megan Fox had a job where she used to dance in the street wearing a giant banana costume to attract customers to a smoothie bar in Florida.

PROFITABLE LUNCH

During one lunch in 1994, Pixar creatives John Lasseter, Pete Docter, and Joe Ranft came up with the ideas that would eventually become the hit movies *A Bug's Life*, *Finding Nemo*, *Monsters Inc.*, and *WALL-E*.

BABY SELFIES

A new crib mobile toy allows babies to take selfies and post the results on Facebook and Twitter. New Born Fame, created by Dutch designer Laura Cornet, features soft toys shaped as a Facebook logo and a Twitter bird, which automatically take a picture or video when the youngster reaches for them.

MAGNETIC SHOES

Inspired by comic book character Magneto, inventor Colin Furze from Lincolnshire, England, created a pair of magnetic shoes that enable him to walk upside-down along metal ceilings. He built the magnets in the shoes using a microwave transformer, with one of the coils removed, and hooked it up to a car battery. Then, he placed the transformer on a shoe-shaped plate and clamped his foot to it before attaching straps to the shoes with switches, which power the flow of electricity and allow him to walk. His only fear was that if there were a sudden power outage while he was walking on the ceiling, he would fall off.

DOG SHOW

Every Thursday at 3 p.m., BBC London 94.9 presents *Barking at the Moon*, the world's only weekly radio show for dogs. It is hosted by dog lovers Jo Good and Anna Webb and their dogs Matilda (an English bulldog) and Molly (a miniature bull terrier). The show has over half a million listeners, from as far away as Hawaii and Australia.

DONKEY CHARGERS

To stay connected to the Internet, village herdsmen in Izmir, Turkey, strap solar panels to the backs of their donkeys and use them as mobile charging points. The farmers stay online during their long overland journeys by plugging their laptop or phone charger into the panels, which can produce up to 7 kilowatts of energy—enough to charge more than 1,000 cell phones.

GOPHER BONES

Kim Kowalski from Pueblo, Colorado, made this ornate pendant from the pelvis of a gopher that a weasel had killed in her backyard. The back of the pendant is decorated with a butterfly wing and a dead finch foot that she obtained from a local aviary. In addition to using animal bones, she also makes unique items of jewelry from bugs and dried plants.

ODD TOGETHER NOW

The Ringling Brothers and Barnum & Bailey Circus ran a successful sideshow in the 1920s and 30s featuring some of the most famous oddities and performers of the era.

Each year, the renowned New York photographer Edward J. Kelty, who specialized in capturing images of the circus, would gather together the sideshow acts, at what he called the "Congress of Freaks," for a photograph at Madison Square Garden, New York City. The 1927 ensemble included more than 35 bizarre characters, including circus legends such as Major Mite the dwarf, giant Jack Earle, and Lionel the dog-faced boy.

CONGRESS of FREAKS WITH

RINGLING BROTHERS AND BARNUM & BAILEY COMBINED CIRCUS.
SEASON — 1927

Image courtesy of Derin Bray American Art & Antiques

1. Lady Olga, Bearded Lady
Born Jane Barnell in North Carolina in 1871 with a hairy face, Lady Olga was sold to a showman by her mother and toured with sideshows from a very young age. She performed in at least 25 circuses, and appeared alongside other sideshow stars in the 1932 movie *Freaks*. Despite her unconventional appearance, she married four times.

2. Daisy Earles, the Dancing Doll Family Harry, Gracie, Daisy, and Tiny were born Kurt, Frieda, Hilda, and Elly Schneider in early 20th-century Germany. Gracie and Harry were taken to California by Bert W. Earles, where they joined a Wild West Show in 1916, changing their names and taking Earles' name. Later joined by the rest of the family, they performed with the Ringling Brothers and Barnum & Bailey Circus for 30 years, riding horses and singing and dancing. All four appeared as Munchkins in the 1939 film *The Wizard of Oz*, and Harry and Gracie played significant parts in *Freaks*.

3. Giant Jim Tarver Jim Tarver, born 1885 in Texas, was described as being 8 ft 6 in (2.6 m) tall, but 7 ft 3 in (2.2 m) is more likely. He was billed as the "tallest man in the world" until Jack Earle (see 17) visited the sideshow and discovered he was even taller!

4. Baron Paucci Baron Paucci, who stood only 27 in (69 cm) tall, was born in Sicily, Italy, in 1894. He performed at Lilliputia—a town full of little people—in Coney Island, New York, for 15 years. He was infamous for his drinking and outrageous behavior, which eventually led to him leaving Lilliputia and joining the Ringling Circus sideshow. Baron Paucci married a woman of normal size, but their marriage was short-lived.

5. & 15. Carlson Sisters Flo and Dot Carlson were billed as the "Boxing Fat Girls" and would spar on stage.

6. "Twisto the Human Knot" Contortionist

7. Lillian Maloney, Fairy Airy Lillian Maloney was a glamorous albino Irish woman, characterized by her bright hair and pale skin. At the time, albinism was not a well-known condition and was regarded as a curiosity.

8. Clico, "The Wild Dancing South African Bushman" Clico was a South African tribesman whose real name was Franz Taibosh. His stage name was inspired by the clicks he used in his native language. Franz's talent for dancing was noticed by Irish settler, Paddy Hepston, who was working in South Africa, and he took Clico to England in 1915 to work as a dancer. He was a sensation and soon caught the attention of American impresarios. He joined Sam Gumpertz's Coney Island sideshow before touring with the Ringling Brothers for many years.

9. Tiny Earles, the Dancing Doll Family (see 2)

10. Miss Londy Eleanor Wagner
Londy Eleanor Wagner was over 7 ft (2.1 m) tall, although she was sometimes billed as being more than 8 ft (2.4 m) tall. She performed at Coney Island, New York, and was known as the "Viennese Giantess," the "German Giantess," and "Miss Londy."

11. Major Mite Standing 26 in (0.7 m) tall and weighing only 20 lb (9 kg), Major Mite was one of the most famous midget performers of the era. The Ringling Brothers and Barnum & Bailey Circus signed him up in 1923, when he was just ten years old, and he starred in the sideshow for more than 25 years. As well as his successful circus career, Major Mite (whose real name was Clarence Chesterfield Howerton) was one of the smallest Munchkins in the movie *The Wizard of Oz* (1939), and had several other Hollywood roles. He died in 1975, aged 62 years old.

12. Koo-Koo the "Bird Girl" Koo-Koo was born Minnie Woolsey in Georgia in 1880, was part of the Ringling Brothers circus sideshow for many years. (See page 26 to read more of her story.)

13. Haig, the Elastic Skin Man

14. The Mighty Ajax, Sword Swallower Joseph Milana was born in Washington, D.C., in 1886, and enjoyed a long career. As a young man he toured with Buffalo Bill's Wild West Show and once performed for King George V of England. He spent years at the Dreamland Circus sideshow at Coney Island and was only with the Ringling Circus for the 1927 season.

15. Carlson Sister (see 5)

16. Harry Earles, the Dancing Doll Family (see 2)

17. Giant Jack Earle Jack Earle, born in 1906, stood 7 ft 7 in (2.3 m) tall, and had a career in the movies until the tumor that caused his extreme height resulted in problems with his eyesight. He performed with the sideshow from the 1920s to 1940.

18. Gracie Earles, the Dancing Doll Family (see 2)

19. Miss Kitty, the Armless Wonder Kitty Smith was born into poverty in Chicago in 1882, and both her arms were amputated at the age of nine after being badly burned. The young Kitty learned to draw, selling her autobiography and drawings to support herself, and eventually found work on the sideshow circuit, performing at Coney Island and the Ringling Circus sideshow.

20. Professor Henri, India-Rubber Man Professor Henri's real name was Clarence H. Alexander. He spent more than 20 years in sideshows as a contortionist who could reportedly stretch his neck 7 in (18 cm) and his limbs out by 12 in (30 cm). Tragically, he killed himself on stage because of his unrequited love for the tattooed lady Miss Mae Vandermark (see 23).

21. Freddie Esele, the Armless Wonder Born without arms in New York in 1888, Freddie was a fixture on the circus sideshow circuit for many years.

22. Jolly Irene Irene was said to weigh almost 700 lb (318 kg) and also performed at Coney Island.

23. Miss Mae Vandermark, Tattooed Woman Born in Pennsylvania, Mae Vandermark Patton trained as a stenographer, but moved to New York in search of adventure. She befriended the tattooed lady Miss Pictoria (see 33), who persuaded her to join the profession, and "Professor" Wagner of the Bowery, New York, completed her full-body tattoos in less than a year. She got a job at Coney Island before landing the role with the Ringling Brothers, marrying a man in the circus business and spending more than 30 years on the road.

24. Unknown

25. & 26. Sadie and Rosie Anderson, "The Spotted Women" African Americans with vitiligo, which causes the skin to turn white in places, were often exhibited as "leopard" or "spotted" people. Sadie, Rosie, and other members of the Anderson family were exhibited in sideshows from an early age, and both girls had long careers with touring circuses.

27. Lionel the Dog-Faced Boy Lionel, the Lion-Faced Man, or Dog-Faced Boy, was born in Poland in 1891 as Stephan Bibrowski. His entire body was covered in long, thick hair, which he claimed was caused by his mother seeing his father killed by a lion while she was pregnant. It is far more likely that he suffered from hypertrichosis, sometimes known as "werewolf disease." Lionel was famous at Coney Island during the 1920s, where he performed a gymnastic act at the Dreamland Circus sideshow.

28. Tom Ton Tom Ton was stage name used for more than one sideshow performer. The man pictured here weighed 645 lb (293 kg) at the age of 21.

29. Ho-Jo, the Bear Boy

30. Madame Adrienne, Bearded Lady Madame Adrienne's real name was Adele Kis, and she was born in

Hungary in 1884. She was married to a circus lion tamer. Adele was touring America when a rival performer cut off her beard while she was sleeping. Adele successfully sued for thousands of dollars in damages.

31. & 32. Eko and Iko, the Albino Twins Eko and Iko, black albino twins, were kidnapped in 1899 by sideshow bounty hunters for their unique appearance. They were variously known as the "Ecuadorian Cannibals," the "Sheep-Headed Men," and the "Ambassadors from Mars," and played saxophone and guitar on stage. They toured unpaid until 1927, the year of this photograph, when their mother tracked them down and demanded that they be freed from performing. They were freed, but soon returned to sideshows with a contract that ensured them a great deal of money, and they played venues such as Madison Square Garden to more than 10,000

people. They toured the world in the 1930s, performing for the Queen of England among others, and returned to the United States to perform right up until 1961.

33. Miss Pictoria Billed as the "Human Art Gallery," Victoria James was a well-known tattooed lady in the 1920s and 30s. Her extensive tattoos, like those of Miss Mae Vandermark, were drawn by "Professor" Charles Wagner in New York.

34. "Baby Bunny" Helen "Baby Bunny" Smith left school to work on sideshows as a fat lady who claimed to weigh more than 500 lb (227 kg). She married the "skeleton man" Peter Robinson (see 35). The unlikely pair had two children and became minor celebrities.

35. "Skeleton Man" Born in 1874, Peter Robinson was said to weigh only 50 lb (26.68 kg). He met his future wife, the "fat girl" Baby Bunny (see 34) in 1919, and they would dance together on stage. A 1924 newspaper described him as "one of the biggest moneymakers in the business," owing to the rarity of "human skeletons," and he spent more than a quarter century in the circus.

36. King Roy, the Scottish Albino King Roy, also billed as a contortionist, was the son of Rob Roy—a famous albino who performed for the Barnum and Bailey Circus in the 19th century— and Annie Roy, a sword swallower. He is said to have had six albino children.

Image courtesy of Derin Bray American Art & Antiques

PEACE, LOVE, AND POTATO SALAD

Ohio's Zack "Danger" Brown won the Internet when his Kickstarter campaign to fund his first foray into making potato salad exceeded his goal of earning just $10—to the tune of more than $55,000! Zack used the cash he'd earned not only to make his salad, but also to throw a huge public party—which was dubbed PotatoStock 2014—benefitting hunger and homelessness charities.

FASHION VICTIM

Mahbub Ali Khan (1866–1911), ruler of Hyderabad, India, never wore the same clothes twice and owned a walk-in closet 120 ft (36.6 m) long.

LONG WAIT

In August 2014, English singer Kate Bush played her first concert in 35 years. Although she recorded eight studio albums during that time, she had not performed live since her first and only tour ended in 1979.

JEDI RAZOR

The handheld communicator that Liam Neeson's character, Jedi master Qui-Gon Jinn, uses in the 1999 movie *Star Wars: The Phantom Menace* is based on a Gillette Sensor Excel female razor.

TOO CLEVER

Essen-based School of Economics and Management, in Germany, sued its student Marcel Pohl for graduating too quickly. The university claimed loss of income after Pohl completed his bachelor's and master's degree studies in about a quarter of the time it takes most of its students to finish.

SURPRISE ENDING

A performance of the musical *Peter Pan: The Never Ending Story* in Glasgow, Scotland, in 2014 had a surprise ending when the actor playing Peter Pan proposed for real to the actress playing Wendy. Dutchman Sandor Sturbl popped the question on stage to Scottish actress Lilly-Jane Young. To a chorus of cheers from the audience, she accepted.

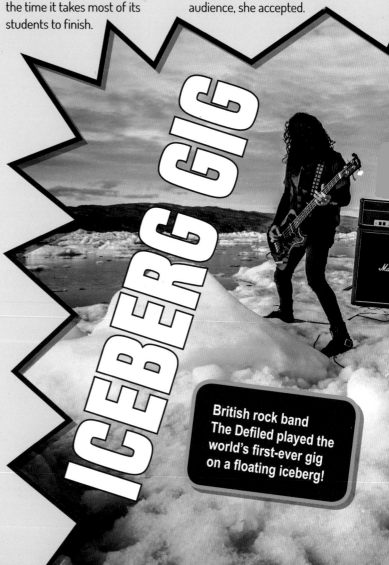

ICEBERG GIG

British rock band The Defiled played the world's first-ever gig on a floating iceberg!

CALIFORNIA DREAMIN'

Rap duo Silibil N' Brains—Billy Boyd and Gavin Bain from Dundee, Scotland—posed as Californians for 4.5 years, fooling record companies, partying with Madonna, and touring with Eminem before their hoax was finally exposed.

TWO NOTES

German vocalist Anna-Maria Hefele can sing two notes at once. The eerie technique is called "polyphonic-overtone singing" and allows her to sustain a constant low note while simultaneously singing a high-pitched scale.

AUTO WRECKERS

More than 500 cars were destroyed in the making of the 2011 movie *Transformers: Dark of the Moon*. All the cars were previously flood-damaged and therefore of no value.

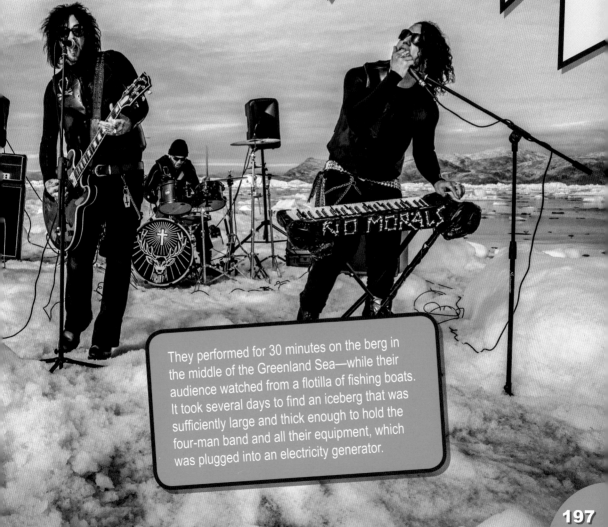

They performed for 30 minutes on the berg in the middle of the Greenland Sea—while their audience watched from a flotilla of fishing boats. It took several days to find an iceberg that was sufficiently large and thick enough to hold the four-man band and all their equipment, which was plugged into an electricity generator.

FAN FAVES

PEAK PLAYER
William Cruz, from Provo, Utah, played the video game *Far Cry 4* for 79 minutes on the summit of the 18,569-ft-high (5,660-m) Himalayan mountain Kala Patthar in freezing temperatures of –17°F (–8°C).

FAMOUS LOGO
Nike paid designer Carolyn Davidson, then a student at Portland State University, Oregon, $35 for their famous swoosh logo in 1971, with Nike cofounder Phil Knight saying of the design: "I don't love it, but maybe it will grow on me."

MISSING LETTER
Los Angeles, California, rap artist Andrew Thomas Huang has recorded a song "Rap Without The Letter E"—which lasts 2 minutes 39 seconds and in which none of the lyrics contain the letter "e."

CONFETTI PARADE
When astronaut John Glenn returned from 1962's Mercury 6 mission, 3,474 tons of confetti were thrown during a New York City parade in his honor.

CARVED CRAYONS

California artist Hoang Tran hand carves beautifully detailed images of characters from *Star Wars*, *Game of Thrones*, *Doctor Who*, and *Breaking Bad* into the tips of ordinary wax crayons. The former dentist uses his old dental tools to do the carving and sometimes adds melted wax from different colored crayons to make the sculptures more realistic.

FOOD FASCINATORS

Israeli designer Maor Zabar uses felt, plastic, and wire to create amazingly realistic models of food dishes, which he then fixes to hats. His fashionable designs include a berry pie beret, a salad sombrero, a prawn salad fascinator, and even a hat in the shape of an inverted, melting ice-cream cone.

HOBBIT VILLAGE

Lord of the Rings fan Svatoslav Hofman, a student from Orlickych Horach, Czech Republic, has created his own accurate replica Hobbit-sized village, complete with a pub—and he did it all from memory.

HISTORIC VIOLIN

The violin that was played to calm passengers as the Titanic sank in the North Atlantic in 1912 sold for $1.45 million in just 10 minutes at a 2013 auction in Wiltshire, England. It was played by the doomed ship's bandleader, Wallace Hartley, who died along with 1,517 others. The violin survived in a leather case found strapped to Hartley's body and was eventually returned to his fiancée, Maria Robinson.

FLYING QUARTET

German composer Karlheinz Stockhausen wrote a piece to be played by a string quartet in four hovering helicopters. The music was first performed in the skies above Amsterdam, the Netherlands, in 1995.

TRACTOR ORCHESTRA

A contemporary music festival in Valencia, Spain, opened with a 30-minute piece played by 12 farm tractors. Swedish conductor Sven-Ake Johansson led the four-wheeled orchestra through a range of diesel-engined whines, groans, and roars.

BEACH BOX

Brian Wilson, lead member of the rock band The Beach Boys, once had a giant sandbox built around the piano in his house so that he could feel sand beneath his feet, which he believed would provide inspiration for his song writing.

EXPENSIVE GUM

A piece of KISS front man Gene Simmons' used chewing gum from his appearance on the U.K. TV sports show *Soccer AM* in September 2013 attracted 29 bids on eBay, eventually selling for £210 ($317) in aid of charity.

PRINGLES SPIDER

The kidney garden spider (*Araneus mitificus*) of Asia gets its name from the dark, kidney-shaped marking on its abdomen—but to many people its markings look just like the Pringles man! However, the arachnid prefers to eat flies and bugs rather than Pringles chips.

TROLL DOLLS

Ray Dyson of Edmonton, Alberta, has a collection of more than 1,750 troll dolls—including Viking trolls, biker trolls, and elephant trolls.

ROOSTER SHOES

Japanese shoe designer Masaya Kushino has created a range of high-heeled footwear inspired by a rooster.

With their metal claw heels, beak-like toes, and uppers made out of feathers and brocade, his "Bird-Witched" stiletto designs certainly look unusual, but he insists they are perfectly wearable.

CHURCH REGULAR

Martha Godwin became the pianist at Macedonia United Methodist Church in Southmont, North Carolina, in 1940 at age 13 and has held the position for more than 74 years.

WHEEL SCREENS

For motorcyclists who want to personalize their rides, Thai company World Moto uses the latest technology to turn bike wheels into full-color, eye-catching LED TV screens. Each Wheelie has 424 LED lights mounted on an eight-spoke wheel, turning the wheel into a spinning screen, although amazingly the image appears static as the wheel turns. A computer tracks the wheel's speed and the position of each spoke, and also controls the lighting of the LEDs.

EARLY JOB

Actor Tom Hanks once worked as a bellboy at the Hilton Hotel in his hometown of Oakland, California, and carried the luggage of stars such as Cher, Bill Withers, and Sidney Poitier.

WHISTLESTOP TOUR

Country music star Hunter Hayes played ten shows in ten cities in 24 hours. He began in New York at 8:17 a.m. on May 9, 2014, and then moved on to Boston and Worcester, Massachusetts; Providence, Rhode Island; New London, New Haven, and Stamford, Connecticut; South Orange and Asbury Park, New Jersey; and finally, at daybreak on May 10, he performed in Philadelphia, Pennsylvania.

KING PONG

Frank Lee, a professor at Drexel University, Philadelphia, Pennsylvania, played a supersized version of the trailblazing 1972 video game *Pong* on the side of a city skyscraper. He recreated the classic Atari game on the 29-story Cira Centre, turning it into a 60,000-ft-sq (5,575-sq-m) screen as hundreds of embedded LED lights replicated the game's ball and paddles, which were controlled by a joystick about a mile away.

FANTASY WEDDING

Kerry Ford and Darren Prew enjoyed a *Game of Thrones*–themed wedding at Eastnor Castle, Herefordshire, England, dressing up as characters from the TV series for a ceremony that was attended by wolves, wildings, and white walkers. The bride arrived on a white horse and the couple sliced their five-tier wedding cake, which featured a chocolate crown, with a 4-ft-long (1.2-m) broadsword.

HIGH CULTURE

On April 23, 2014, British actors Simon Cole, Gary Fannin, and William Meredith, members of the Reduced Shakespeare Company, performed a selection of the Bard's plays at an altitude of 37,000 ft on board a flight from Gatwick, West Sussex, to Verona, Italy. Using the length of the airplane as their stage, they performed the "Shakes on a Plane" routine for almost an hour to mark the 450th anniversary of Shakespeare's birth.

FONDUE FOOTWEAR

Inspired by people dipping vegetables into melted cheese, Japanese designer Satsuki Ohata has created fondue footwear. By dipping his or her feet one at a time into colorful melted PVC, the wearer creates an exact foot mold. Once dry, the mold can be peeled off and on.

FUTURISTIC DRESS

Dutch designer Daan Roosegaarde has created a futuristic dress that becomes transparent if the wearer encounters someone they find attractive. The dress has leather strips that are embedded with electronic foils. Beneath the garment, tiny, hidden sensors are placed to detect changes in the wearer's body temperature and heart rate, and when those readings increase, the foils change the color of the dress.

PIPE MUSIC

Busker Jake Clark of Adelaide, Australia, plays music ranging from techno to covers of hits by The White Stripes and Iggy Azalea—by hitting plumbing pipes with his rubber flip-flop shoes. His avant-garde music proved so popular that YouTube videos of his performance went viral.

1,290 SHIRTS

Between July 2011 and January 2015, Isac Walter from Los Angeles, California, wore a different rock band T-shirt for 1,290 consecutive days—without repeating a single band.

FRIENDS REUNITED

When young Phoebe Simpson from Yorkshire, England, accidentally left her favorite teddy bear, Roar, on a train in London, she feared she would never see him again—but passenger Lauren Bishop Vranch found the bear and launched a campaign on Twitter and Facebook, which soon reunited Roar with his owner.

SEWER CONCERT

The sewerage system of Cologne, Germany, hosts jazz and classical music concerts. Built by the Romans in the 1st century AD, the system's Kronleuchtersaal space was later fitted with chandeliers and can accommodate audiences of up to 50 people.

SATNAV SHOES

In Hyderabad, India, Anirudh Sharma and American Krispian Lawrence have developed a range of GPS footwear that will help the wearer find their way home. The shoes are fitted with a Bluetooth link that connects to the mapping system in a cell phone, calculating which route the wearer should take and sending discreet vibrations to the feet telling them when they need to make a turn. The technology, called Lechal, comes either ready-fitted in a special shoe or as an insole that can be inserted into any shoe.

JACKSON TRIBUTE

The 225-piece Ohio State University Marching Band moonwalked across the football field during half-time at an OSU game against Iowa in October 2013 while playing a selection of Michael Jackson hits and forming a giant silhouette of him.

BEARS' AUTOGRAPHS

Superfan Glenn Timmerman has 126 autographs of Chicago Bears players past and present tattooed on his body. He started in 2005 when he met former Bear Otis Wilson and asked him to sign his body. Timmerman then drove straight to his favorite tattoo parlor and had Wilson's signature inked permanently into his skin.

POP PLATES

Los Angeles, California, artist Angela Rossi buys "orphaned and unloved" vintage decorative plates and turns them into fun, contemporary artworks by applying portraits of TV and movie characters and icons.

Using a special heat technique, she seals onto the plates images of the likes of Yoda and R2-D2 from *Star Wars*, Mr. T from *The A-Team*, and the Starship Enterprise from *Star Trek*.

A dancer supports his sleeping dance partner at a 1930 Chicago dance marathon. If a competitor's knees touched the floor, they were disqualified. Contestants used a range of tricks to keep each other awake and upright, including pinpricks, pinching, smelling salts, and ice packs. In extreme cases, exhausted partners were fastened together with chains to prevent them from drifting apart.

PHOTOS SOLD HERE MADE BY
'Rdm' Studio
OPEN DAY & NIGHT.

DANCE MARATHONS

In a Chicago ballroom on April 1, 1931, exhausted dancers Mike Ritof and Edith Boudreaux struggled to stay on their feet after winning an epic dance contest.

Since the event began on August 29, 1930, they had danced nonstop for an unbelievable 5,154 hours 48 minutes—that's 214 days, or seven months. Couples were required to remain in motion for 45 minutes every hour. During the 15-minute rest period, men and women retired to separate sleeping quarters for a nap. Any dancer who failed to wake up in time was either slapped or dunked in a tub of ice water.

Couples compete in a marathon event on a ship off the coast of California. The dance was halted by authorities concerned for the health of participants.

WALKATHONS

Some dance contests, known as "walkathons," resembled modern marathon races, with dancers traveling several miles between locations on public roads. In 1927 hundreds of couples danced 20 mi (32 km) around Los Angeles, California, accompanied by an orchestra on wheels.

ROYAL TREKKIE

While still a prince, King Abdullah bin al-Hussein of Jordan appeared as an extra in a 1996 episode of *Star Trek: Voyager*. A huge fan of *Star Trek*, he asked his aides to arrange for him to make a cameo appearance as an unnamed, uncredited ensign briefly glimpsed in a corridor.

SILENT GIGS

U.K. death metal band Unfathomable Ruination played a series of 2014 London gigs inside an airtight, soundproof steel box—so that nobody could see or hear them—until the oxygen inside ran out, usually after about 15 minutes. The 6-ft (1.8-m) cube was an art installation by a Portuguese artist named João Onofre.

CELEBRITY HUNTER

New York City bar worker Vanessa Sky Ellis spends up to 12 hours a day hunting for celebrities and has had selfies taken with more than 10,000 stars, including Brad Pitt, Al Pacino, Katy Perry, Johnny Depp, and Lady Gaga.

STREET JAM

In 2013, a street musician from Berlin, Germany, was performing Bronski Beat's 1984 hit song "Smalltown Boy" and couldn't believe his eyes when Scotsman Jimmy Somerville, the former Bronski Beat frontman, wandered over and joined in. Somerville, 52, happened to be walking his dog in the area.

GAME PROPOSAL

Robert Fink from Oregon City, Oregon, created a video game to propose to his girlfriend. He and two friends devised *Knight Man: A Quest For Love*, in which a knight collects a gold ring that he uses to propose to his princess. Robert proposed by asking his partner Angel White to test the game.

ROLE MODELS

When Japanese video game maker SEGA launched *Sonic the Hedgehog* in 1991, they gave him red-and-white sneakers based on a pair of boots worn by Michael Jackson. They modeled his adventurous character on future U.S. President Bill Clinton.

ZOO JEANS

A new line of distressed jeans has been "designed" by lions, tigers, and bears. To raise funds for the Kamine Zoo in Hitachi, Japan, volunteers wrap the animals' favorite toys in a sheet of denim and let them rip it apart. Humans then collect what remains of the denim and cut and sew it into shape to form a pair of unique Zoo Jeans.

FLOWER POWER

Experiments conducted by British horticultural students show that plants thrive when played heavy metal music—particularly by the band Black Sabbath—developing larger flowers and becoming more resistant to disease.

LITERARY TUSK

A narwhal whale tusk was engraved with the name Cornelius Fudge—the same name as the Minister for Magic in the Harry Potter books—more than a century before author J.K. Rowling first wrote about the boy wizard. The tusk's owner, John Jeffries from Cornwall, England, assumed that Rowling must have somehow heard of sailor Cornelius Fudge, to whom it was originally presented in 1881, but she said she had made the name up and that it was just an amazing coincidence. The ivory with literary links sold at an auction for $60,000 in 2013.

TREKKIE MANSION

When entrepreneur Marc Bell bought an eight-bedroom mansion in Boca Raton, Florida, he converted the 2,000-sq-ft (185-sq-m) ballroom into an arcade with more than 60 games, and in another room built an exact replica of the bridge of the Starship Enterprise from *Star Trek*.

MOVIE MOTOR

Movie fan Brian O'Neill of Sussex, England, spent two years and thousands of pounds creating a replica of the silver Delorean car from the 1980s' *Back to the Future* trilogy. He even wears a wig and white coat to dress up as the character Doc Brown while driving the car.

ANTIQUE BOOK

A copy of the *Bay Psalm Book*, the first book printed in America, in 1640, was sold for $14.2 million in November 2013. Sold at Sotheby's auction house, the book is one of only 11 surviving copies.

BIRD WATCHING

The population of the world has collectively spent more than 200,000 years playing *Angry Birds*—about the same length of time that modern humans have existed.

WEIRD WHEELS

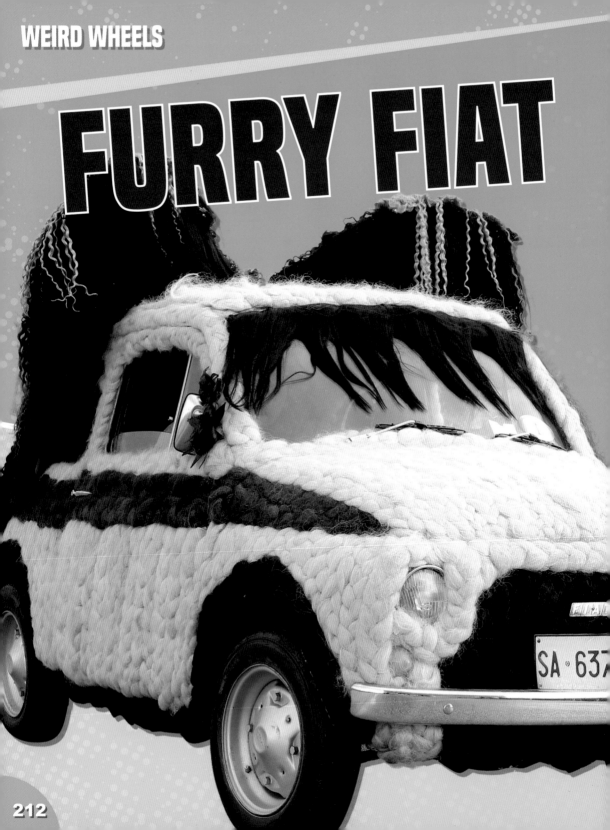

FURRY FIAT

SA·637

DRIVEABLE SUITCASE

He Liangcai from Changsha, China, has invented a drivable suitcase. The electric suitcase has a small motor that allows it to be ridden and can transport two adults at 12 mph (20 kmph) for up to 37 mi (60 km).

DENTAL CAR

Rex Rosenberg from Great Bend, Kansas, covered a Subaru with more than 140 lb (64 kg) of dentures and dental impressions to create his art car ChewBaru. He found the dentures online, soaked them in bleach, and glued them to the car along with toothpaste tubes and dental tools. He also found a discarded mannequin, cut it into pieces, inserted LED lights into the eyes, and stuck the head to the roof of the car.

WATER BIKE

Judah Schiller rode a bike 4 mi (6.4 km) across San Francisco Bay on September 27, 2013 on two pedal-powered inflatable pontoons. The following week he took his contraption to New York City and rode across the Hudson River in just 15 minutes.

CONTINENTAL TREK

Stopping only to collect roadkill to make stew, British couple Katharine and David Lowrie trekked the length of South America pulling a 220-lb (100-kg) trolley. It took them more than a year to travel the 6,400 mi (10,300 km) from the southern tip to the Caribbean, a journey that took them across rain forests, mountains, and windswept pampas.

EIGHT WHEELS

The Overland Octo-Auto, invented by U.S. automobile pioneer Milton Reeves in 1911, had eight wheels and was 20 ft (6 m) long. When it failed to sell, he replaced it the following year with a six-wheel version, the Sexto-Auto, which proved equally unsuccessful.

TUBE CHALLENGE

In August 2013, Geoff Marshall and Anthony Smith, both from the U.K., visited all 270 London Underground stations in 16 hours 20 minutes and 27 seconds. They were helped by a team of friends who warned them of possible obstacles along their route.

Italy's Maria Mugno has spent 150 hours covering her Fiat 500 car in 265 lb (120 kg) of human hair.

Using hair imported from India, because it is stronger, she sewed the different-colored strands to both the exterior and interior, including the seats, dashboard, and steering wheel. She still drives the car, which is now worth around $100,000, although she usually needs to comb it before hitting the road.

PIZZA-COPTER

Dirk Reich from Hamburg, Germany, created a radio-controlled "pizza-copter" by attaching four engines and a flight controller to a regular pizza box. In a trial run at his home, his flying pizza box lifted off the ground and glided through a doorway before landing on a table. He hopes to improve the prototype by making the box lid open automatically as it lands.

PROUD MARY

Launched in 2013, the Danish-registered Mary Maersk cargo ship holds 18,000 containers and would be 250 ft (76 m) taller than the Eiffel Tower if stood on end.

RECUMBENT RIDE

Riding a recumbent bike, 48-year-old Bruce Gordon from Halfmoon Bay, British Columbia, cycled 18,100 mi (29,000 km) around the world in 153 days.

BURIED FERRARI

In 1978, cops working on a tip dug in the mud outside a house in Los Angeles' West Athens district and uncovered a dark green Ferrari Dino 246 GTS completely buried in the soil. Investigators revealed that the car, which was in surprisingly good condition and would be worth more than $300,000 today, had been stolen in 1974 as part of an elaborate insurance scam.

PUMPKIN VOYAGE

Artist Dmitri Galitzine from London, England, sailed 4 mi (6.4 km) across the Solent seaway from Hampshire to the Isle of Wight in a boat made from an 800-lb (363-kg) pumpkin. The voyage took him nearly two hours in the hollowed-out pumpkin, which was fitted with a small outboard motor.

FARM FORDS

Auto mechanic Spyros Droulias from Elis, Greece, converts abandoned family cars into farm machinery. More than a million cars have been discarded by their owners in cash-strapped Greece because they can no longer afford to run them and are unable to sell them. The enterprising auto-shop owner has set up a lucrative sideline that uses his mechanical skills to modify unwanted Fords and Toyotas into useful milking machines and ploughs.

GIGANTIC JAMS

New York, U.S.A., August 1969–Revelers traveling to the Woodstock music festival caused a 20-mi (32 km) jam on the nearby New York Thruway, and drivers abandoned their cars to enjoy the event.

Tokyo, Japan, August 1990–Holiday traffic and a typhoon caused an 84 mi (135 km) jam between Hyogo and Shiga, trapping 15,000 cars.

Germany, April 1990–18 million cars lined up at the border between East and West Germany during the first Easter holiday after the fall of the Berlin Wall.

France, February 1980–The Lyon-Paris road was brought to a standstill by a 109-mi-long (175-km) jam caused by skiing vacationers returning to Paris in bad weather.

England, April 1985–Good Friday 1985 saw a giant traffic jam on the M6 motorway in Lancashire, involving 50,000 vehicles.

MIND THE GAP

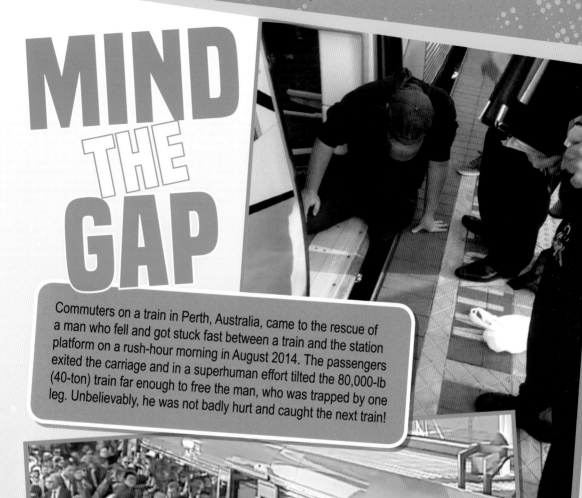

Commuters on a train in Perth, Australia, came to the rescue of a man who fell and got stuck fast between a train and the station platform on a rush-hour morning in August 2014. The passengers exited the carriage and in a superhuman effort tilted the 80,000-lb (40-ton) train far enough to free the man, who was trapped by one leg. Unbelievably, he was not badly hurt and caught the next train!

TRAM ON STILTS

In 1896, engineer Magnus Volk opened an electric tramline that actually ran through the sea for 2.8 mi (4.5 km) between Brighton and Rottingdean in Sussex, England.

Advertised as "a sea voyage on rails," it consisted of a single tramcar raised on four 23-ft-high (7-m) tubular legs, which contained wheels plus a set of scrapers to sweep seaweed, crabs, and shingle from the track. The rails were supported by concrete blocks embedded at 2.5-ft (0.8-m) intervals along the shore. Able to carry 160 passengers, the *Pioneer* (or "Daddy Long-Legs" as it was known) was equipped with a lifeboat and life preservers, but although it operated successfully in shallow water, it came to a near standstill at high tide. A violent storm badly damaged the tramway just a week after opening, but it trundled on for another few years before finally closing in 1901.

OLD HOUSE
While piloting a light aircraft over Northglenn, Colorado, Brian Veatch accidentally crashed into a house he had once owned. Brian, who was unhurt in the crash, sold the house in 2003 and now lives about a mile away.

BOTTLE BOAT
To celebrate their graduation, four science and technology students from Chongqing, China, spent two months building a working rowboat from 1,528 used plastic bottles. The 16-ft-long (5-m) vessel can hold the weight of five adults. Armed with oars, the four students took the boat out onto the river to show that it was fully functional and would not sink.

217

WEIRD WHEELS

WOODEN BIKE
Russian carpenter Yuri Hvtisishvili made a life-sized replica of a classic IZH-49 Soviet motorbike—entirely from wood. It took him four months of carving to create the detailed model, on which even the tires look real.

ABSENT MINDED
After police issued a Facebook appeal to trace the owner of a $108,000 boat that had been moored in Stromstad Harbour, Sweden, for two years, a wealthy Norwegian man came forward and said it was his, explaining that he had somehow forgotten all about the luxury vessel.

SUBMARINE HOTEL
British company Oliver's Travels rents out a submarine that has been converted into a luxury hotel 650 ft (200 m) under water. "Lovers Deep" is staffed by a crew of three—captain, chef, and butler—and can be harbored anywhere in the world from a starting price of $268,000 per night.

TIGHT FIT

Driver Chen Zhongliang somehow managed to squeeze his 4×4 into a tiny parking space outside his home in Quanzhou, China, that was just a few inches bigger than his vehicle. More impressive still, he reversed into the gap in a single maneuver.

NO STEERING WHEEL

A 38-year-old man stopped by police in Adelaide, Australia, was found to be driving without a steering wheel. The car was controlled instead with just a set of vise grips, which had been attached to the steering column.

CHEAP TRAVEL

Students in Nantes, France, have invented the Microjoule, a superlight car that could be driven around the world on just $26 of fuel. Made of carbon fiber, the vehicle accommodates only a driver—lying horizontally—but can travel more than 2,000 mi (3,200 km) on 0.25 gal (1 l) of fuel. It has an internal combustion engine and achieves its fuel efficiency by its aerodynamic shape and low resistance—when you spin its wheels, they revolve for several minutes without stopping.

DESTINATION ERROR

Edward Gamson and Lowell Canaday of Washington, D.C., thought they had booked vacation tickets to Granada in Spain, but instead British Airways took them to the Caribbean island of Grenada. The couple realized the error only when their connecting flight from London began heading west

FUN RIDE

After a trip to a theme park, Will Pemble built his children Lyle and Ellie a 180-ft-long (55-m) roller coaster in the back garden of the family home in San Francisco, California. It cost him more than $3,000 and took 300 hours to construct.

TOY STORY

A six-year-old boy was rescued by motorists after driving a miniature battery-powered ATV on to a busy six-lane highway in New York City. Three motorists slowed their vehicles and formed a shield around the toy car to protect it from traffic traveling at 50 mph (80 kmph) on the

TRAIN CROSSING

The runway at New Zealand's Gisborne Airport, which handles more than 17,000 flights and 130,000 passengers a year, has a railway track running straight across it.

MECHANICAL SHEPHERD

Instead of a dog, Marty Todd uses a remote-control miniature helicopter to herd the sheep on his farm in Nelson, New Zealand. The sheep react to the movement and sound of the whirring blades as the helicopter flies back and forth.

BONE TRUCK

Indian artist Jitish Kallat creates giant, gruesome vehicles that appear to be made of old dinosaur bones.

He uses resin, steel, and paint to create his large-scale sculptures of trucks, buses, motorcycles, cars, and three-wheelers, which are deliberately designed to look like prehistoric skeletons.

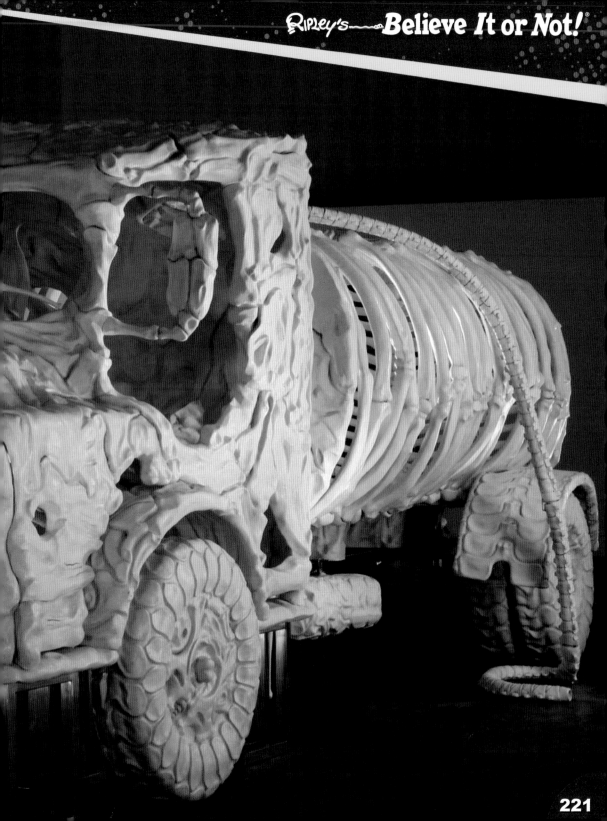

SHEEPDOG CAR

Farmer Dave Isaac from Sussex, England, covered his station wagon in fur so that it looked just like his favorite sheepdog, Floss.

He built a timber frame around the chassis and recreated Floss to the last detail, giving her a top speed of 40 mph (64 kmph). The replica was so accurate that when he drove it around his farm to round up the sheep, they did not appear to notice any difference.

WRONG CAR

A shopper in Stansbury, South Australia, accidentally drove home in the wrong car. The man got into a gray Hyundai hatchback instead of his nearly identical Toyota that was parked in the next lot and only realized his mistake when stopped by police officers. Both vehicles had been left in the parking lot unlocked with the keys in the ignition.

FOLDING SCOOTER

Engineering student George Mabey from Southampton, England, has invented a scooter that folds up to the size of a standard piece of paper—small enough to fit in a woman's handbag. The lightweight scooter works by linking aluminum parts with a cable that, when tightened, pulls them together to support the weight of an adult.

BIKE CRAZY

Twenty-seven percent of all journeys taken in the Netherlands are on bicycles—compared with under 2 percent in the U.K. and North America.

ICONIC CAR

Gordon Grant of England spent 12 years building an exact replica of Chitty Chitty Bang Bang, the iconic car driven by Dick Van Dyke in the 1968 movie of that name.

HUBCAP CREATURES

Artist Ptolemy Elrington from Brighton, England, creates incredible wildlife sculptures from car hubcaps. He has collected thousands of lost hubcaps from U.K. roadsides and turned them into imaginative sculptures of owls, dogs, wolves, lizards, sea creatures, and chickens. A 33-ft-long (10-m) dragon that he built from 200 hubcaps sold for around $5,000. He cuts the hubcaps to shape with a craft knife and a hacksaw and joins them together with salvaged wire.

PEDAL PORSCHE

Johannes Langeder of Linz, Austria, built a full-size, gold foiled Porsche sports car with a top speed of just 5 mph (8 kmph). The car took six months and $20,000 to build and is operated by pedal power.

OLYMPIC ODYSSEY

Farmer Chen Guanming said he rode a three-wheeled rickshaw for more than two years all the way from his remote Chinese village to London, England, in time for the 2012 Olympics. His 37,500-mi (60,000-km) journey took him through 16 countries, floods, war zones, mountains, and temperatures of –22°F (–30°C).

DUAL POWER

The Varibike, designed by Martin Kraiss from Ülm, Germany, can be propelled by both arms and legs. The bicycle has foot pedals and arm cranks connected to the wheels, thereby increasing the machine's power and speed by more than 30 percent.

TOO HEAVY

Four new submarines costing $3.2 billion commissioned by the Spanish Navy were found to be too heavy and, if launched, would have sunk like stones.

STATIONARY WARSHIP

In 1803, the British Navy registered a 575-ft-high (175-m) rock off Martinique as a British warship—HMS *Diamond Rock*—and hoisted guns on top.

VANISHING TRICK

Artist Laurent La Gamba from Paris, France, makes human models disappear by blending them in with high-performance sports cars.

Using BMWs and Porsches as his backdrop, he spends up to two hours painting his models with acrylics before photographing them so that they are perfectly camouflaged against the bodywork of the car and the surrounding landscape.

ART TRUCKS

Japanese truckers love to customize their vehicles with steel, chrome, and gold, topped with brightly colored neon and ultraviolet lighting for a dazzling display at night.

Many *Dekotora* ("decorated trucks") also have landscapes, pictures of celebrities or images of characters from popular Japanese animation, and comic books painted on the sides.

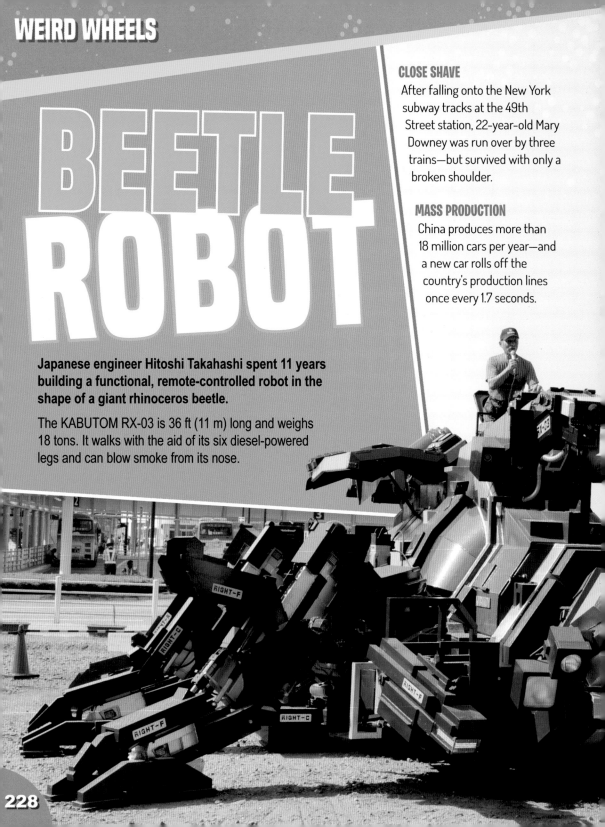

BEETLE ROBOT

Japanese engineer Hitoshi Takahashi spent 11 years building a functional, remote-controlled robot in the shape of a giant rhinoceros beetle.

The KABUTOM RX-03 is 36 ft (11 m) long and weighs 18 tons. It walks with the aid of its six diesel-powered legs and can blow smoke from its nose.

CLOSE SHAVE

After falling onto the New York subway tracks at the 49th Street station, 22-year-old Mary Downey was run over by three trains—but survived with only a broken shoulder.

MASS PRODUCTION

China produces more than 18 million cars per year—and a new car rolls off the country's production lines once every 1.7 seconds.

ROMANTIC CROSSING

Harry Martin-Dreyer of London, England, rowed 3,000 mi (4,800 km) across the Atlantic Ocean to Barbados in a charity race so he could propose to his girlfriend, Lucy Plant. The voyage took him and crew mate Alex Brand more than 50 days, battling 50-ft-high (15-m) waves in places. At one point Harry, who carried the diamond engagement ring in a waterproof bag, was hit in the face by a flying fish. Luckily it was all worth it as Lucy said yes.

JET TRUCK

Neal Darnell of Springfield, Missouri, has built a jet-powered truck that can reach speeds of nearly 380 mph (612 kmph), making it faster than a Japanese bullet train. Named Shockwave, the 4-ton truck has three jets taken from a U.S. Navy trainer aircraft, which generate 36,000 horsepower. It can cover a 0.25 mi (0.4 km) in just 6.5 seconds and has to be stopped by using two military parachutes.

MISSING PLANE

A Boeing 727 airplane was stolen from an airport in Luanda, Angola, on May 25, 2003, and it has never been found.

EMERGENCY STOP

A pilot landed a light airplane on a highway in Sichuan Province, China, and then taxied to a nearby gas station to refuel. He climbed onto the wing of the plane to reach the fuel cap and, with the help of staff, managed to extend the gas pump nozzle far enough to fill up.

HOME RAILROAD

Todd Miller has built mini working steam locomotives, 11,000 ft (3,353 m) of track, and a 400-ft-long (122-m) tunnel on the grounds of his home outside Portland, Oregon. It took him eight years to build some of the locomotives for the railroad, which is so big that up to 40 passengers can ride on it at a time.

DETECTOR SEAT

Researchers at Nottingham Trent University, England, have developed a car seat that detects when drivers are falling asleep at the wheel. An electrocardiogram sensor system embedded into the fabric of the seat interprets heart signals, which indicate when a driver is becoming less alert. The system then issues a warning, and if that is ignored, active cruise control technology is deployed to slow down the vehicle.

LEFT-F

LEFT-F

WILD STUNTS

NOSE PULL

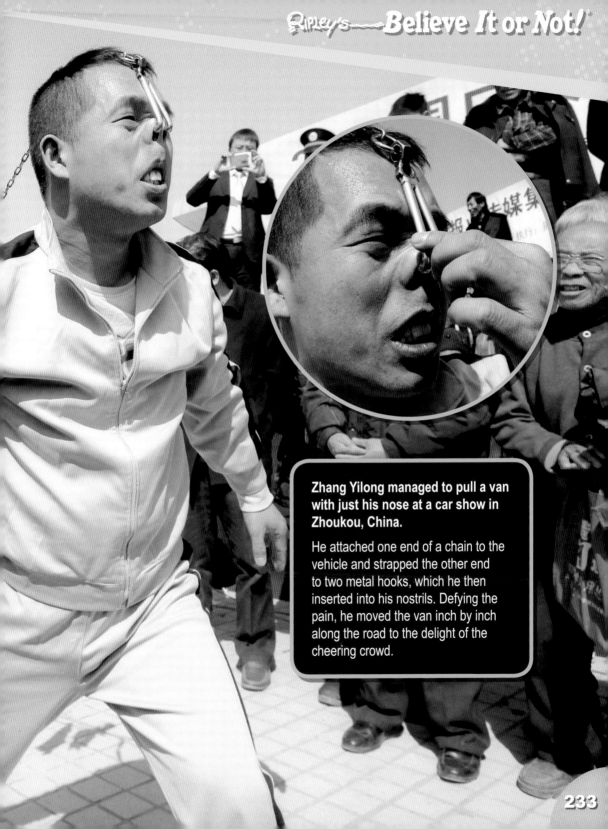

Zhang Yilong managed to pull a van with just his nose at a car show in Zhoukou, China.

He attached one end of a chain to the vehicle and strapped the other end to two metal hooks, which he then inserted into his nostrils. Defying the pain, he moved the van inch by inch along the road to the delight of the cheering crowd.

SPEEDING WAKEBOARDER

Five-time British wakeboard champion Jorge Gill was pulled along a flooded field in Lincolnshire, England, by a $1.7-million Ferrari at speeds of up to 84 mph (135 kmph). The thrill-seeking 19-year-old attached himself by a cord to the supercar's spoiler, jumped into the water-filled ditch, and, as the Ferrari accelerated along an adjacent country lane, he clung on as it dragged him at speeds more than four times faster than he usually travels on a wakeboard.

DOUBLE CLIMB

Twenty-nine-year-old Nepalese mountaineer Chhurim Sherpa climbed Mount Everest twice in a week in May 2012—the first woman to climb the world's highest mountain twice in a season. She made her first ascent on May 12, and then returned to base camp for a couple of days' rest before scaling the peak again on May 19.

QUICK ARROWS

Master archer Lars Andersen, from Denmark, is so fast and accurate he can throw a ring pull from a can into the air and hit it with an arrow before it falls to the ground. He can even hit other arrows as they are fired at him,

SKATER GIRL

Nine-year-old Sabre Morris from Newcastle, Australia, can land an awesome 540-degree skateboard spin—but she still can't ride a bike! She learned to skate when she was six because her parents would not allow her to have a bicycle, as their house has no garage.

OLDEST CLIMBERS

Esther Kafer, 84, and her husband Martin, 85, of Vancouver, British Columbia, became the oldest people to reach the summit of Tanzania's 19,340-ft-high (5,895-m) Mount Kilimanjaro on September 30, 2012. The couple have been climbers for

BOOK CHAIN

To promote reading, a chain of 4,845 second-hand books was tumbled in domino fashion along a 2,014-ft-long (614-m) pathway at Belgium's 2013 Antwerp Book Fair. It had taken a team of 40 volunteers two hours to set up the lines of books so that they would fall in sequence.

BOWLING BACKWARDS

Andrew Cowen of Rockford, Illinois, scored 280 points in a game bowling backwards. Facing away from the pins, he bowled ten straight strikes, and except for a second-frame spare, he would have bowled a backwards

DARING BACKFLIP

After speeding down a sheer drop, New Zealand mountain biker Kelly McGarry performed a sensational backflip across a 72-ft-wide (22-m) canyon gap in Utah during the 2013 Red Bull Rampage.

SPRING SENSATION

Sixteen-year-old gymnast Mikayla Clark, a student at Westlake High School, Atlanta, Georgia, can perform 44 consecutive back handsprings, or backflips.

RIVER WALK

French tightrope walker Denis Josselin defied gravity by balancing on a thin rope 82 ft (25 m) above the River Seine in Paris, France, and walking nearly 500 ft (150 m) to the other side—without a harness or safety net. The walk took him 30 minutes to complete and halfway across he put on a blindfold for a short distance to make the stunt even more dangerous.

URBAN GOLFER

Detroit, Michigan, news reporter Charlie LeDuff turned the city into an 18-mi-long (29-km) golf course by playing from one end of town to the other through abandoned houses, grassy fields, and crumbling landmarks. Carrying only four clubs and playing each shot where it lay, he took 2,525 strokes.

PAINFUL SLEEP

China's Zhou Jie suffered for her art for 36 nights by sleeping almost naked on an unfinished bed and pillow made of harsh, skin-piercing iron wire as part of a painful performance piece.

Visitors to the Beijing, China, exhibition hall watched her work to complete her stark wrought-iron bedroom, which, in addition to the bed, featured toy animal sculptures made from rough metal wire.

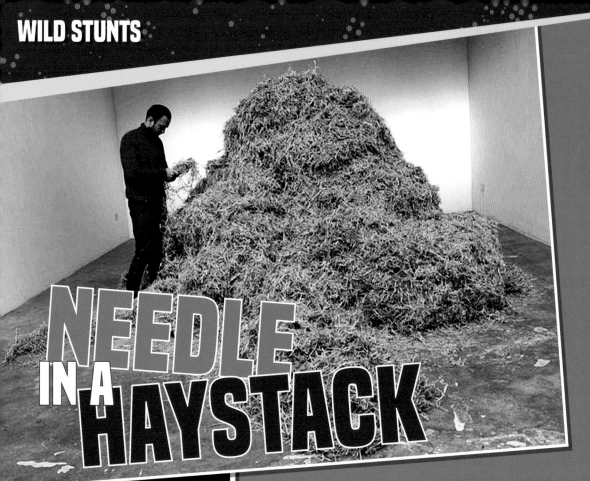

NEEDLE IN A HAYSTACK

New York–based Italian artist Sven Sachsalber achieved the supposedly impossible by finding a needle in a haystack.

He had given himself 24 hours to locate with his bare hands a single silver needle that had been pre-inserted into an enormous haystack by the president of a Paris museum—but he managed to find it with six hours to spare. His previous performances have included sawing the branches off a tree while still sitting in it and spending 24 hours in a room with a cow.

BRAINS AND BRAWN

Michael Kotch of Upper Milford Township, Pennsylvania, solved a Rubik's Cube with one hand in 25 seconds while simultaneously doing push-ups with the other arm.

FAST FIZZ

Frank Esposito, a restaurant manager in Long Island, New York, can use a saber to open 48 bottles of champagne in one minute.

DARING DORIS

Great-great-grandmother Doris Long from Hampshire, England, celebrated her 99th birthday in May 2013 by abseiling down the side of a 110-ft-high (34-m) building.

BIKE CLIMB

Without his feet ever touching the ground, Italian Vittorio Brumotti cycled up 3,700 steps to the top of the tallest building in the world—the 2,715-ft-high (828-m) Burj Khalifa in Dubai. He jumped his way up the 160 floors in 2 hours 20 minutes.

PRAM PUSHER

Dougal Thorburn from Dunedin, New Zealand, ran 6 mi (9.6 km) in 32 minutes 26 seconds—while pushing a pram containing his two year old daughter, Audrey. His time was only six minutes slower than the world record for the same distance for athletes not pushing a pram!

MOUTH JUGGLER

In June 2013, entertainer Mark Angelo from Hudson, Ohio, juggled two ping-pong balls using nothing but his mouth, for a total of 212 spits and catches in 2 minutes 8 seconds. Mark, who first discovered his unusual talent by tossing popcorn in the air and catching it in his mouth, can also balance a golf club on his chin with a golf ball on top of it and another club spinning on top of the ball!

POGO FLIPS

In Tokyo, Japan, on December 18, 2013, Fred Grzybowski from the United States performed 17 consecutive backflips on a pogo stick.

TUNNEL VISION

James Wilson from Surrey, England, solved a Rubik's Cube in 3 minutes 16 seconds while freefalling in an artificial wind tunnel where he fought wind speeds of 125 mph (200 kmph).

TOE WRESTLING

One of England's craziest sports events is the World Toe Wrestling Championships, which takes place each year in Derbyshire, England. Competitors sit barefoot facing each other and lock their big toes together, the aim being to pin the opponent's big toe on the platform for three seconds. During the contest, hands must be kept flat on the floor and the non-fighting foot must stay in the air. The championships were devised in the 1970s by George Burgess, who wanted to give England the chance to be world champions in at least one sport!

WINNING STREAK

Pakistani squash player Jahangir Khan won 555 consecutive matches over a period of five years and eight months between 1981 and 1986.

TOTAL FLIP

At the 2012 Winter X Games at Aspen, Colorado, Heath Frisby of Middleton, Idaho, became the first person ever to front-flip a snowmobile, completing a 360-degree revolution in midair before landing safely.

BED OF NAILS

At Fremont, Indiana, Amy Bruney skipped rope 117 times on top of a 125-lb (57-kg) board that was fitted with 3,000 upturned nails, the points of which were painfully pressing onto the chest and stomach of her husband, Pastor Jon Bruney.

ARMLESS STAR

Ibrahim Hamadtou of Egypt lost his arms in a train accident when he was ten years old, but that didn't stop him from becoming a world-class table-tennis player.

He began playing three years after the accident and at first tried holding the bat under his arm, but now he holds it in his mouth and serves by flicking the ball up with his foot. His technique has proved so successful that he won the silver medal at the African Para Table Tennis Championships.

RHESUS NEGATIVE

Tim Flock drove in eight NASCAR races in 1953 with a rhesus monkey, "Jocko Flocko," as his codriver. He retired the monkey after Jocko was hit by a pebble during a race and the resultant pit stop cost him a victory.

GIANT SNOWMAN

Greg Novak from Gilman, Minnesota, used farm equipment to build a 50-ft-high (15.2-m) snowman. It took him hundreds of hours to construct the snowman, who had plywood eyes, a barrel for a nose, garbage can covers for buttons, an 80-ft-long (24.3-m) scarf, and carried a 35-ft-high (10.6-m) broom.

REVERSE SPEAKER

Schoolboy Cameron Bissett from Bo'ness, Scotland, can speak fluent English backward. He started by imagining what words would sound like backward before progressing to full sentences. He can even pronounce the title of the *Mary Poppins* song "Supercalifragilistic-expialidocious" backward!

EGG BALANCING

Cui Juguo from Changsha, China, can balance eggs on the points of needles—even ostrich eggs. He can also balance forks, toothpicks, and eggs on a pin—all at the same time.

HIGH CATCH

In 1938, Henry Helf of the Cleveland Indians caught a baseball that was dropped 708 ft (215 m)—and thought to be traveling at 138 mph (222 kmph)—from the top of Cleveland's Terminal Tower.

KNITTING MARATHON

David Babcock, a professor at the University of Central Missouri, ran the 2013 Kansas City Marathon in 5 hours 48 minutes—while knitting a scarf that became more than 12 ft (3.6 m) long.

DEFYING THE ODDS

In 2007, Geoff Holt, who is paralyzed from the chest down following a diving accident, sailed solo 1,400 mi (2,253 km) around the coast of Great Britain on a voyage that took 109 days.

In 2011, soldier Joe Townsend, who lost both legs in Afghanistan, completed the arduous Ironman U.K. challenge. It took him 13 hours to swim 2.4 mi (3.86 km), cycle a 112-mi (180-km) ride, and run a marathon.

Matt Stutzman of Fairfield, Iowa, won the silver medal at the 2012 Paralympic archery competition despite being born without any arms. Using his left foot to load the arrow, he pushes the bow with his right foot and releases it with a special apparatus strapped to his body.

Dutch wheelchair tennis player Esther Vergeer did not lose a single match between 2003 and her retirement in 2013. She ended her career with an unbroken winning streak of 470 matches.

South African Natalie du Toit lost her left leg in a road accident when she was 17, but went on to win 13 Paralympic swimming gold medals and was so fast she became the first amputee to qualify for the regular Olympics, in 2008.

WILD STUNTS

For 70 years, three generations of the legendary Zacchini family risked life and limb by defying gravity as human cannonballs. Audiences gasped as the Zacchinis were blasted into the air from a cannon at speeds of 90 mph (144 kmph) toward a net that was more than 150 ft (46 m) away!

The Zacchinis were already long-established circus performers when Maltese-born inventor Ildebrando Zacchini suggested to the Italian government that his new human cannon would be a good way of propelling soldiers into enemy lines during World War I. After the proposal was rejected for being too risky, Ildebrando decided to use the cannon in a family act, involving seven brothers and two sisters.

Ildebrando's eldest son, Edmondo, was the first to try out the spring-loaded cannon. It hurled him just 20 ft (6 m) and put him in hospital with a broken leg. In the 1920s the Zacchinis replaced the crude contraption with a cannon that enabled them to fly greater distances.

The famous Hugo Zacchini atop his cannon outside the Ringling Brothers and Barnum & Bailey Circus in Brooklyn, New York, in 1933.

HUGO ZACCHINI—HUMAN PROJECTILE RINGLING BROTHERS and BARNUM & BAILEY COMBINED CIRCUS

HUMAN
CANNONBALLS

During World War II, when her brothers Hugo and Mario were sent to fight, 18-year-old Victoria Zacchini took their places in the cannon. Here she is in Chicago in 1943 being blasted outward.

Here, Egle Zacchini is seen inside the cannon, wearing her suit, crash helmet, and asbestos mask just before a launch in the 1940s.

YOU'RE FIRED!

OTHER HUMAN CANNONBALLS

In 2005, former math teacher David "Cannonball" Smith Sr. was fired over the Mexico-U.S. border, taking off in Tijuana and landing in Imperial Beach, California. As he soared over the border fence, he waved his passport in the air.

Since 1987, Long Island native Jon Weiss, a clown-turned-human cannonball, has been shot a total distance of 125 mi (200 km) through the air in the course of more than 5,500 career performances.

Owing to the extreme G-force of being fired from a cannon (as much as nine times normal gravity), some human cannonballs have been known to black out in midair.

Hugo Zacchini being shot out of a specially constructed cannon at Starlight Park in the Bronx, New York, circa 1929.

The first recorded human cannonball was a 14-year-old girl—acrobat Rosa Richter, a.k.a. "Zazel" (1862-1922)—who was shot 30 ft (6 m) into the air by a spring-loaded cannon in London, England, in 1877.

DEADLY TRICK

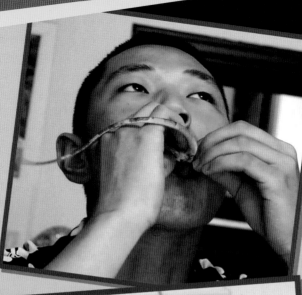

Li Peng entertains crowds by putting live venomous snakes, scorpions, and spiders into his mouth before pulling them back out again!

The showman from Jilin Province, China, trained for the trick by being locked in a room with 30 deadly snakes. Although he has been bitten many times, he says he has learned how to neutralize the snakes' venom.

DOMINO TOWER

Graduate engineer Tom Holmes from Bristol, England, spent 7.5 hours building a free-standing domino tower from 2,688 dominos. The tower stood 17 ft 4 in (5.3 m) tall—taller than a double-decker bus.

ACROBATIC SWORDSMAN

Nick Penney of Augusta, Maine, can swallow three swords and then turn two consecutive cartwheels while keeping the swords in place. He has also swallowed three swords at once while suspended upside down

TANDEM JUMP BASE

Jumpers Julie Wentz and Ramon Rojas pulled off a daring piggy-back tandem wingsuit jump in Kjerag, Norway. The pair leaped from a 3,000-ft-high (900-m) cliff with her perched on his back and flew through the air before gliding safely to the ground.

900-MILE SWIM

Sean Conway from Gloucestershire, England, swam the length of Britain from Land's End, Cornwall, to John O'Groats, Scotland, in 135 days. Between June and November 2013, he swam 900 mi (1,448 km) up Britain's west coast, during which he made an estimated three million strokes and was stung ten times by jellyfish. Cold weather forced him to stay out of the water for 45 days overall, and, while swimming, his jaw became so numb he was unable to chew solid food and had to have his meals pureed.

MUSICAL GENIUS

After receiving a blow to the head while playing lacrosse when he was 12 years old, Lachlan Connors of Denver, Colorado, became a musical genius. He had shown no interest or ability in music before the accident, but within a few years of the dramatic blow, he had taught himself to play 13 different instruments, including the piano, guitar, and bagpipes, entirely by ear.

TALL ORDER

Kevin Schmidt, of Rapid City, South Dakota, climbed 1,500 ft (457 m) to the top of the KDLT-TV antenna near Salem just to change a light bulb. He has scaled hundreds of towers in his job as a communications company engineer, sometimes in 60 mph (96 kmph) winds.

OLD REF

Harry Hardy from Derbyshire, England, still referees local amateur soccer matches at age 87. He started refereeing in 1959 and says, "I can still run a bit."

SHARP SHUCKERS

Using sharp knives, a team of ten Canadian oyster shuckers opened 8,840 oysters in one hour during the 2014 Tyne Valley Oyster Festival on Prince Edward Island.

FIN FUN

Wearing a snorkel and cumbersome swim fins that were more than twice the length of his foot, New Yorker Ashrita Furman ran 1 mile (1.6 km) in just under 8 minutes. Furman, who has been performing crazy athletic feats for 35 years, has also run 3.1 mi (5 km) in swim fins while juggling three objects in just over 32 minutes.

LOOP-THE-LOOP

Scottish trials cyclist Danny MacAskill performed a gravity-defying loop-the-loop around a colossal 16-ft-high (5-m) loop erected on a barge floating on the River Thames, London, England, in front of the London Eye ferris wheel.

After practicing the stunt for hours, he rode down a 60-ft (18-m) ramp to build up enough momentum to complete the terrifying loop, the biggest he had ever conquered.

MATCHBOX COLLECTION
Steven Smith of Norfolk, England, has more than 20,500 matchboxes and more than one million matchbox labels from 130 different countries.

TWO SPORTS
Deion Sanders is the only athlete to play in both the Super Bowl, for the San Francisco 49ers (1995) and the Dallas Cowboys (1996), and the World Series, for the Atlanta Braves (1992).

STRONG SHINS
Martial arts expert Dr. Mak Yuree Vajramuni from Bangladesh has shins that are as strong as steel, and he can use them to shatter a bundle of three baseball bats with a single shin kick. To break each bat requires 740 psi of force.

ONE-ARMED WEIGHTLIFTER
Within a year of losing her right arm in a car crash, Krystal Cantu of San Antonio, Texas, could lift 210 lb (95 kg) clear above her head with her remaining arm.

LONGEST MOONWALK

At an event organized by the Ripley's Believe It or Not! museum in Pattaya, Thailand, on June 24, 2014, 16-year-old Niwat Otthon stepped backward in a continuous Michael Jackson-style moonwalk for a record-breaking distance of 0.75 mi (1.2 km).

247

MOTORBIKE YOGA

Gugulotu Lachiram performs impressive, death-defying yoga exercises on the back of a motorbike traveling at 40 mph (64 kmph) along roads in Telangana, India.

The 40-year-old farmer can sit, stand, or lie down on his moving bike for a distance of more than 3 mi (4.8 km), and although disaster is just a slip away, he has never had an accident.

STILT WALKER
Neil Sauter completed the 2013 Grand Rapids Marathon in Michigan in 5 hours 56 minutes 23 seconds—on 3-ft-high (0.9-m) stilts. As he has a mild case of cerebral palsy, Neil's feet turn inward, making it difficult for him to walk normally, but when he wears stilts his feet are strapped in tight, with the result that he is much more coordinated on a pair of stilts than on his own two feet!

TEDDY TOSS
In the 19th year of the annual Teddy Bear Toss, where Canadian hockey fans take stuffed toys to a game and throw them onto the ice when the home team scores its first goal, supporters of the Calgary Hitmen flung 25,921 toys onto the rink on December 1, 2013, after Pavel Padakin had opened the scoring against the Medicine Hat Tigers.

REVERSE RIDE
Australian Andrew Hellinga rode a bicycle backward for 209.77 mi (337.6 km) in 24 hours in October 2013 at an average speed of 8.75 mph (14 kmph). He first started riding backward to impress girls when he was a teenager!

MODERN MERMAID
Wearing a mermaid-like monofin for greater speed, Rebecca Coales of Bristol, England, held her breath underwater for two-and-a-half minutes as she swam nearly four lengths of an Olympic-sized pool in July 2014. She swam the 587 ft (179 m) without a breathing device and without coming up for air at the pool in Stockport, Greater Manchester.

SENTIMENTAL SKYDIVE
In November 2013, 93-year-old Jack Hake from Dorset, England, carried out a tandem skydive from an altitude of 10,000 ft (3,000 m) while carrying the ashes of his late wife Veronica, to whom he had been married for 70 years.

HUGE HAMMOCK
Bay Hammocks, a small company based in Seabright, Nova Scotia, created a giant handmade hammock, which measured 52 ft (16 m) long and 16 ft (5 m) wide, from 62 pieces of rope. It took more than 1 mi (1.6 km) of rope to make the hammock, which is 11 times the size of a regular hammock.

BURNING DESIRE
Ridip Saikia from Ratanpur, India, can swallow 30 pieces of burning charcoal in a minute—without suffering any injury.

HOOVER FAN
Nine-year-old Harry Burrows from the West Midlands, England, has a collection of more than 40 vacuum cleaners. He has been fascinated by the vacuums ever since his parents used one to soothe him to sleep when he was a baby, and he now spends his pocket money buying old or rare models.

Russian BASE jumper Stanislav Aksenov leapt from a 1,300-ft-high (400-m) cliff near Bern, Switzerland, and glided to the ground with a parachute attached to metal piercings hooked into the flesh on his back.

Although his skin stretched under the strain of his body weight and he was left hanging by his flesh for more than two minutes, he still managed to land safely in a field.

HOOKED UP

СЕВЕРНЫЙ ПОЛЮС

МУРМАНСК - 2349 км.

МОСКВА - 3840 км.

ЯКУТСК - 3108 км

Земля ФРАНЦА-ИОСИФА - 1100 км.

ДУДИНКА - 2282 км.

OTTAWA - 4960 км.

STOCKHOLM - 3552 км.

WASHINGTON - 5717 км.

Н.НОВГОРОД -3920 км.

УЛЬЯНОВСК

Signposts indicate that this is a marathon far from civilization.

A wind chill of -50°F (-45°C) can cause frostbite in just five minutes! To help stop vital organs from losing heat, our extremities—nose, fingertips and toes—will lose their blood and become cold to keep us alive.

NORTH POLE MARATHON

Labeled the world's coolest marathon, the North Pole Marathon has been run since 2003 by intrepid athletes who have braved sub-zero temperatures, polar bears, and a course that is constantly on the move beneath their feet.

The 26.2-mi (42.2-km) race is run in temperatures as low as –25°F (–32°C) across snow and thick ice covering the Arctic Ocean—and although the runners are unable to feel it, the ground beneath their feet is forever shifting with the ocean current.

The event is the brainchild of Irishman Richard Donovan, who won the inaugural South Pole Marathon in Antarctica in 2002. Before establishing the North Pole contest, he ran a solo marathon there himself to see if it could be done and so became the first person to complete marathons at both poles.

Runners have to wrap up to survive freezing temperatures.

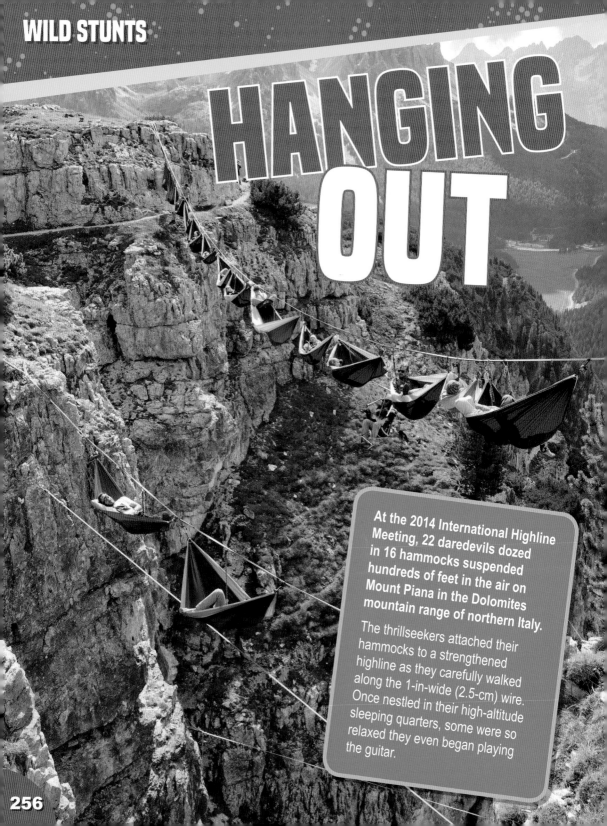

HANGING OUT

At the 2014 International Highline Meeting, 22 daredevils dozed in 16 hammocks suspended hundreds of feet in the air on Mount Piana in the Dolomites mountain range of northern Italy.

The thrillseekers attached their hammocks to a strengthened highline as they carefully walked along the 1-in-wide (2.5-cm) wire. Once nestled in their high-altitude sleeping quarters, some were so relaxed they even began playing the guitar.

LONG SCARF

Helge Johansen from Oslo, Norway, has spent 30 years knitting a scarf that is 3.1 mi (5 km) long and weighs around 1,100 lb (500 kg). When he started work on the garment, at age 17, he did not know how to knit and had to be taught by his mother.

YOUNG VOLUNTEER

Jimmie Foxx (1907–67), "the right-handed Babe Ruth," who played Major League baseball from 1925 to 1945, was the only ten-year-old to volunteer during World War I. He tried to enlist in the U.S. military as a drummer boy, but the recruiting officer explained to him that drummer boys carried firearms.

HIGH JUMP

Wearing no safety gear, extreme trampolinist Greg Roe of Brampton, Ontario, can jump from a height of 180 ft (55 m)—equivalent to the 25th floor of an apartment building—and perform incredible twists and somersaults in midair before landing on a huge airbag.

MARATHON GAME

Two teams in the Philippines played a basketball game that lasted for 120 hours 1 minute 7 seconds—just over five days. The final score saw Team Bounce Back beat Team Walang Iwanan by 16,783 points to 16,732.

SOFT LANDING

On the 18th hole of the 2013 PGA Championship at Oak Hill Country Club, Rochester, New York, Swedish golfer Jonas Blixt's tee shot landed in the back pocket of a spectator's pants—yet he still went on to make a birdie!

LIVING DOLL

Robyn Amato of Tampa, Florida, has been collecting Raggedy Ann dolls for more than 20 years and now has over 3,000. She has spent more than $20,000 on her hobby, and even dresses up as Raggedy Ann and takes some of her dolls out on day trips.

ARTISTIC VISION

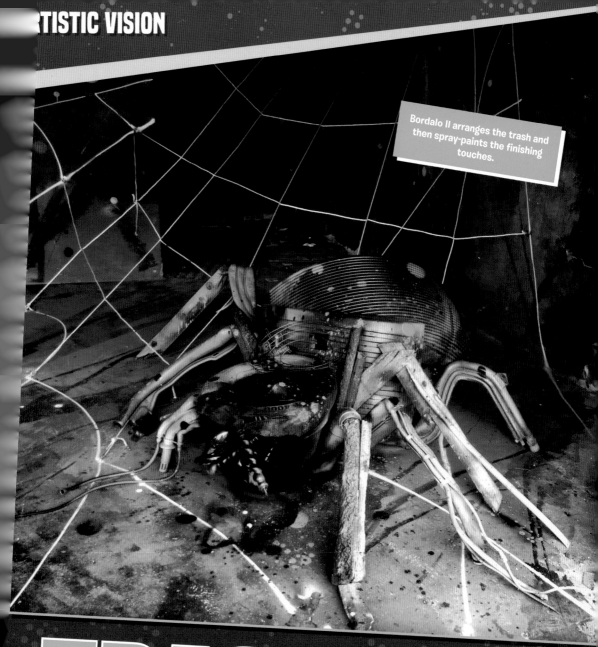

Bordalo II arranges the trash and then spray-paints the finishing touches.

TRASH ZOO

Portuguese artist Bordalo II is turning the city of Lisbon into a giant trash zoo. He scours the streets in search of pieces of garbage, which he then builds into huge sculptures of brightly colored mammals, birds, and insects.

He tours dumpsters and dumps in search of discarded plastic sheeting, scrap metal, old tires, shingles, cardboard boxes, and lengths of electrical cable. Once he has the basic materials for his artwork, he painstakingly positions the individual pieces in the shape of the creature before spray-painting it. His technique enables him to turn an urban environment into a fantasy wilderness populated with huge crocodiles, parrots and owls, and ladybugs the size of cars.

The grandson of an artist called the Real Bordalo, who also painted parts of Lisbon, Bordalo II says his aim is not only to promote recycling, but to show that we often have nice things that are based on junk without realizing it. He first had the idea for his urban zoo when he began gluing together some of the garbage that had collected in his studio to see if he could make anything from it.

Ripley's ASK

Have you always been a graffiti artist? I've been a graffiti writer since the age of 11, painting illegal stuff in the street. However, the artwork I'm presenting now is different—it's more like street art, contemporary art, or big-scale assemblage.

How did you come up with the idea to create art from junk? I had a lot of junk in my studio, so I started to glue small pieces to a canvas. I liked the effect, so I painted over the collages. Then, I started to explore various techniques using different materials.

What are some of the most unusual items you've used in your designs? I like to think there's nothing unusual about the objects I use, because they are just the city's waste—objects that we all use (and throw away) every day.

How long does each piece take and do you create the pieces on your own? I have two production assistants who help me with big-scale pieces, which might take three or four days, depending on the size and materials. I make my canvas pieces alone.

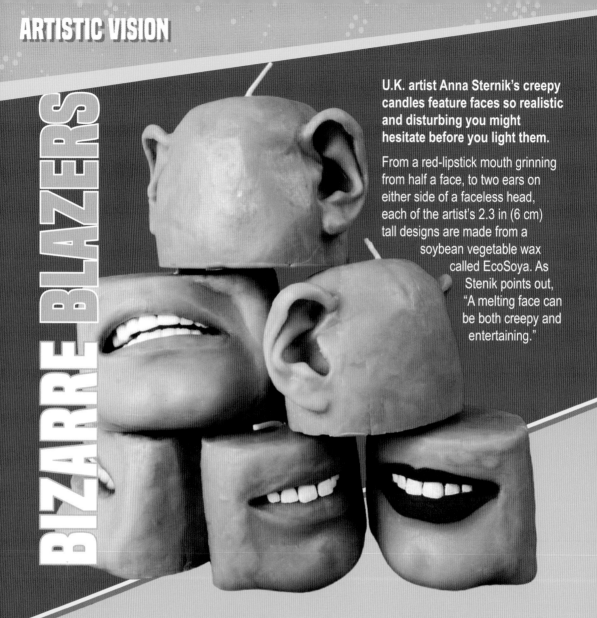

BIZARRE BLAZERS

U.K. artist Anna Sternik's creepy candles feature faces so realistic and disturbing you might hesitate before you light them.

From a red-lipstick mouth grinning from half a face, to two ears on either side of a faceless head, each of the artist's 2.3 in (6 cm) tall designs are made from a soybean vegetable wax called EcoSoya. As Stenik points out, "A melting face can be both creepy and entertaining."

SOCCER NUT

Using a scalpel and a magnifying glass, micro-artist Quentin Devine from Surrey, England, celebrated the 2014 World Cup by carving tiny sculptures of five England soccer legends from individual Brazil nuts.

MONEY BOAT

Sergei Nikolayev Knurov, a chef from Mykolaiv, Ukraine, made a model of a ship from 17,000 coins, with banknotes for sails. The coins are held together by silicate glue, and it took him six months to collect enough coins to build the 30-lb (13.6-kg) ship.

ANTIQUE DOORSTOP

A woman used an old wooden pot as a doorstop at her cottage in Hertfordshire, England, for more than 40 years before discovering it was a rare 18th-century Chinese ornament. She sold it an auction in 2014 for a staggering £150,000 ($250,000).

BEAR NECESSITIES

For 13 days and 13 nights in April 2014, French performance artist Abraham Poincheval lived inside the hollowed-out carcass of a dead bear. He ate, drank, slept, and lived inside the sterilized carcass while being filmed by two cameras at the Hunting and Wildlife Museum in Paris, France. He previously spent a week in an underground hole beneath a Marseille bookshop.

BLACK MAGIC

Using the pseudonym "Roadsworth" (suggesting a poet of the roads), stencil artist Peter Gibson has transformed the streets, sidewalks and parking lots of Montréal, Quebec, into large-scale works of art. He creates huge paintings on black asphalt so that it looks as if flocks of geese are swooping along the city's streets and schools of sardines are swimming happily along busy roads.

FAKE FOOD

New York artist Roxy Paine spent six months building a replica of a fast-food restaurant entirely out of birch wood, maple, and glass. It featured order screens, cash registers, soft-drink dispensers, a frozen yogurt machine, straw dispensers, coffee brewers, deep fryers, and stacked-up containers for burgers and fries.

SAND DRAWINGS

Using a device called a Focused Ion Beam, Brazilian artist Vik Muniz and researcher Marcelo Coelho etch detailed, microscopic drawings of sandcastles onto individual grains of sand.

ROYAL TOAST

Nathan Wyburn from Cardiff, Wales, created an image of the Duchess of Cambridge from 35 slices of toasted white bread and a pot of Marmite yeast extract.

LIPSTICK LOOK-ALIKES

May Sum from Hong Kong, China, carves expensive lipsticks into small, lifelike 3-D busts of such fashion icons as Lady Gaga, Audrey Hepburn, Elizabeth Taylor, and Madonna. Some of the lipstick sculptures take more than a week because she goes into great detail, even capturing English model Twiggy's individual eyelashes.

BARBIE PARTS

For her "Plastic Body" series, Margaux Lange makes unique items of wearable jewelry from the parts of old Barbie dolls.

The New York–born artist, who always loved Barbie as a child, has thousands of secondhand Barbies in her studio and uses their hands, arms, ears, mouths, breasts, eyes, and legs to make necklaces, earrings, brooches, and rings. One neckpiece is made up of 29 Barbie mouths; another contains 20 Barbie arms!

PRISON MURAL

While serving a 70-month jail sentence, artist Jesse Krimes created an impressive, 39-panel mural from prison bedsheets, newspapers, and hair gel. He burnished thousands of high-quality images from *The New York Times* onto the bedsheets with just a plastic spoon and using hair gel as a transfer agent. He worked on one sheet at a time, and after he had finished each one, he shipped it to his home in New Jersey. It was only when he was eventually released that he saw the complete work.

UNDERWATER ARTIST

Wearing full diving gear, Ukrainian artist Alexander Belozor paints landscapes underwater—at depths of up to 85 ft (26 m). He paints on canvases covered in an adhesive waterproof coating to prevent the colors running.

CANDY MAP

Seventeen-year-old Jackson McKenzie of Nampa, Idaho, used more than 70,000 M&M candies to create a vast mosaic of Idaho and its state counties. The mosaic, which took ten months to plan and six days to complete, covered an area of 124 sq ft (11.5 sq m) on the bottom floor of the Idaho Statehouse.

PENCIL TOWER

Gandhavalla Umasankar from Andhra Predesh, India, took two months to build a model of the Eiffel Tower from 600 pencil leads.

RECYCLED HOMES

Gregory Kloehn, a designer from Oakland, California, has turned recycled and reclaimed materials found on streets into mobile homes for homeless people, featuring washing machine doors for windows and minivan tops for roofs.

INCENDIARY SCULPTURE

A $500,000 public art sculpture, *Wishing Well*, in the shape of a giant, halved steel ball, was removed from display in Calgary, Alberta, Canada, after the sun's rays bounced off its mirrored concave interior and burned a hole through a visitor's clothing. People had been encouraged to step inside the shiny object's 16-ft-high (5-m) hollow hemispheres and send text messages that would then be translated into a light display.

PAPER PLANES

Xu Shuquan from Chengdu, China, has spent 60 years folding 10,000 paper planes, using an origami technique called "Zhezhi."

VICTORY CELEBRATION

When the University of Mississippi football team, the Ole Miss Rebels, beat Alabama for the first time in 11 years in 2014, fans swarmed onto the field at the Vaught-Hemingway Stadium in Oxford, dismantled the goalposts, and paraded them through the streets.

IRON MAN

Zhongkai Xiang, a young artist from Taiwan, spent 12 months of his spare time making an incredible full-size Iron Man suit out of cardboard. He has also created life-size sculptures of horses, dragons, and birds from cardboard. As a break from working with cardboard, he made a sculpture of an alien out of drinking straws.

TONGUE PAINTING

Artist Ani K from Kerala, India, has painted more than 1,000 artworks—including an 8-ft-wide (2.4-m) version of Leonardo da Vinci's *The Last Supper* and this portrait of Jesus—with his tongue. He uses his tongue as a palette on which to mix new colors and then licks the paint onto the canvas before twisting his head to form different strokes, even though the process often leaves him with headaches and jaw pain.

DIRTY WORK

Parking attendant Rafael Veyisov uses just his fingers to draw amazing pictures of birds, buildings, and landscapes in the layers of dust and dirt that collect on vehicles in the streets of Baku, Azerbaijan.

ICE HORSES

Artists in Russia spent nearly two months sculpting 400 ice horses on Siberia's Lake Baikal—the world's deepest freshwater lake. Each horse was modeled from a 2-ton block of ice cut out of the lake's frozen surface.

GLASS PLANTS

Glassblower Jason Gamrath of Seattle, Washington, makes 12-ft-tall (3.6-m) flowers from glass—even though it sometimes means climbing inside a burning hot oven.

The biggest of his beautifully detailed flowers was made from one solid piece of molten glass, but his usual equipment was not big enough so he had to build a special 10 × 12 ft (3 × 3.6 m) oven heated to 1,832°F (1,000°C). Covered in flameproof Kevlar and a silver aluminum suit, he then climbed inside the red-hot oven and sculpted the flower, aware that he could remain inside only for so long. He still got a little burned—but reckons it was worth it.

CHAIR TOWER

To mark the 125th anniversary of the completion of the Eiffel Tower, French company Fermob built a Paris art installation from 324 red Bistro chairs in recognition that the real tower stands 324 m (1,063 ft) tall. The 43-ft-high (13-m) model was held together by 5,184 rivets and contained 3,888 separate welding points.

FILM COLLAGE

Korean photographer Seung Hoon Park makes collages of famous buildings and landmarks from dozens of strips of 8-mm or 16-mm camera film. He takes hundreds of photos at a chosen location, places the film strips in rows, and then weaves them together to give the impression of a single large print.

BABY BELT

Seventy-one-year-old Mary Jane François of Yellowknife, Canada, spent two years making a 21-ft-long (6.5-m) baby belt—the longest baby belt in the world. The belt—a traditional aboriginal garment which mothers use to carry their babies—consisted of 26 beaded flowers, each about the size of a person's hand, with a rainbow in the middle.

HOLE PUNCHING

Norwegian artist Anne-Karin Furunes makes black-and-white portraits by punching thousands of tiny perforations into large canvases. She covers the canvas with a layer of black acrylic paint and then punches the holes—making each one by hand and using 30 different sizes— to form an image.

CARDBOARD DRAGON

British artist Chris Gilmour has created a sculpture that retells the story of the patron saint of England, St. George, slaying the dragon. Measuring 10 ft (3 m) tall, the statue is made entirely from cardboard and glue using boxes and cigarette cartons found on the streets.

WEEPING STATUE

Thousands of worshipers descended on a house in the small Israeli town of Tarshiha in February 2014 after a statue of the Virgin Mary, bought by Osama and Amira Khoury a few months earlier, appeared to be weeping oil.

TOP MAN

Bob Wheeler of Webster Groves, Missouri, reached the summit of Africa's 19,340-ft-high (5,895-m) Mount Kilimanjaro on October 2, 2014—at age 85.

COSTLY PRANK

Pranksters painted cheap, red nail varnish on the white marble toes of the statue of *Satyr Playing the Flute* in the grounds of the Gatchina Palace Museum, Russia—but because of the way the varnish reacted with the marble, it cost the museum $70,000 to have it removed.

STRAW MOSAIC

Fier, Albania, artist Saimir Strati made a mosaic from more than 150,000 plastic drinking straws. The artwork, titled *Adam's Apple*, represents the bitten apple from the Garden of Eden and measures 325 sq ft (30 sq m).

PUZZLE DESK

Kagen Schaefer, a woodworker from Denver, Colorado, crafted a desk with an internal pipe organ and more than 20 puzzles and secret compartments.

SHELL SKULL

Artist Gregory Halili has carved delicate human skulls on black- and gold-lipped mother of pearl shells collected from his native Philippines.

After the carving process is finished, he adds oil paint with such finesse that it is difficult to see where nature ends and the artist begins. Also known as nacre, mother of pearl is a blend of minerals secreted by oysters and some other mollusks as an inner shell layer to protect them from parasites.

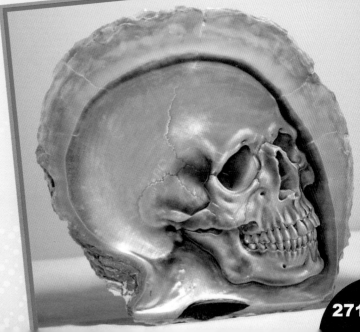

PIXEL PAINTING

It can take him up to 500 hours to finish each work.

272

Bradley Hart injects plastic bubble wrap with paint to create pictures that appear to be made up of thousands of pixels.

The painstaking process involves loading acrylic paint into up to 2,500 syringes and then injecting each tiny air-filled bubble individually. For his recreation of Johannes Vermeer's masterpiece *Girl with a Pearl Earring*, Bradley filled 25,488 individual bubbles, while his portrait of the late Apple cofounder Steve Jobs required 15,764 bubbles to be injected with 89 of the 121 different colors of paint he has in his palette.

Just filling the syringes may take up to a week, so it can take him up to 500 hours to finish each work. "If you inject too fast, you're going to destroy the bubble," he says. "But if you go too slow, it doesn't fill properly."

Completed artwork

The New York–based artist was inspired to use bubble wrap after finding a roll left over from wrapping his first solo exhibition. Researching the history of the product, he found that it was originally invented in 1957 as a modern form of wall covering. So he has not only taken it back in that direction; he is also flipping it from its popular use as a protective covering for art into art itself.

He even manages to create a second collection of paintings from the actual injection process. As the bubbles are injected, the excess paint drips down the back of the piece. Upon completion, the drippings are peeled away to reveal an imprint of the work, which becomes part of his *Impressions* series.

Part of his *Impressions* series.

Made of bubble wrap!

ASK

How did you start getting into bubble wrap art?
That's a big question, and there were a bunch of ideas leading up to it. I was trying to find the quintessential dumb material, and to make something from everyday material. My first pieces were a number of signs that said "Don't touch the art!" But, as it was bubble wrap, everyone wants to touch it! Then I spray-painted over it, saying "Touch me!" But if you did touch it, it is solid once the paint injected into the bubbles has dried, so I was playing with your senses. If you did work up the courage to touch the art, you thought "Oh, I can't pop this."

What is the largest bubble piece you've created?
The biggest piece I have done, which took me over 500 hours, is the old master, *The Ladies*, which is 7 × 6.5 ft (2.1 × 2 m) and contains more than 40,000 bubbles.

What do you do if you make a mistake? I invented a tool to remove damaged bubbles, a cylinder that can cut around the bubble remove it and replace it with a fixed bubble. The process is so seamless that even I cannot find the replaced bubble!

Your favorite piece? I can't answer this; it's really hard, because I love them all. Although sometimes some do turn out better than I expected, but I love all my babies equally!

For this re-creation of Johannes Vermeer's masterpiece *Girl with a Pearl Earring*, Bradley filled 25,488 individual bubbles! He has also re-created other classic artworks with bubble wrap, including Leonardo da Vinci's *Mona Lisa* and Vincent Van Gogh's self-portrait.

MATCHSTICK GLOBE

Over a period of almost two years, Andy Yoder of Falls Church, Virginia, built a 43-in (109.2-cm) diameter, 200-lb (90-kg) world globe from 300,000 matchsticks. He made his Earth's core from plywood, cardboard, and expanding foam, and then covered it in rice paper. Each colored match was carefully marked so he could replicate the image of 2012's Hurricane Sandy approaching the east coast of the U.S.A. He painstakingly hand-painted the matchsticks five at a time—blue for sea, green for land, and white for clouds.

TREE LIKENESS

The natural markings on a tree stump in Lillehammer, Norway, have formed a remarkable replica of artist Edvard Munch's famous painting *The Scream*.

PLASTIC FANTASTIC

Instead of using a brush, Sandy Byers paints beautiful landscapes with plastic credit cards. Her unusual technique started by accident when, on a 2013 painting trip to Marymere Falls in Olympic National Park, Washington, she realized that she had forgotten her brushes. Rather than go back, she took out her credit card and began painting with it. Since then, she has never used a brush, preferring to scrape the paint onto the canvas with her large array of cards.

REAL TEETH

An 18th-century Mexican statue of Jesus Christ contains real human teeth. Restoration experts made the shocking discovery from X-rays, which showed that the teeth in the statue of the Lord of Patience in a church in San Bartolo Cuautlalpan once belonged to an adult human before being inserted into the mouth of the Christ figure. The teeth of statues are often made of animal bone, but rarely human teeth.

RECLAIMED TOYS

Marlyn Pealane from Manila, Philippines, has a collection of hundreds of thousands of toys, many of which were found in local garbage.

COIN MOSAIC

Swedish company Sandvik Coromant unveiled a coin mosaic covering more than 840 sq ft (78 sq m) in Chicago, Illinois. It used 214,000 dollars and coins, worth more than $65,000.

HANDMADE CAVES

For over 25 years, sculptor Ra Paulette has used a pickaxe to scrape and shape New Mexico's sandstone cliffs into a series of 14 ornately decorated caves. One of his artistic caves, *Tree of Human Kindness*, located between Santa Fe and Taos, covers 208 acres (84 ha) and is valued at $795,000.

1,000 BRICKS

For more than two decades, 78-year-old Neil Brittlebank, from Leeds, England, has traveled the length and breadth of the U.K. collecting old and rare house bricks—and he now has more than 1,000 of them in his collection.

HIGHLINE WALK

Battling wind and rain, slackliner Alexander Schulz, from Rosenheim, Germany, after three days of trying and failing, finally managed to walk the incredible distance of 1,230 ft (375 m) along a highline in China. The line was anchored between two cliffs 330 ft (100 m) above the ground.

CD PORTRAITS

Italian artists Mirco Pagano and Moreno De Turco spent more than 200 hours lining up 6,500 compact disks to create portraits of seven world famous musicians—Michael Jackson, Bob Marley, Jim Morrison, Jimi Hendrix, James Brown, Freddie Mercury, and Elvis Presley—from copies of their own CDs.

CARD MURAL

Los Angeles–based artist Glenn Kaino made a large mural featuring a sculptural portrait of magician Ricky Jay from several decks of playing cards.

SEWER STUNTS

Wakeboarders Matt Crowhurst, Lee Debuse, Christian Koester, and Ollie Moore performed stunts in a sewer in Surrey, England. They swapped their boat for a rope attached to a portable petrol winch to show off their skills in the drain.

New York artist James Haggerty makes portraits of iconic Star Wars characters from tens of thousands of multi-colored staples!

He has fashioned Darth Vader from 10,496 staples and C-3PO from 33,580 staples. He punches each staple individually onto a painted board and can take six months to complete a work.

Made using 10,496 staples!

STAPLE PORTRAITS

TINY PEOPLE

London-based artist Jonty Hurwitz creates nanosculptures of humans that are so tiny they can fit in the eye of a needle and can be viewed only through an electron microscope at 400x magnification. He uses over 200 cameras shooting simultaneously to scan life-size models and then prints his tiny sculptures using a special micro-sized 3-D printing technique. Then, over several hours, the sculptures are assembled, pixel by pixel and layer by layer.

Eye of a needle!

DUST DRAWINGS

Using just one finger as his brush, artist Ben Long from London, England, draws beautiful pictures in the layers of dust that accumulate on the rear doors of commercial trucks. If the drivers don't wash their trucks, his artworks can last for six months.

TINY COMIC

German artist Claudia Puhlfürst designed a comic strip, "Juana Knits the Planet," which Andrew Zonenberg etched onto a strand of human hair. He burned the dozen 25-micrometer frames into a single hair using focused ion beam etching.

FISHY BUSINESS

French artist and photographer Anne-Catherine Becker-Echivard recreates scenes of everyday life using real fish heads. She obtains the open-mouthed fish heads from a market and, once she has come up with an idea, asks her mother to make the costumes. She then photographs the dressed fish as puppets. The whole creative process can take her three months per picture.

BONE CHINA

Charles Krafft from Seattle, Washington, makes fine bone china—out of human bones! He mixes cremation ash with clay to create unique mementoes of the dead.

PAPER SHIPS

Since 1968, Peter Koppen from Munich, Germany, has folded more than 200,000 tiny paper ships to make colorful collages. To create his "microships," he makes 15 folds into pieces of paper that are about one-fifth the size of a postage stamp.

ZOMBIE BALLS

German spray-gun artist Oliver Paass designed a series of zombie bowling balls to promote 13th Street, the country's popular horror TV channel. Oliver and his team snuck into bowling alleys all over Germany and swapped ordinary balls with ones depicting gruesome images of decapitated heads.

GARBAGE
PORTRAITS

Zac Freeman of Jacksonville, Florida, has created a series of portraits of family members and friends from recycled garbage.

He incorporates up to 5,000 items of trash in each picture, including buttons, bottle tops, key caps, and even old computer keyboards. He works from photographs of his subject, gluing the objects onto his canvas, and each portrait takes him up to two years to complete.

SWEET ART

Instead of using paint, Othman Toma of Baghdad, Iraq, creates colorful pictures from ice cream, including an impressive portrait of a lion from a chocolate ice cream bar. He places his chosen flavors of ice cream on a plate until they melt and then puts the sugary liquid onto a brush and applies it to the canvas. When the work is finished, he takes a photograph of it, along with the ice creams used in the picture's making.

40 FRUITS

By using pieces of tape to graft together different fruit-bearing trees, Sam Van Aken, an art professor at Syracuse University, New York, has created a single tree that produces 40 types of stone fruit—including peaches, plums, cherries, nectarines, almonds, and apricots. The process took him over nine years to develop.

TO DIE FOR

Adam Brown of Grandview, Missouri, incorporates his dead clients' ashes into beautiful prints. People send him a small amount of the cremated remains of their loved ones and he then mixes the ashes with paints, glues, and resins to form a mixture used to create anything from the deceased's favorite place to a portrait of that person during life.

BONE JEWELRY

Kristin Bunyard of Austin, Texas, makes pieces of jewelry from old animal bones. She sources dead animals from farms or pet stores, and after removing the organs and excess flesh, she slow boils the bones for a few hours. She then soaks the bare bones in a peroxide mixture until they are clean, before turning them into elegant necklaces, bracelets, and earrings.

CLOUD SHAPER

For his series titled *Shaping Clouds*, Argentinian artist Martin Feijoó took pictures of clouds on a visit to Mexico and drew on top of them what he imagined from their outline. The shapes of the clouds he photographed inspired him to create illustrations of a dinosaur, a dog, a turtle, a crocodile, a duck, a fish, and even the "Father of Evolution," Charles Darwin.

JEDI TAPESTRY

Sci-fi fan and artist Aled Lewis from London, England, has hand-stitched the entire *Star Wars* story onto a 30-ft (9-m) Bayeux-style tapestry. He watched and rewatched the movies and read up on the major plot lines and characters before creating his *Coruscant Tapestry*, the border of which features quotes from each film written in Aurebesh—the writing system used in the *Star Wars* universe.

BOTTLE TREE

Dalius Valukonis, a Lithuanian policeman, built a 13-ft (4-m)-tall Christmas tree from 1,100 empty bottles of champagne and sparkling water. A non-drinker, he spent three years obtaining the bottles from restaurants, bars, family and friends.

CHEWED GUM

Ukrainian artist Anna-Sofiya Matveeva creates portraits of celebrities such as Elton John and the late Steve Jobs from hundreds of pieces of gum chewed by her friends. After separating the gum into different colors, she warms it up in a microwave. Each finished artwork can weigh up to 11 lb (5 kg).

GLASS KNITTING

This sculpture by Seattle-based artist Carol Milne makes it appear as though she is able to knit with glass, but it is really the result of a four-week process. She first builds the sculpture with wax, out of which she makes a mold. After filling the mold with glass pieces and heating it to 1,500°F (815°C), she waits days for it to cool and then gently chips away at it to reveal the glass sculpture.

GIANT DRAWING

Working five hours a day for eight days, Singapore's Edmund Chen single-handedly created a drawing of koi fish and lotus flowers on a giant roll of paper that measured more than 1,968 ft (600 m) long—that's six times the length of a soccer field.

LEGO SANTA

A team led by Duncan Titmarsh used 750,000 Lego bricks to construct a Santa Claus, in a sleigh with a sack of presents, and nine reindeer.

Pop artist Jason Mecier spent more than 30 hours creating a candy tribute to Robin Williams.

Mecier, from San Francisco, California, created the amalgam of some of Williams's most famous characters—Mork, Mrs. Doubtfire, and Patch Adams—from pieces of candy, including jelly beans, gum balls, black licorice, and gummy bears.

CANDY TRIBUTE

LIFE IN A

Nathalie Alony from Mantova, Italy, makes the most of small spaces, using clay to craft lots of tiny, everyday apartment scenes, which she then places within the confined space of empty sardine cans.

She has named the humorous series "Home Sweet Home" or "The Sardinas," and describes her cozy creations as being "all these different lives, different stories, different histories and futures, all that intimacy, condensed between four walls, one next to the other, in little apartments, little boxes that each of us calls home."

Soon after starting the project, Nathalie began miniaturizing almost everything she saw!

SARDINE CAN

Nathalie started the series after thinking about people "squeezed in like sardines" in apartment buildings.

Nathalie finds humor and intrigue in everyday scenes.

Nathalie started "The Sardinas" in 2006 after thinking about people "squeezed in like sardines" in apartment buildings, hearing their neighbors' lives in these enclosed spaces. She captures the scenes of people's daily lives within 2.4-by-4-in (6-by-10-cm) tins, despite the fact that the tins once housed small salty fish, which she feeds to her cats.

She has completed hundreds of sardine-can scenes, portraying a large array of scenarios. Most are inspired by her own life, but sometimes other people commission her to place their own stories within a can. Nathalie sees the cans as her own biography—in 3-D comic frames that reveal her life.

It takes about three days for Nathalie to create a scene.

Nathalie feeds the tiny fish from the tins to her cats!

ASK

How long does it take to create one scene? It takes about three days—including molding, cooking, carving, sanding, painting, and doing the interior.

Why in a sardine can specifically? When too many people are tightly sharing a small space we use the expression "squeezed in like sardines," so when the idea came up of making condo-buildings with cans, the medium served the metaphor.

What tools do you use to create the scenes? I use small cutters and professional modeling tools. I also have a kit bought in a dentist market in Delhi, India, which is extremely useful.

How do you come up with the ideas for each scene? I began with the most simple activities people do in their houses: have dinner, argue, go to the toilet, and so on. Soon enough, "The Sardinas" took me over and I started miniaturizing every situation I had in mind, everything I saw, heard, imagined, or fantasized. It became an instinct, an impulse, a new and amusing communication form.

PAPER LAYERS

Beijing-based Chinese artist Li Hongbo creates sculptures that look like Roman plaster busts but are really made from as many as 8,000 layers of thin paper.

The layers are carefully glued together and then carved into shape. As these paper layers are flexible, the sculptures can be stretched and twisted in almost any direction, like a giant slinky, and then compressed back together into their original form.

CON-HORSE-TIONIST

Jockey Stefanie Hofer "rides" a team of ten painted acrobats contorted into the shape of a racehorse at the winning post at Ascot Racecourse in Berkshire, England, in July 2014. The unusual creature, which celebrated the Shergar Cup, was created in seven hours by the make-up artists Civilised Mess.

TO BOLDLY GROW

As part of his Exobiotanica project, Japanese artist Azuma Makoto launched a bonsai tree into space at Black Rock Desert, Nevada. Tied to a large helium balloon, the tree soared for 100 minutes, reaching an altitude of 91,900 ft (28,000 m) before the balloon popped and the tree plummeted back to Earth. He also launched a bouquet of flowers 87,000 ft (26,500 m) into space.

MINI LISA

Scientists at the Georgia Institute of Technology created a copy of Leonardo da Vinci's *Mona Lisa* that is just a third of the width of a human hair in size. They used an atomic force microscope and heat-based nanotechnology to make the tiny painting, and by varying the amount of heat applied at each pixel, they were able to control the picture's shades to accurately replicate the original famous artwork.

POWDERED MUMMY

The paint color known as "mummy brown," which was popular with the Pre-Raphaelite artists of the 19th century, was made from powdered Egyptian mummies, both human and feline. Colormen could satisfy the demands of their artist customers for 20 years with the contents from a single mummy.

SINGLE STROKE

Using a 100-year-old technique called Hitofude Ryuu, the Sumie painters from the Kousyuuya Studio in Nikko, Japan, can paint the body of a dragon with a single stroke of the brush. Starting from the ornate head, it takes them just a matter of seconds to sweep a large brush across the canvas to paint the dragon's body, depicting all its scales and diverse shading.

SCRAP ROBOTS

A scrap metal yard in Jinan, China, built and displayed more than 20 Transformer robots—including Optimus Prime, Bumblebee, and Megatron—from leftover material. The tallest robot is more than 52 ft (16 m) tall and weighs 5 tons.

MISSED OPPORTUNITY

Original signed canvases by famous British street artist Banksy were sold from a stall in New York City's Central Park during October 2013 for just $60 each—despite being worth up to $30,000. Over a period of seven hours, only three people bought anything in the sale, the day's takings coming to just $420, with many valuable pieces remaining unsold.

A large sheet of paper is vacuum-sucked onto a table, keeping the artwork perfectly flat.

Ted's blood feeds into the machine.

Blood flows as if it were ink, mapping out the illustration.

BLOOD SELFIE

Brooklyn-based artist Ted Lawson drew a life-size, nude self-portrait, titled *Ghost in the Machine*, from his own blood.

Ted fed his blood, as if it were ink, intravenously into a preprogrammed robotic arm attachment, which dispensed the blood onto a huge sheet of paper to form the illustration. He prepared for the three-hour blood selfie by eating a large cheeseburger, as he says fatty foods improve his blood flow.

BOTTLE MOSAIC

A team of artists in Dubai, United Arab Emirates, created a mosaic from 12,844 plastic dishwasher liquid bottles. The mosaic, which took 30 hours to make and spelled out the brand name of the dishwasher liquid, was 38 ft (11.5 m) long and 22 ft (6.6 m) wide.

TWINKIE FAN

Inspired by Andy Warhol, artist Nancy Peppin from Reno, Nevada, has created dozens of artworks featuring America's iconic, cream-filled Twinkie snack cakes. When makers Hostess Brands closed in 2012, she created *The Last Snack*, a nod to Leonardo Da Vinci's famous painting *The Last Supper*, featuring a Twinkie in place of Jesus.

LOOKING UP

Visitors to the Beaverbrook Art Gallery in Fredericton, New Brunswick, often view the large Salvador Dali painting *Santiago El Grande* by lying on the floor in the middle of the lobby. It is said that if you lie down and look at the painting from below, the horse appears to be jumping out of the canvas in 3-D.

PUMPKIN DINOSAURS

The 2013 Great Jack O'Lantern Blaze at Croton-on-Hudson, New York, featured sculptures made from 5,000 individually carved pumpkins. They included life-sized dinosaur skeletons made entirely from hundreds of pumpkins stacked together.

PIANO BUTTONS

Augusto Esquivel from Buenos Aires, Argentina, spent more than two months making a life-size 3-D sculpture of an upright piano from 30,000 black and white buttons. He suspends hundreds of strings from the ceiling and then threads differently colored buttons onto those strings in the required order. When he brings the strings together, they form an image. The Miami-based artist has also used the technique to create portraits of movie stars including Audrey Hepburn, Marilyn Monroe, and James Dean.

BONE FLOWERS

Believe it or not, these delicate flowers are made from the bones of dead animals. Sculptor Hideki Tokushige from Tokyo, Japan, buys frozen rats and mice from pet stores, defrosts them, cuts away the flesh, and spends more than a month dissecting the skeleton. He then glues the individual bones together to create beautiful flowers, each one containing at least 100 rodent bones.

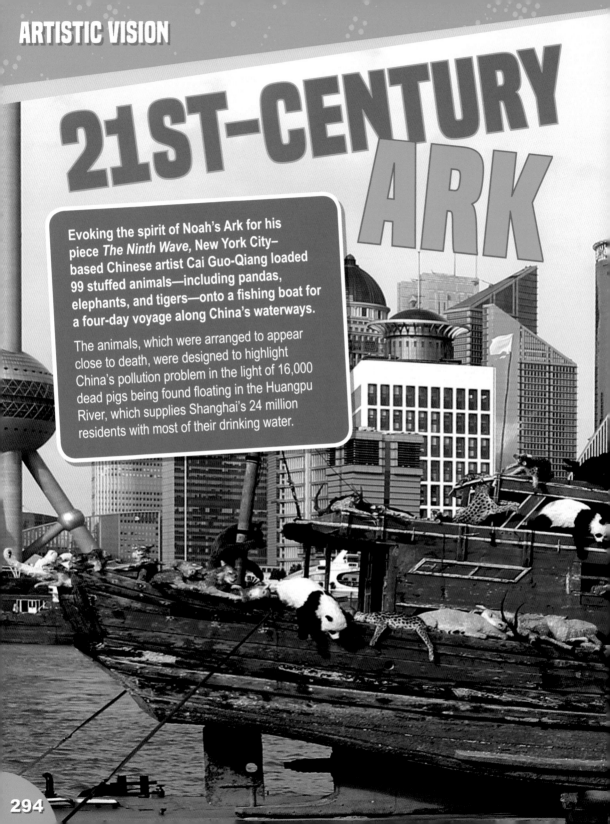

21ST-CENTURY ARK

Evoking the spirit of Noah's Ark for his piece *The Ninth Wave*, New York City–based Chinese artist Cai Guo-Qiang loaded 99 stuffed animals—including pandas, elephants, and tigers—onto a fishing boat for a four-day voyage along China's waterways.

The animals, which were arranged to appear close to death, were designed to highlight China's pollution problem in the light of 16,000 dead pigs being found floating in the Huangpu River, which supplies Shanghai's 24 million residents with most of their drinking water.

PAINTING PREMONITION

Artist Chloe Mayo from Surrey, England, painted a near-perfect likeness of herself with her husband—months before she even met him! In 2009, she created the image of herself holding hands with her dream partner, a man with a dark beard. Weeks later, she joined an online dating website and spent two months messaging 30-year-old Michael Goeman before finally meeting him face to face. After they had been dating for six weeks, she thought his face looked familiar and remembered her oil painting. Seeing the similarity in the two men, she was so worried about being accused of stalking Michael that at first she hid the picture under her bed—but once they married in 2012 she could hang it proudly in their home.

MAN ON LEASH

For his performance art piece *Hipster on a Leash*, Chinese artist Guo O Dong rode a Segway while walking a bearded man on a leash around the streets and parks of the Williamsburg neighborhood of New York City. The artist had looked on Craigslist to find someone who would allow himself to be rented out for the day.

SPOON STATUE

Sculptor Alfie Bradley built a 12-ft-high (3.6-m) statue of a gorilla from 40,000 metal spoons for spoon-bending entertainer Uri Geller. Hand-welding every spoon individually to the statue at the British Ironworks Centre in Shropshire, England, it took almost five months to finish the gorilla, using spoons donated from as far away as China, Kenya, and India.

STREET PAINTING

A team of artists led by Yang Yongchun created a 3-D street painting on the campus of the Communication University of China in Nanjing that measured nearly a quarter of a mile long. The 1,200-ft-long (365-m) painting, called *Rhythms of Youth*, covered a total area of 29,466 sq ft (2,737 sq m) and took 20 days to complete.

PIGEON POOP

Frances Wadsworth-Jones makes £2,500 ($3,767) designer brooches that deliberately look like pigeon poop. The artist, from London, England, took hundreds of pictures of bird poop to inspire the original design for "Heaven Sent," a line of jewelry consisting of black diamonds and sapphires arranged so that they replicate the shape, size, and color of pigeon poop.

EXTREME EXHIBITIONS

Abstract artist Edgy (real name Edward Fraser), from Alice Springs, Australia, staged his first exhibition at the Singing Sand Dunes of the Qatari Desert, where the temperature was above 122°F (50°C). By contrast, his second exhibition was a cold one, held at the base camp of Mount Everest at an altitude of 17,598 ft (5,364 m).

DUNG HEAPS

The Oriel of the Blue Horses, a 2012 installation by Austrian artist Martin Gostner, consists only of four piles of fake dung. Each dung heap corresponds to one of the horses in Franz Marc's expressionist painting *The Tower of Blue Horses*, which the Nazis seized in 1937 for being "un-German" and has since vanished. It is not known whether or not the painting still exists.

MATCHSTICK MODELS

Djordje Balac from Gospic, Croatia, has made a fully functional model of the world's largest crane—a Liebherr LTM 11200—from 175,518 matchsticks, 44 lb (20 kg) of glue, and 17.6 lb (8 kg) of varnish. Working every day from 8 a.m. to midnight, it took him three months to make the crane, which, just like the real thing, has a moveable extending arm. He has also made amazingly detailed matchstick models of trucks, complete with detachable cabins.

Bart refers to his art style as "pugilist expressionism."

HAND PUNCHED ART

Dutch boxer and artist Bart van Polanen Petel paints with his fists.

Bart, who owns a gym in Tilburg, puts on boxing gloves, dips them in paint, and throws punches at a blank canvas wrapped around a punching bag until it is daubed in a brightly colored abstract pattern. He says he just keeps punching until he is happy with what's in front of him, and sometimes adds finishing touches with his fingers. He needs to stay in peak physical fitness, as each of his pieces take between one and three hours of boxing to complete.

BLOOD SCULPTURE

Shihan Hussaini, an artist and archery teacher from Chennai, India, sculpted a bust of J. Jayalalitha, Chief Minister of the Tamil Nadu state, from 23.2 pints (11 l) of frozen blood.

For more than eight years, Shihan has had his blood drawn every three months and stored ready to be used as a medium for a sculpture, but he had only 13.7 pints (6.5 l) of his own blood put by, so he had to ask his archery students to supply the rest. To create his blood sculpture, Shihan first made a likeness from clay, and then created a silicone mold and filled it with the blood. Finally, the mold was frozen at –17°F (–27°C) for two months before being unveiled to the public.

ARTISTIC LEAVES

Iranian-born artist Omid Asadi from Manchester, England, uses a craft knife, needle, and magnifying glass to turn dry, fallen leaves into intricate works of art. He carves beautiful silhouettes into the fragile brown leaves, including portraits of John Lennon, Bob Marley, and Jimi Hendrix, and an impression of Edvard Munch's painting *The Scream*. Each image can take him up to a month to create, after which he carefully presses the finished leaf onto a sheet of white paper with wood glue.

EGG CARTONS

Charlotte Austen and Jack Munro used 6,500 egg cartons to create a life-size replica of a World War II Spitfire fighter plane at Duxford Imperial War Museum in England. The cartons were attached to a wood and steel frame, which was broken down into 12 sections for transportation by truck.

TAPE ARTIST

Emanuel Pavao shared with Ripley's these pictures of his artwork. The Toronto-based artist replicates photographs of storefronts, people, and scenes of urban decay using different types of tape—including duct, electrical, and masking—applied to paper or canvas board. He seals the final artwork with a clear resin for protection.

CRAZY CRAVINGS

Pie inside!

John Clarkson of Lancashire, England, created a burger that was 5 ft 4 in (1.6 m) tall—only 2 in (5 cm) shorter than himself.

Called the "pie-scraper," it featured ten cheeseburgers, sausage rolls, a bacon sandwich, pizza, Spam, and pies, all encased in 18.7 lb (8.5 kg) of beef. Racking up 30,000 calories, it was enough to feed someone for nearly two weeks. It took John and his wife Corinne an hour and a half to assemble the burger on a specially made metal stand to make sure the tower did not topple.

PIE-SCRAPER

IRON TEETH

Chen Fengzhi, a 63-year-old Chinese woman, smashes lightbulbs and then chews the shards of glass with her "iron teeth." After swallowing the glass, she likes to bite down hard on a stone.

WHOSE TOOTH?

Jane Betts of Cambridge, England, bit into a slice of cheese she had bought from a supermarket and discovered a piece of tooth. She frantically checked her own teeth to see where it had fallen from, but finding that they were all intact, she took it to her dentist, who confirmed that it belonged to someone else.

EDIBLE LANDMARKS

Food artist Prudence Staite from Gloucestershire, England, re-created some of the U.K.'s most iconic landmarks—including the London Eye, Big Ben, Stonehenge, and the White Cliffs of Dover—from French fries and mushy peas. Her version of the statue *The Angel of the North* required 240 fries and took 12 hours to make.

HIP DINNER

Norwegian artist Alexander Wengshoel boiled and ate his own hip. He took the body part home after undergoing a hip replacement operation, boiled it to loosen the meat, and then ate it with potato gratin and a glass of wine. He said it tasted like "wild sheep." "First I just had a little taster, but since it tasted good, I made a full dinner of it. It was very exciting and stimulating. It was so personal."

WHALE ALE

An Icelandic brewery has released a new brew made from fin whale testicles smoked in sheep dung!

CHRISTMAS TREAT

A successful 1970s ad campaign led to it becoming popular in Japan to eat a bucket of KFC chicken on Christmas Eve—and orders are now taken months in advance.

NOODLE NIGHTMARE

Jun Chia of China was knocked over by a scooter while snacking—lodging his chopsticks into his neck. Miraculously, there was no damage to any key organs!

BUG SATAY

Among the tasty dishes on sale at the Shenyang Summer Food Festival in China was centipede satay served on a skewer.

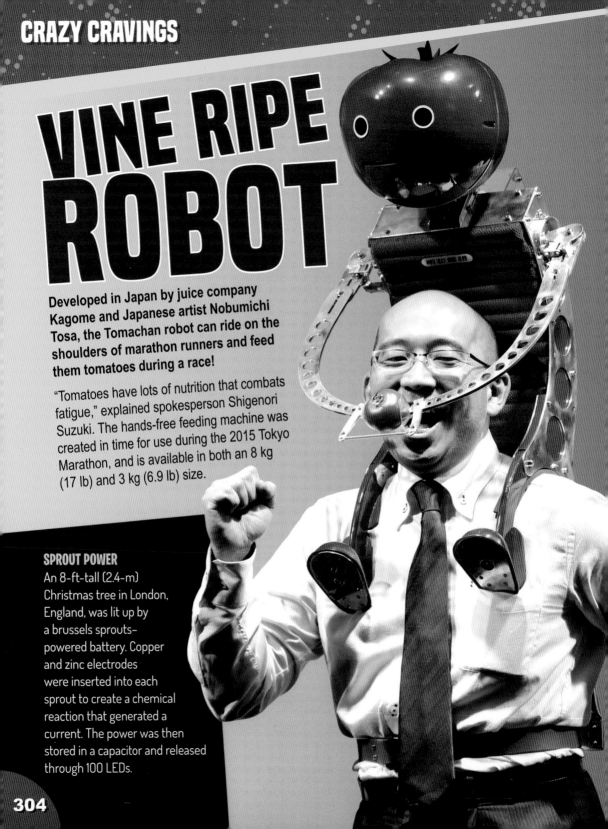

VINE RIPE ROBOT

Developed in Japan by juice company Kagome and Japanese artist Nobumichi Tosa, the Tomachan robot can ride on the shoulders of marathon runners and feed them tomatoes during a race!

"Tomatoes have lots of nutrition that combats fatigue," explained spokesperson Shigenori Suzuki. The hands-free feeding machine was created in time for use during the 2015 Tokyo Marathon, and is available in both an 8 kg (17 lb) and 3 kg (6.9 lb) size.

SPROUT POWER

An 8-ft-tall (2.4-m) Christmas tree in London, England, was lit up by a brussels sprouts–powered battery. Copper and zinc electrodes were inserted into each sprout to create a chemical reaction that generated a current. The power was then stored in a capacitor and released through 100 LEDs.

SILENT SUPPER

Jawdat Ibrahim, who owns the Abu Ghosh restaurant 6 mi (10 km) outside Jerusalem, Israel, offered customers a 50 percent discount if they turned off their cell phones during their meal.

KING NOODLE

Zhao Mingxi, chef at a noodle restaurant in Chongqing, China, can make a noodle that is 1,000 ft (300 m) long—more than 12 times the length of a tennis court. He regularly makes 200-ft (60-m) noodles and spends up to ten hours preparing and swinging them.

ZOMBIE BEER

The Dock Street Brewing Company based in Philadelphia, Pennsylvania, created a zombie beer brewed with real smoked goats' brains. The company said of its zombie beer: "Don't be surprised if its head doesn't hang around forever!"

PASTA STRAND

Lawson's Pasta Restaurant in Tokyo, Japan, created a single strand of pasta that measured an incredible 12,388 ft (3,776 m)— that's almost 2.5 mi (4 km) long!

CHILI PIE

At the State Fair of Texas in Dallas, cooks made a 1,325-lb (601-kg) Fritos chili pie, containing 635 bags of Fritos corn chips, 660 cans of chili, and 580 bags of shredded cheese.

SWEET MUSIC

Chocolatier Ben Milne and the Scottish band Found cooked up sweet music with the creation of their edible, playable chocolate records!

BLACK TOMATO

By crossbreeding red and purple tomato plants, Professor Jim Myers of the University of Oregon created a black tomato. The Indigo Rose tomato starts green as normal but ripens to jet black, and apart from its unique color, it is also believed to be beneficial in fighting obesity and diabetes.

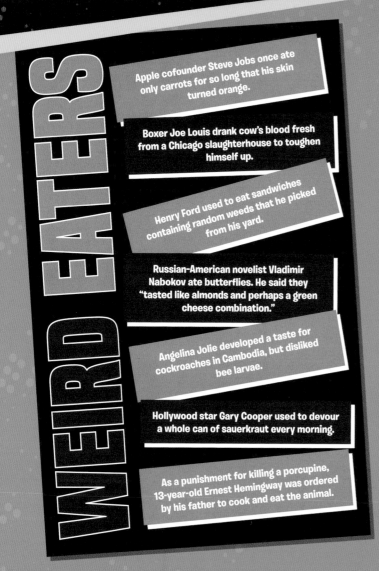

WEIRD EATERS

Apple cofounder Steve Jobs once ate only carrots for so long that his skin turned orange.

Boxer Joe Louis drank cow's blood fresh from a Chicago slaughterhouse to toughen himself up.

Henry Ford used to eat sandwiches containing random weeds that he picked from his yard.

Russian-American novelist Vladimir Nabokov ate butterflies. He said they "tasted like almonds and perhaps a green cheese combination."

Angelina Jolie developed a taste for cockroaches in Cambodia, but disliked bee larvae.

Hollywood star Gary Cooper used to devour a whole can of sauerkraut every morning.

As a punishment for killing a porcupine, 13-year-old Ernest Hemingway was ordered by his father to cook and eat the animal.

ANCIENT CHEESE

Cheese has been found on the bodies of mummies buried in China's Taklamakan Desert that is more than 3,500 years old, dating back to around 1615 BC. The combination of dry desert air and salty soil prevented the cheese from decaying. It remains a mystery why the people were buried with pieces of cheese on their necks and chests, but the food may have been intended as cheesy snack for the dead to enjoy in the afterlife.

FAST FOOD

To promote the variety of restaurants in the small Philadelphia, Pennsylvania, suburb of Jenkintown, Mayor Ed Foley ate in all 24 of them in one day—April 19, 2014.

CHICKEN POPSICLES

During a 2014 heatwave in Tokyo, Japan, the Zenyaren restaurant served iced chicken popsicles. The frozen skewers of grilled meat wrapped in collagen were snapped up by customers who said the ice pops not only kept them cool, but also improved their skin.

SWEET MEATS

Grundhofer's Old Fashioned Meats of Hugo, Minnesota, makes more than 100 flavors of bratwurst, including Bloody Mary, Cherry Kool-aid, Blueberry, and even Gummy Bear.

7 UP

In 2013, Joey "Jaws" Chestnut from San Jose, California, ate a record 69 hot dogs and buns in 10 minutes to win the Nathan's July 4th Hot Dog Eating Contest at Coney Island, New York, for the seventh consecutive year. In 2017, he won by downing 72 hot dogs!

MILK VODKA

Farmer Jason Barber from Dorset, England, produces vodka from pure cows' milk by fermenting the whey using a specialist yeast that turns milk sugar into alcohol. It took him three years to perfect the recipe for his Black Cow vodka.

BEER ICE CREAM

Atlanta, Georgia, firm Frozen Pints has created beer-flavored ice cream. The strongest tub has an alcohol level of 3.2 percent, and so customers must be of legal drinking age to buy and eat it. The quirky concept came about by accident when someone spilled beer near an ice-cream maker.

DUMPSTER MISSION

To protest against food waste, Baptiste Dubanchet of Tours, France, cycled 1,875 mi (3,000 km) from Paris, France, to Warsaw, Poland, eating only from dumpsters along the route.

COW URINE

Hindu worshipers in Agra, India, believe that drinking fresh cow urine first thing in the morning can cure stomach problems, cancer, and diabetes.

They also claim that cow pee is the only effective treatment for baldness. Hindus regard the cow as holy, and so dozens of people gather every day to drink the animals' urine, although apparently for the medicine to work, the cow must not have given birth. Jairam Singhai has been drinking cow pee for more than ten years and says it has brought his diabetes levels under control.

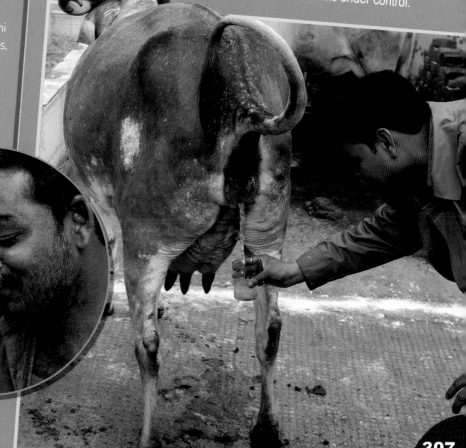

WARTIME RATIONS

Carolyn Ekins of Nottingham, England, lost 80 lb (36 kg) over a 12-month period from 2013 to 2014 by following a ration-book diet from World War II. She weighed 350 lb (159 kg) at her heaviest, but saw the pounds fall off after sampling wartime favorites such as mock turkey and Spam fritters. Her food bill was also reduced by 80 percent, saving her nearly $5,000.

PET FOOD

Dorothy Hunter, owner of pet stores in Richland and Kennewick, Washington, ate only dog, cat, and bird food for a month to demonstrate their nutritional value. She had the idea when, not having time to go out for a snack, she grabbed a bag of pet treats from the counter and was surprised how good they tasted. One of her favorite pet foods was Tiki Cat brand chicken, which she ate straight from the can.

TASTY WORM

The 12-inch-long (30-cm) Teredo worm, extracted from rotten mangrove trees, is considered a delicacy and is eaten raw by the Aboriginal people of Australia.

FREE FOOD

At The Picture House, a pop-up restaurant in London, England, customers pay for their food with photographs. The restaurant belongs to frozen food company Birds Eye, and serves two-course meals that customers do not have to pay for if they take a picture of the meal and then share it online via the social media site Instagram.

COCKROACH TEA

Tea made from cockroaches was a traditional remedy for tetanus in 19th-century Louisiana. Powdered roaches were also used to cure indigestion, while a crispy, fried cockroach tied tightly over a wound was said to relieve the pain of a bad cut.

COLOR CHANGE

Physicist Manuel Linares of Barcelona, Spain, has invented an ice cream that slowly changes color from blue to pink as it melts. Called Xamaleon, its exact recipe is secret, but it is made with strawberries, cocoa, almonds, banana, pistachio, vanilla, and caramel, and it tastes like tutti-frutti.

BANNED FRUIT

The ackee fruit, which is popular in Jamaica, can induce a deadly vomiting sickness if eaten when unripe. Its raw form is restricted in the U.S.A.

CHOCOLATE HEART

This isn't any ordinary chocolate heart— it's an anatomically correct 1 lb (0.4 kg) solid chocolate heart, complete with tasty valves and ventricles. It is made by long-standing Illinois chocolate manufacturer, Morkes, who also produce chocolate skulls and a chocolate brain.

RECEIPT TATTOO

Teenager Stian Ytterdahl from Lørenskog, Norway, will never forget one particular visit to his local McDonald's restaurant—because he has had the receipt tattooed onto his right arm.

The inked artwork features his order, which included a Coke, three cheeseburgers, and a cheeseburger Happy Meal, as well as the time and date, plus the restaurant's address and phone number.

GUMMY HUMANS

For around $60, FabCafé, a dining and designing destination in Tokyo, Japan, offers customers the chance to make mini gummy replicas of themselves using 3-D body scanning technology.

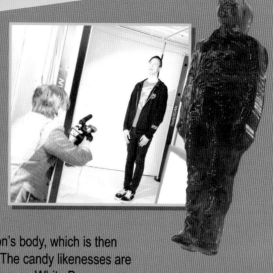

A full-body scan takes just six seconds, after which the café uses its own 3-D printer to create a hollow mold of the person's body, which is then filled with the sweet gummy mix. The candy likenesses are intended as a unique gift to partners on White Day, an Asian holiday held a month after Valentine's Day.

RICH DIET

Tests on the body of King Richard III of England, who died in 1485 and whose remains were discovered under a parking lot in 2012, show that he drank up to a bottle of wine a day in the last years of his life. Samples taken from a femur, rib, and tooth also reveal that he ate exotic bird meat, including swan, crane, heron, and egret.

JESUS PANCAKE

A pancake served up on Good Friday at Cowgirl Cafe, Norco, California, bore what looked like the face of Jesus Christ. Manager Karen Hendrickson was so moved by the religious image, she would not allow it to be eaten and instead preserved it in a freezer.

SUBWAY MEAL

To demonstrate that a new model of vacuum cleaner kills bacteria and germs, brand manager Ravi Dalchand ate a meal off the floor of a subway station used for filming in Toronto, Ontario. After cleaning the floor area with the Bissell Symphony, he tipped pasta onto the platform, pulled out a fork, and ate his meal, even mopping up the sauce with bread.

BLOODY SUNDAE

Washington, D.C., eatery The Pig serves a chocolate ice-cream sundae made with real pig's blood. The dessert, called "Sundae Bloody Sundae," uses blood instead of egg yolks in the ice-cream-making process to give a subtle mineral taste to the dark chocolate.

Your Uploads

MELON MONSTER

Ripley's was delighted to hear from Vancouver-based food sculptor Clive Cooper, who carves ordinary watermelons into fantastic shapes, including human faces, sharks, frogs, monkeys, and this scary alligator.

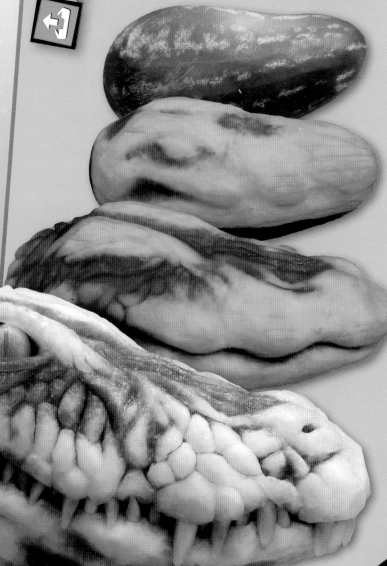

KING CAULI
Peter Glazebrook of Nottinghamshire, England, grew a cauliflower that measured 6 ft (1.8 m) wide and weighed a whopping 60 lb (27 kg), making it 30 times bigger than a regular cauliflower. The vast vegetable would make 120 portions of cauliflower cheese, but would require 6 lb (2.7 kg) of cheese as an accompaniment.

FRENCH FRIES
Chef Daan Vernaillen cooked French fries continuously for 125 hours—more than five days— at Sint-Katherina-Lombeek, Belgium, serving up around 2,000 portions to customers.

ANTIQUE BUN
A hot cross bun owned by Andrew and Dot Munson and kept in a cardboard box at their home in Essex, England, is more than 200 years old. They were given the bun 30 years ago by a neighbor, along with paperwork stating that it was baked in 1807. A traditional Easter food, hot cross buns were often stored for luck instead of eaten.

Dried, salted, and cooked field mice are strung on sticks in Malawi and sold as a tasty snack at markets or roadside stalls.

The mice are hunted in cornfields after the harvest when they are at their plumpest. Young boys either chase and catch them with their bare hands or lure them with food into water-filled clay pots where the rodents then drown. The most commonly eaten species is known locally as *kapuku* and is gray with a shorter tail than a rat.

MOUSE KEBABS

FINGER COOKIES

At The V in Beijing, China, customers can eat cookies that look frighteningly like severed fingers—complete with fake blood. The vampire-themed bar also serves chocolate in the shape of an eyeball and cocktails in syringes and blood bags.

DOG HAIR DIET

Dog lover Wang Jing of Heilongjiang Province, China, eats dog hairballs every day as a snack. She has eaten 1,000 hairballs over the last two years and says they taste especially nice— "sweet, like chocolates"—after she has given her pet poodle Kuku a bath. She began eating dog hair when Kuku shed some fur while she was washing her. Out of curiosity she put it in her mouth and immediately fell in love with the taste. Wang's obsession with dog hair has actually improved her health because it led her to quit her stressful job as a graphic designer and start designing clothes for dogs.

GARLIC COLA

The city of Aomori, known as the garlic capital of Japan, has produced such novelties as garlic beer, garlic ice cream, and Jats Takkola, a garlic cola.

LONG LIFE

English-born American chemist Robert Chesebrough, the inventor of Vaseline, attributed his longevity to eating a spoonful of the petroleum jelly every day right up until his death in 1933 at the age of 96.

PURRFECT PERK

In Indonesia, palm civet cats—also known as toddy cats—that prowl around coffee plantations ingest only the ripest beans, and their excretions are used to create a smooth, uniquely flavored $75 cup of coffee!

EXPLOSIVE FISH

Oilfish and escolar are popular seafood dishes in many Asian countries, but if you eat more than 6 oz (170 g) of them at a single sitting, they cause explosive, oily, orange diarrhea between 30 minutes and 36 hours later.

GOLDEN DELICIOUS

Should you prefer some glitzy gluten, visit the Pan Piña bakery in Andalusia, Spain, where you can taste a loaf of bread sprinkled with 250 mg of gold dust. Loaves cost a sparkling $140.

ROADKILL CRAVINGS

Here Alison is enjoying Japanese gyoza stuffed with her roadkill findings, a dish she calls "feral fusion."

Taxidermist and artist Alison Brierley of Harrogate, England, cooks and eats roadkill!

She usually turns the dead animals she finds on local roads into jewelry, but when she became pregnant, she developed cravings to eat the roadkill instead. Her flattened feasts include animals such as pheasant, rabbit, pigeon, deer, and owl. She wants to try fox and badger, but unfortunately, they are almost always too squashed to go into the cooking pot.

SCORCHING SAUCE
A sauce made by chef Muhammed Karim at the Bindi Restaurant in Lincolnshire, England, is so hot he has to wear a gas mask while preparing it. Called Atomic Kick Ass, the sauce scores 12 million units on the Scoville scale of hotness, making it nearly three times more fiery than police pepper spray.

GARLIC BEER
Japanese company Aomori has created a garlic-flavored dark beer—Garlic Black Beer—with a spicy aftertaste. Black garlic is achieved by fermenting normal garlic in a hot room until it turns charcoal black in color.

TEARING TREE TRUNK
A retired gardener was surprised to find that the thundering crash he heard from his Worcester, England, backyard was his 150-year-old apple tree splitting down the middle! The tree cracked under the enormous weight of all its apples.

MARSHMALLOW ART
Cake artist Michelle Wibowo of Sussex, England, made a life-sized reproduction of Michelangelo's famous Sistine Chapel fresco The Creation of Adam from 10,000 marshmallows and half a billion sprinkles.

DIET OF WORMS
Three volunteers in Beijing, China, ate worms for more than three months in a sealed laboratory to test whether astronauts could use them as their principal source of protein. The researchers fattened up the worms on plants grown inside the Moon Palace One biosphere and then ate them with a bean sauce.

COBRA EGGS
Snake breeder Huang Kuo-nan from Tainan, Taiwan, sells boiled fertilized cobra eggs as health food.

CHEESY STREET
As an alternative to salt, the city of Milwaukee, Wisconsin, has been experimenting with cheese brine—used in cheesemaking—to keep their streets from freezing in winter. Brine is particularly effective because it works at a lower temperature than normal salt.

COAL™

The first all-black
charcoal cheddar cheese
Deliciously creamy mature
cheddar blended with

The first all-black
charcoal cheddar cheese
Deliciously creamy,
mature cheddar blended
with charcoal

Char Coal™

Deliciously creamy,
mature cheddar
blended with charcoal

Char Coal™

Deliciously creamy,
mature cheddar
blended with charcoal

Char Coal™

Deliciously creamy,
mature cheddar
blended with charcoal

BLACK CHEESE

These may look like lumps of charcoal, but they are cheese!

Char Coal Cheese is made by British company Michael Lee Fine Cheeses. It is a mature cheddar that has been mixed with real charcoal. Despite its appearance, it has a creamy, cheddary taste.

HELPING HOMELESS

Narayanan Krishnan, from Tamil Nadu, India, gave up his career as a chef at top hotels to help poor people—and since 2002 he has served more than 1.5 million meals to India's homeless.

CHEESE FRIES DIET

A teenager living in Scotland suffers from an extreme food phobia, where she becomes severely nauseous if presented with new or feared food. To combat this, she subsists on a diet of French fries topped with cheddar cheese.

SILVER CARROTS

German food company The Deli Garage has invented a tasteless edible spray paint called Food Finish to give meals an exciting splash of color—it comes in shades of gold, silver, red, or blue.

RABBIT PIZZA

New Zealand restaurant chain Hell Pizza promoted its new rabbit pizza for Easter 2014 with giant billboards covered in real rabbit skins. Rabbits are considered a major pest in New Zealand.

MASSIVE MUSHROOM

A huge fungus found in Yunnan Province, China, was made up of as many as 100 individual caps attached at the base of their stems. It weighed more than 33 lb (15 kg) and measured 36 in (90 cm) in diameter.

SPECIAL TORTILLA

In Vitoria-Gasteiz, Spain, chef Senen Gonzalez and his team cooked up a 3,300-lb (1,500-kg) tortilla that measured 16 ft (5 m) wide and was large enough to feed more than 10,000 people. A giant pan and a complex heating mechanism were engineered specially for the event, allowing the gargantuan tortilla—made from eggs, potatoes, onions, and 40 gal (150 l) of olive oil—to be cooked on both sides without needing flipping.

CHOCOLATE ROOM

This is every chocolate-lover's dream—a hotel room where nearly everything, including the book, lamp, candlestick and candles, vase of flowers, slippers, toothbrush, toothpaste, and even the "Do Not Disturb" sign, is made of chocolate. The edible room was created by students from almost 220 lb (100 kg) of Callebaut chocolate and was installed for one night at London's Cavendish Hotel. The room was kept at a constant temperature of 61°F (16°C) to prevent the contents from melting.

INSECT PASTA

Absente, an Italian-style café in Kinshicho, Japan, serves a spaghetti dish topped with a generous helping of cooked locusts! Although they may look disgusting, locusts are packed with protein, calcium, and vitamin A, and were widely eaten in Japan during World War II to help combat malnutrition.

PITCH POTABLE

Taking everyone's healthy zero-calorie drink to the next level, Blk is an electrolyte-infused mineral water that just happens to be completely—and naturally—black!

VEGAN VICTUALS

Siblings Aubrey and Kale Walch raised $60,000 in a Kickstarter campaign to create The Herbivorous Butcher, the first American vegan butcher store that sells only meatless meat.

CARDBOARD RESTAURANT

At Taiwan's Carton King restaurant, everything—except for the food, the waiters, and some cutlery—is made of cardboard. Customers sit on cardboard chairs, drink from cardboard cans, and eat out of cardboard bowls at a cardboard table.

FRUIT BABIES

Farmer De He of Nanchang, China, grows fruit in the shape of babies. He was inspired to grow the fruit in little human-shaped molds by a Chinese fairy tale about a baby-shaped fruit that makes whoever eats it immortal.

The restaurant La Cocinita de San Juan in Mexico City sells tacos filled with Maguey worms, a species of edible caterpillar.

Highly nutritious—a 3.5-oz (100-g) portion contains calories equal to two plates of rice—the worms can be eaten alive and raw, or braised and served with a spicy sauce. The moth larvae are also used in bottles of the Mexican liquor *mezcal* to give added flavor to the drink.

WORM TACO

GOLDEN CUPCAKE

The Sweet Surrender candy store in Las Vegas, Nevada, sells a cupcake that costs $750. The "Decadence D'Or" is handcrafted from rare, expensive Venezuelan chocolate and Tahitian gold vanilla caviar, topped with Louis XIII Cognac—100 years in the making—and edible gold flakes.

SLUGFEST

Competitive eater Matt Stonie from San José, California, wolfed down 43 slugburgers—a traditional southern patty made of meat and soybeans served in a bun—in 10 minutes at the 2014 World Slugburger Eating Championships in Corinth, Mississippi.

TWIN DINER

At the Twin Stars diner in Moscow, Russia, the waiters, bartenders, and chefs are all identically dressed twins. Restaurant-owner Alexei Khodorkovsky was inspired to hire only twins by a 1964 Soviet film in which a schoolgirl crosses into a parallel world and finds her twin.

BUTTER CUP

Nick Monte, owner of the Village Chocolate Shoppe in Bennington, Vermont, made a giant peanut butter cup that was almost 5 ft (1.5 m) wide and weighed nearly 230 lb (104 kg). It was made up of 70 lb (32 kg) of chocolate and 160 lb (72 kg) of peanut butter.

FLY BURGERS

Villagers living near Lake Victoria in East Africa coat saucepans with honey to catch the trillions of flies that swarm around the area; they then make the trapped insects into nutritious flyburgers.

FOOD DROP

Adam Grant, David McDonald, and Huw Parkinson have founded a business in Melbourne, Australia, called Jafflechutes, which delivers toasted sandwiches by parachute from high-rise balconies to customers on the street below.

FRIED CAT

At the now defunct Gastronomical Festival of the Cat in La Quebrada, Peru, townsfolk feasted on hundreds of specially bred domestic cats for two days. They believed that eating cat burgers, fried cat legs, and fried cat tails could cure bronchial disease.

DELISH DISH

After hosting a party that left a mountain of dirty dishes in its wake, two Belgian designers invented edible dishes. Biodegradable and neutral tasting, the dishes are even oven safe!

SUPERSIZED SAUSAGE

Kazakh horsemeat butcher Timur Omarova made a 700-ft-long (213-m) sausage that weighed 2,770 lb (1,256 kg)—more than a ton. He used the intestines and thigh meat from 38 horses to make the colossal sausage in Yining, China.

CHEESE SHOES

Lisa Dillon, a fashion student from Bath Spa University, England, designed and made this pair of shoes out of cheese!

She sculpted a block of cheddar to form the heel of her "Jimmy Cheese" shoes, incorporated a stale cheese sandwich into part of the platform sole, and melted more cheese to create the embellishments on the top.

DRIED BLADDERS

Isinglass, a substance obtained from the dried swim bladders of tropical fish, is commonly used by breweries to make their beer less cloudy.

COFFEE WINE

Florida beverage company Fun Friends Wine has created a new drink that combines coffee and wine in the same can. The company sells flavors such as Cabernet Coffee Espresso and Chardonnay Coffee Cappuccino.

BARBECUE MARATHON

Lee De Villiers and Simon Clarke kept a barbecue going for more than 29 hours at the Old Sergeant pub in the Wandsworth borough of London, England, during which time they cooked 500 pieces of meat.

SURPRISE STUFFING

When Linda Hebditch from Dorset, England, opened a packet of supermarket-bought sage mix from Israel, a 3-in (7.6-cm) exotic praying mantis leaped out at her.

COFFEE CRAZY

French writer and philosopher Voltaire (1694–1778) got his regular caffeine fix by drinking 50 cups of coffee a day.

SKUNK MEAT

A Bolivian man who died in 2014 aged 107 said he owed his longevity to a diet of skunks. Carmelo Flores Laura, a herder from the mountain village of Frasquia, never ate pasta or sugar, preferring a wild grain crop called canahua, and skunk meat.

COOL STUFF

SCARY SELFIES

Self-taught mother-of-three Nikki Shelley uses face paint to transform herself into scary monsters, zombies, and ghouls that look as if they have stepped straight out of a horror movie.

Her creepy characters have proved so popular that her pictures have gone viral on Facebook, winning her thousands of likes, and also impressing Neill Gorton, the acclaimed prosthetics designer on *Doctor Who*.

The 34-year-old home care worker from Warwickshire, England, started by painting the faces of her children—Taylor, Leah, and Kaiden—for Halloween and was soon able to paint as many as 12 children's faces in an hour. She also painted her husband Craig, but realized that she could not rely on her family to be human canvases all the time, so she began experimenting with designs on her own face.

"I didn't think anything would come of it, but the reaction to my work has been incredible," she says. "I don't really have an idea in mind when I start to paint. I just start and see what happens."

325

Ripley's ASK

How did you discover your incredible talent for face painting? I first started as most moms do, with a small set of Snazaroo face paints, painting the kids' faces for Halloween. Then once, while I was painting children's faces at my nephew's birthday party, the other parents were asking me if I had any business cards for their kids' parties! I started practicing more and more on my own children, but they soon got bored with being my canvas, so I started to paint my own face!

How do you come up with your ideas? There are so many talented face/body artists out there, and I wanted to find a way to make my work stand out. I am a HUGE fan of horror movies, so took my inspiration from movie characters and from masks that I found on the Internet, taking ideas from a number of different characters and making them my own. Each time I started something new, I was pushing my skills to try something a little harder, a little more unusual.

What's your process for creating a painting? I start by outlining any major shapes such as eyes or mouth, but I use my own facial structure to do this, it just makes it look that bit more natural. Then, once I know where everything is going, and I'm happy with the placement, I start with the base layer. Once the base layer is on, and any blending is done, I can go in with the detail and shading to complete the look.

How long can it take for you to complete a painting? It's time-consuming, with an average painting taking around an hour and a half, depending on the detail.

With her clever use of face paint, Nikki can create the incredible illusion that she has a giant gaping mouth with sharp teeth or big yellow eyes like a wolf, and can even make herself look as though she's been beheaded!

HIGH WIRES

When the 164-ft-high (50-m) SAT Telefontornet, or Phone Tower, opened in Stockholm, Sweden, in 1887, 4,000 separate wires led from it to homes across the city.

The wires created such darkness in the sky that locals complained that the sun was blocked. At the time Stockholm had more telephones (5,500) than any city in the world, and these required 3,107 mi (5,000 km) of overhead wire. The tower was demolished in 1953 following a fire.

HUMPTY'S FALL

When two men climbed onto a wall in 2014 to pose for a photograph at the Enchanted Forest theme park in Salem, Oregon, they accidentally knocked Humpty Dumpty off his perch. The cement Humpty crashed to the ground where he smashed into pieces, leaving his creator, artist Roger Tofte, with the task of putting him back together again. Humpty had sat on the wall ever since the park opened in 1971.

ROOF TRACK

With space on the ground in short supply, an elementary school in Taizhou, China, decided to build its running track on the roof. The 200-meter track fits perfectly on the roof of the oval-shaped, four-story building at the TianTai No. 2 school.

BELOVED PLANT

Ronna Scoratow of Pittsburgh, Pennsylvania, is leaving $5,000 in her will to a friend on condition that Phil, her 7-ft-tall (2.1-m) philodendron house plant that she has kept for more than 40 years, is lovingly fed and watered for the rest of its life.

BARBIE WANNABE

Blondie Bennett of California has spent more than $40,000 on surgery in an attempt to replicate her heroine Barbie's physique.

GOOSE PULLING

Goose pulling—a man on horseback attempting to pull the greased head of a live goose from its body—was a traditional European and North American sport from the 17th to 19th centuries. It is still practiced today, using a dead goose, in parts of Belgium, Germany, and the Netherlands.

SCHOOL DRAG

When floods made it impossible to use a nearby suspension bridge in 2014, young students in Sam Lang, Vietnam, had to get to school by crossing a swollen river inside giant plastic bags. Adults put the children inside the bags to keep their uniforms dry, and then pulled them through the raging torrent before unwrapping them on the other bank.

KISSED PIG

To fulfill a promise he made to his young students if they stopped dropping litter, Hong Yaoming, deputy head teacher of Xianning Experimental Elementary School in China, kissed a 44-lb (20-kg) pig.

In an art performance at a Beijing music festival, dozens of Chinese teenagers treated cabbages as pets by taking them for walks on lengths of string.

The stunt was arranged by artist Han Bing, who has been walking humble cabbages across the world for over 14 years as a reflection upon materialistic society. The walkers said that cabbages are more suitable for walking than dogs because they don't bark, need food, or leave a mess on the sidewalk, and they don't start fights with other cabbages.

CABBAGE WALKERS

CARTWHEEL BAN

Sixty-five-year-old Dianne Barker, of Phoenix, Arizona, has been banned from doing cartwheels at public meetings held by the Maricopa Association of Governments. A former college cheerleader, she says the cartwheels are her way of expressing passion, but the association claimed they were disruptive and a danger to public safety.

DUMMY MUMMY

A skeleton found in 2013 in an attic in Diepholz, Germany, that was originally declared by scientists to be a 2,000-year-old mummy has instead been exposed as a worthless plastic dummy. "The Mummy of Diepholz" had been sprayed with a chemical that made the bones appear real to experts.

DEATH SCENT

Raychelle Burks, a chemist at Doane College, Crete, Nebraska, has developed a perfume to help people survive a zombie apocalypse. Eau de Death features putrescine, cadaverine and methanethiol to create a scent that stinks of rotten eggs and boiled cabbage but works on the principle that zombies are attracted by the smell of the living.

Your Uploads

CLIP ART

New Yorker Mike Drake sent Ripley's this paperweight he made containing a year's worth of his fingernail and toenail clippings (nearly 500 in total) encased in acrylic. He had hoped to build up a collection of nail paperweights, but his wife was so disgusted by the idea she threw out a lot of the clippings that he had been carefully keeping since 2001.

LAME EXCUSE

A 67-year-old Canadian man who was stopped while driving at 112 mph (180 kmph) near Black Diamond, Alberta, told Mounties he was speeding so that he could dry his newly washed car. He was fined $800 and suspended from driving for 45 days.

FLY KILLER

Eighty-year-old Ruan Tang of Hangzhou, China, devotes her life to exterminating flies and estimates that she kills up to 1,000 of the disease-carrying insects every day. She has been a one-woman pest control operation for 15 years and spends eight hours a day prowling the city with her swatter.

PERMANENT BRIDE

When Xiang Junfeng of Shandong Province, China, married Zhu Zhengliang in 2004, it made her so happy that she has refused to wear anything but her wedding dress ever since. To ensure that she could wear one all year round, she had three more wedding dresses made, and she even wears her bridal gown while working in the fields.

GOOD TIMING

Nicollette Brynn Anders was born in Missoula, Montana, at 2.15 p.m. on November 12, 2013, meaning that she was born on 11-12-13 at 14:15.

EXTRAVAGANT GIFT

As a gift to his future bride, Meng Huang hired 18 drivers and a fleet of luxury cars to deliver bamboo baskets filled with $1.5 million in cash to her home in Zhejiang, China.

FLASH MOB

Tim Bonnano, a student at Aptos High School, California, enlisted a flash mob consisting of hundreds of fellow students to persuade Gabriella DeNike to accompany him to the school prom. While he played the guitar, his accomplices held up signs begging Gabriella to be his date.

EDIBLE CARDS

Believe it or not, this business card is made out of meat! Chris Thompson, head of Philadelphia, Pennsylvania, company MeatCards, creates the distinctive name cards by laser-etching the customer's details into 2-by-4-in (5-by-10-cm) pieces of dried beef jerky. Not only are the cards impressively different; they remain edible for up to a year.

ELF EARS

Convinced that she was an elf in a past life, Melynda Moon, a 24-year-old model from Guelph, Ontario, had surgery to give herself pointed ears.

The tops of her ear cartilages were skinned, and pieces were cut from the tips to form points. She often dresses like an elf, too.

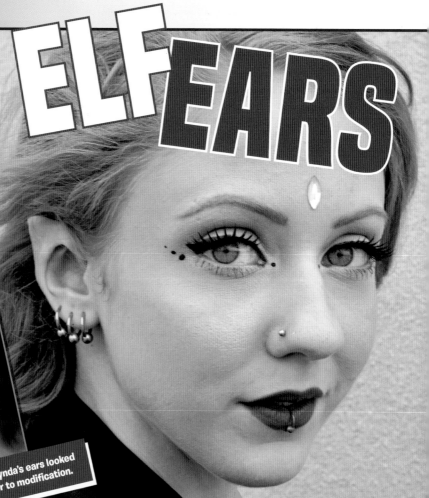

What Melynda's ears looked like prior to modification.

FLYING CAR

This white SUV somehow ended up stuck in a tree over 10 ft (3 m) above ground in a hillside forest close to a zoo in Wenzhou, China.

SNEEZE LOG

Since 2007, Peter Fletcher from Birmingham, England, has carefully logged every one of his sneezes—more than 4,000 in total. Whenever he sneezes, he makes a note of the time and date, where he is, and what he is doing. Looking back through his records, he realized that he has never sneezed while on the toilet and is particularly proud of sneeze number 42, which, although powerful, he managed to avoid getting on a quiche.

UNLUCKY SHOT

U.S. sea captain John Kendrick was killed in Hawaii in 1794 while having dinner on board his ship, *Lady Washington*, when a British vessel accidentally used a live shot to fire a cannon salute in his honor.

BOTTLE COFFIN

Anto Wickham, a 48-year-old former soldier, has spent $5,000 on a 10-ft-long (3-m), custom-made casket shaped like a bottle of Jack Daniel's whiskey, which he wants to be buried in when he dies.

LOST GOLD

French athlete Mahiedine Mekhissi-Benabbad was stripped of his gold medal for the 3,000 meters steeplechase at the 2014 European Championships in Zurich, Switzerland, because he ripped off his running vest 100 meters from the finish. In doing so, he violated the rule that athletes' bibs must be visible throughout the race.

WEEPY PAPER

Notebook manufacturer Magnus Ferreus has launched the Onion Note, a pad that makes you cry whenever you write on it. The pages are treated with compounds found in onion oil, and the heat caused by the friction of pen on paper evaporates these compounds, releasing a tear-inducing gas.

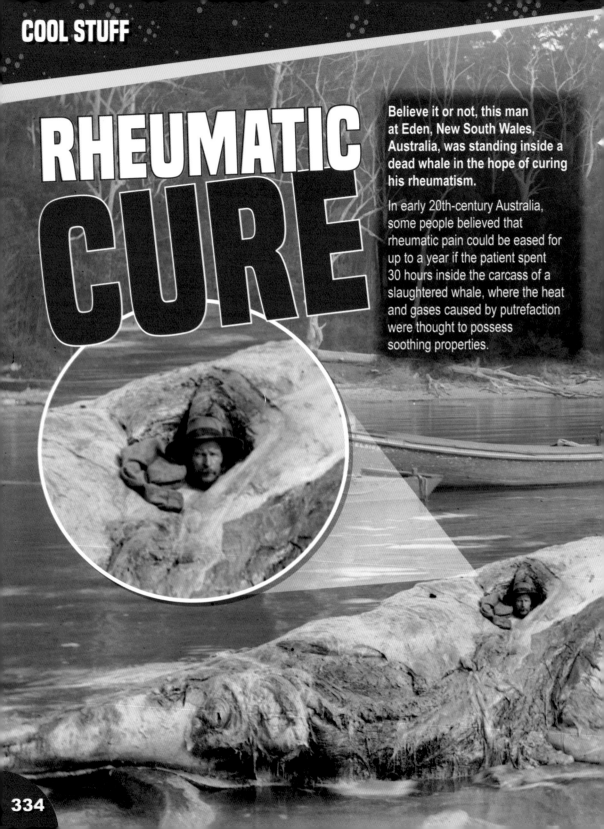

RHEUMATIC CURE

Believe it or not, this man at Eden, New South Wales, Australia, was standing inside a dead whale in the hope of curing his rheumatism.

In early 20th-century Australia, some people believed that rheumatic pain could be eased for up to a year if the patient spent 30 hours inside the carcass of a slaughtered whale, where the heat and gases caused by putrefaction were thought to possess soothing properties.

TOILET TALK

The Miraikan science museum in Tokyo, Japan, staged a three-month exhibition devoted to toilets—including a choir of singing toilet seats, poop jokes, and explanations about how feces are made. Visitors could also flush themselves down a 16-ft (5-m) toilet slide.

FACEBOOK BLUNDER

A burglar who broke into a house in St. Paul, Minnesota, was easily apprehended after checking his Facebook profile on the homeowner's computer, but forgetting to log out.

SKIN THEFT

A man was charged with stealing more than $350,000 worth of human skin from Mercy Philadelphia Hospital, Pennsylvania. Prosecutors say he repeatedly stole skin grafts from the hospital between November 2011 and July 2013.

CLEAN RACE

Before the 2014 Fredagsbirken, a major cycle race held in Rena, Norway, a liquid detergent company handed out free samples of its product to all the competitors so that they could wash their outfits in it afterward. However, during the race, six thirsty cyclists mistook their sample for an energy drink, gulped it down, and had to be rushed to hospital.

BACK TO LIFE

Several hours after being pronounced dead, 78-year-old Walter Williams of Lexington, Mississippi, woke up in a body bag. Workers at a funeral home opened his body bag in preparation for embalming him—but stopped in their tracks when he suddenly began kicking. It is thought his pacemaker had stopped working and then started again.

ACCIDENTAL DISPLAY

Pensioner Hung Feng inadvertently started a spectacular blaze in a fireworks factory in Wuhan, China, by cooking sausages in the building. The explosion destroyed the building as well as hundreds of thousands of fireworks, but it gave locals a dazzling display.

KNEE SHRAPNEL

World War II veteran Ronald Brown lived with 6 oz (170 g) of metal shrapnel in his left knee for 68 years. His family only learned the extent of his injury after he died in 2012 at age 94 and a pile of metal was found among his cremated ashes. He had stepped on a booby-trap device while serving with the British Army in France in 1944.

HERE COMES THE PUN

The George Harrison memorial tree in Griffith Park, Los Angeles, California, has been killed by—beetles! Planted in memory of the Beatles bandmember in 2004, the pine tree had grown to a height of 10 ft (3 m) until an infestation of tree beetles killed it in 2014.

DOWN THE DRAIN

Fire crews had to rescue 16-year-old Ella Birchenough when she became stuck in a storm drain while trying to retrieve her cell phone. She jumped into the drain in Dover, England, after accidentally dropping her phone down it, but then became wedged up to her waist.

BORN SURVIVOR

Bill Hillman, a Chicago-based co-author of the book Fiesta: *How to Survive the Bulls of Pamplona*, was hospitalized in Spain after being seriously gored during the 2014 Pamplona bull run. When he tripped and fell, the horn of a 1,320-lb (600-kg) bull sliced through his thigh, just missing his femoral artery. If the artery had been severed, he could have bled to death in seconds.

DEEP POOL

The Deep Joy, a swimming pool at the Hotel Terme Millepini in Montegrotto Terme, Italy, reaches a depth of 130 ft (40 m)—equivalent to the height of nine double-decker buses stacked on top of each other.

STRAY BULLET

A moose hunter on the Norwegian island of Vesteroy shot at a moose, but accidentally hit an elderly man sitting on the toilet in a nearby wooden cabin. The wayward bullet hit the senior in the abdomen, but his injury was not serious. The moose escaped unharmed.

FOUR MANAGERS

The Boston Red Sox baseball team used four different managers during their game with the Tampa Bay Rays on May 30, 2014. John Farrell, Torey Lovullo and Brian Butterfield were all ejected by umpires after arguing over pitchers targeting batters, leaving Greg Colbrunn to coach the Red Sox to a 3–2 victory.

LAST POST

On the run for two months in Freeland, Pennsylvania, Anthony Lescowitch Jr. was finally captured by police after making the mistake of posting a wanted picture of himself on his own Facebook page. Posing as a woman, a policeman began chatting online about the post with the fugitive, who readily agreed to a meeting at which he was arrested.

ANIMAL COSTUMES

When a drunk man started threatening women in the street in Coventry, England, he was arrested by two off-duty policewomen dressed as a monkey and a zebra. Officers Terri Cave and Tracy Griffin were on their way to a costume party.

BAT BOMB

During World War II, the U.S. Army tested incendiary bombs attached to 6,000 Mexican free-tailed bats.

ESCAPE ARTIST

Wayne Carlson of Canada has escaped from different North American prisons 13 times since the 1960s.

IRON SHOES

Every day, Zhang Fuxing goes for a walk while wearing iron shoes, each weighing more than 440 lb (200 kg)!

For over seven years, the 53-year-old from Tangshan, China, has walked 50 ft (15 m) a day in his pair of homemade iron shoes—to cure his back pain. It takes him over one minute just to walk ten paces with the blocks strapped to his shoes.

KISSED TO DEATH

A young man in 1909 died while trying to escape birthday kisses.

A gravestone in New York City's Woodlawn Cemetery recounts the sad demise of George Spencer Millet, who died on his 15th birthday while trying to escape six young women intent on giving him a birthday kiss. The women did not realize that he was carrying an ink eraser—a sharp, 6-in-long (15-cm) metal tool—in his pocket, and as they moved in for their kisses, he fell forward and the point of the eraser drove into his heart, killing him.

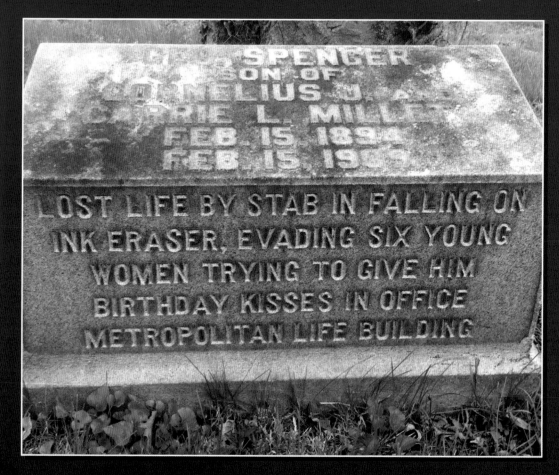

LEG MISSILE

A flight from Tunisia to Edinburgh, Scotland, was diverted after a female passenger threw her prosthetic leg at the cabin crew. She also demanded cigarettes and a parachute so that she could jump off the plane.

POISON PLOT

During World War II, the British Secret Service attempted to "poison" German leader Adolf Hitler with female hormones—a side effect of which would be his mustache hair falling out.

MISHEARD CALL

A dog walker sparked a major search-and-rescue operation in Stirlingshire, Scotland, because her pet was called Yelp. A fellow walker mistook her calls for cries of "Help," prompting 20 police officers, many with dogs, and three mountain rescue workers to scour the area for hours, fearing that the woman may have fallen down an old copper mine.

NO DYING!

In 2012, Giulio Cesare Fava, mayor of Falciano de Massico, near Naples, Italy, banned its 4,000 residents from dying because of a dispute with a neighboring town over how to expand the local cemetery. The mayor asked the residents to keep living until he had built them a new cemetery elsewhere.

UNHAPPY ENDINGS

Hans Steininger died in Braunau, Austria, in 1567 by **tripping over his beard.** He was in such a hurry to escape a fire that he forgot to roll up his 4.5-ft-long (1.4-m) whiskers!

Sir Arthur Aston, a Royalist leader during the English Civil War, was **beaten to death with his own wooden leg** by Oliver Cromwell's soldiers at the siege of Drogheda, Ireland, in 1649.

Acting as a pallbearer at a cemetery in London, England, in 1872, Henry Taylor stumbled on a stone, fell, and was **crushed to death by the coffin** he had been carrying.

Czech housewife Vera Czermak was so distraught to learn of her husband Franz's infidelity that she **jumped out of the window** of her third-story Prague apartment in 1978—just as Mr. Czermak happened to be walking along the street below.

Wesley Parsons, a farmer from Laurel, Indiana, died laughing in 1893. After being told a joke, he was seized by **fits of uncontrollable laughter** for nearly an hour, and when he was finally able to stop, he began hiccupping. Two hours later he died of exhaustion.

MEASURE FOR MEASURE

Founded by New Yorker Scott Griffin, the Drunk Shakespeare Society puts on performances of Shakespeare's plays in the city's bars—and each night a different member of the cast is genuinely drunk.

HUMAN PUNCHBAG

Forty-eight-year-old Xie Shuiping earns $3,500 a month by letting strangers punch him. He tours the bars and clubs of Wuhan City, China, charging people to hit him hard in the stomach three times. Any challenger who manages to hurt him receives free drinks.

MUDDY MARRIAGE

Jared Baylor and Taylor Ratcliff got married in a giant sloppy mud pit at the 2014 Toronto Days Mud Run in Kansas. The bride's white dress was spattered in mud after the groom drove his pick-up truck into the center of the competition bog for the ceremony. Both are fans of the filthy sport of mud bogging, which challenges drivers to plow through a deep mud pit in the fastest possible time.

CARDBOARD COMPANION

After her father died in 2012, Jinna Yang of Norfolk, Virginia, traveled the world with a life-size cardboard cut-out of him to show him the places he had always wanted to visit. She took photos of herself with the cardboard replica at such locations as Iceland's Blue Lagoon, the Louvre in Paris, and the Leaning Tower of Pisa in Italy.

LUCKY PAIR

Calvin and Zatera Spencer of Portsmouth, Virginia, won the state lottery three times in March 2014—including two $1 million prizes.

LEAP YEAR

Betty Flemming, of Springfield, Virginia, celebrated her 22nd birthday in 2012—even though she was born in 1924. Her birthday is February 29, so she has a "real" birthday only every four years—on which basis she became legally old enough to buy alcohol only in 2008, at age 84!

RUNNING OF THE BALLS

A new festival in the Spanish town of Mataelpino features runners racing downhill trying to outpace giant 275-lb (125-kg) polystyrene balls. The balls have replaced traditional live bulls, following complaints that the event was cruel.

LIZARD MIMICS

The Australian sport of goanna pulling gets its name because the rival competitors adopt the pose of goanna lizards. A strap is tied around the necks of the two fighters, who get down on all fours opposite each other with their stomachs touching the ground and their heads held high. The game is like tug-of-war, but instead of their hands, the competitors use their heads to pull each other over a line and win the fight. The National Goanna Pulling Championships have been held in Wooli, New South Wales, since 1985.

RARE QUADS

Sharon Turner of Berkshire, England, gave birth to amazing quadruplets—a pair of identical twin boys and identical twin girls—at odds of 70-million-to-one.

TATTOOED COUPLE

Husband and wife Victor and Gabriela Peralta from Buenos Aires, Argentina, have 90 and 65 percent of their bodies covered in tattoos, respectively.

Victor had his first tattoo at age 13. The couple also has 77 body modifications between the two of them, including 50 piercings, five dental implants, four ear expanders, two ear bolts, and one forked tongue.

SECRET MUSEUM

Hidden behind unmarked doors in the Tribeca district of Manhattan lies New York's most secret museum—an abandoned elevator shaft packed with quirky, random objects.

Founded by Alex Kalman and brothers Benny and Josh Safdie, "Mmuseumm" contains such diverse items as a copy of the shoe thrown at George W. Bush during a 2008 press conference, a homemade antenna, an assortment of tip jars, papers accidentally left behind in copy machines, newsstand paperweights, and a collection of plastic vomit from around the world.

5 OTHER CRAZY EXHIBITS AT MMUSEUMM

- Homemade weapons of defense
- Objects made for prisoners or by prisoners
- Potato chips from around the world
- Disney bullet-proof backpacks
- Misspelled food-container labels

DOZY SUSPECT

Burglary suspect Dion Davis was found fast asleep on a bed next to a bag of stolen jewelry after allegedly breaking into a house in Nokomis, Florida. A cleaning lady who discovered him called the police, and Davis remained asleep even while deputies took pictures of him lying on the bed.

CRAZED LAWYER

Angry at the way an inheritance case was going for his client, Evgeniy Tankov, a lawyer from Karaganda, Kazakhstan, suddenly pulled out a flyswatter in court and started hitting the judge with it in a fit of rage. After the lawyer had delivered the third blow, the judge jumped up from behind his desk and wrestled with Tankov, who was immediately barred from practicing law and faced a ten-year prison sentence for assault.

DISSATISFIED CUSTOMER

Tonya Ann Fowler of Commerce, Georgia, was arrested for wasting police time after calling 911 to complain about the quality of the mugshot of her that was issued following a previous arrest.

CRAZY NAME

After losing a bet in a poker game, a 22-year-old man from Dunedin, New Zealand, has legally changed his name to Full Metal Havok More Sexy N Intelligent Than Spock And All The Superheroes Combined With Frostnova. The name had been chosen for him by his fellow card players.

BITE BET

Norwegian soccer fan Thomas Syverson won almost $900 after placing a $5 bet that Uruguayan international soccer player Luis Suarez would bite an opponent during the 2014 World Cup.

BIG ROLL

This giant toilet-paper roll made by Charmin measures 9.73 ft (3 m) in diameter and contains more than 1,000,000 sq ft (92,903 sq m) of toilet paper—enough to make 95,000 standard-sized rolls.

Normal toilet roll!

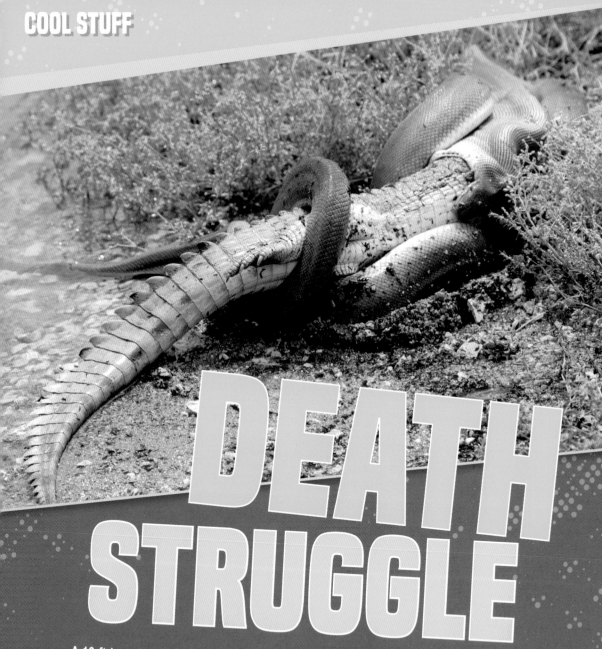

DEATH STRUGGLE

A 10-ft-long (3-m) water python swallowed a crocodile whole after a five-hour struggle in front of startled onlookers at Lake Moondarra in Queensland, Australia.

After slowly constricting the 3.3-ft-long (1-m) freshwater croc to death, the snake dragged it ashore before devouring it headfirst in just 15 minutes. Afterward, the exhausted and overstuffed snake lay still, while it digested its dinner, with the crocodile's ridges and legs clearly visible inside its belly.

Snakes have flexible jaws that allow them to swallow prey much larger in width than their own bodies!

SHOWER SIREN

Nineteen-year-old Kiyuu Oikawa, of Japan, converted his showerhead into a creepy "girlfriend," with water flowing from her mouth.

To create the doll, he taped a human mask with a wig onto the showerhead, attached clothing stuffed with a balloon for the body, and made spindly arms out of packing tape and wire.

SATANIC CHEESE

Polish exorcist Elzbieta Gas warned shoppers at her local supermarket to avoid buying packets of goat's cheese priced at 6.66 zlotys ($2.24), citing that 666 is the sign of the devil. Her fears were fueled further by the goat horns, which, not unreasonably, appear on the packaging.

RAT BOUNTY

Businessman Gareth Morgan has introduced a plan to offer students at the Victoria University of Wellington, New Zealand, a reward of free beer for every rat they catch—dead or alive.

FRESH AIR

As a protest against pollution in his home country, artist Liang Kegang gathered a jar of French fresh air in Provence during a trip and sold it for $860 in Beijing, China.

ROOFTOP GRAZING

Passersby in city of Bern, Switzerland, did a double-take when they looked up and saw a cow standing precariously on the steep roof of a farmhouse. The inquisitive animal had climbed on to the roof in search of new pastures but, not finding any, calmly made her way back to her field unharmed, leaving her owner Dieter Mueller to pay for the tiles she had smashed.

CLUB BADGE

Bulgarian builder Zdravkov Levidzhov is such a big fan of English soccer club Manchester United that he has officially changed his name to "Manchester United" and has had the club's red-and-yellow badge tattooed onto the center of his forehead as a permanent reminder of his allegiance.

SMALL DEMAND

A month after Alastair King emigrated from the U.K. to New Zealand, he received a tax demand from his former council—South Somerset District Council—for just 2 pence, which they said he could pay in installments.

INDOOR SLIDE

Trisha Cleveland from Minneapolis, Minnesota, has come up with a device that entertains children by converting a staircase into an indoor slide in just a few minutes. The SlideRider consists of a series of foldable mats with safety rails.

IDIOT SIGN

After impatient driver Shena Hardin mounted the curb in Cleveland, Ohio, because she did not want to wait behind a school bus, a judge fined her and ordered her to stand at an intersection for two days with a sign saying, "Only an idiot would drive on the sidewalk to avoid a school bus."

NATURAL GAS

French inventor Christian Poincheval has come up with a range of pills that make human gas smell like roses, violets, or chocolate. The capsules, which are made from natural ingredients such as fennel, seaweed, vegetable coal, and blueberries, also ease indigestion and reduce the amount of flatulence.

QUICK SALE

The flawless, 59.6-carat Pink Star diamond—at 0.8 × 1 in (2.69 × 2.06 cm) the world's largest cut diamond—sold for $83 million at an auction in Geneva, Switzerland, in 2013, but the sale never went through.

Snail eating colored paper.

SNAIL CARPET

Believe it or not, these brightly colored floor tiles are made from snail poop!

Dutch artist Lieske Schreuder discovered that when snails eat colored paper their feces retain that color because the snail's digestive system does not absorb the pigments. So she set up a small laboratory where the malleable excrement from 1,000 snails was collected and fed into a machine that mixed and ground it into a 5-mm-thick (0.2-in) thread. She then wove the thread to form speckled floor tiles. The process moves at a snail's pace because it takes nine snails five days to produce enough poop for just 3.3 ft (1 m) of thread.

Snail poop floor tiles.

Untreated snail poop.

Snail poop made into thread.

Woven snail poop.

WHO LOO

Customers wanting to use the toilet at the Warmley Waiting Room Café near Bristol, England, must step into a replica of the TARDIS, *Doctor Who*'s time machine.

Justin and Claire Hoggans paid £1,800 ($3,000) for the TARDIS on eBay and spent almost as much again converting it into a functioning "Who Loo" fitted with a toilet, sink, and hand dryer. Whenever anyone enters or leaves the cubicle, lights flash courtesy of a motion sensor, while TARDIS sound effects are operated via a doorbell in the café.

POLICE PUBLIC CALL BOX

Your Uploads

LONG HAIR

Tom Wilson of Lino Lakes, Minnesota, sent Ripley's this image featuring his one gray chest hair, which measures an incredible 9 in (22.5 cm) long.

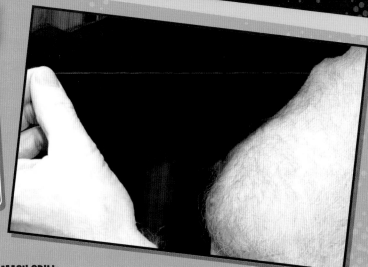

LUCKY TOILET

The Kalamazoo Christian prep baseball team from Michigan carries a portable toilet to every game to bring the players good luck. The toilet is said to symbolically represent the team flushing away its past losses in order to move onto future victories.

HOLLYWOOD HERO

Danielle Davies of Ocean City, New Jersey, lives with a full-size cardboard cutout of Hollywood star Bradley Cooper. She shops with him, cooks, eats and mows the lawn with him, and takes him to bed—even though she is happily married with children. Danielle, who has her own website, "My Life With Bradley Cooper," where she documents her adventures, actually met her hero during her sophomore year at Villanova University when they appeared in a play together.

MASH SPILL

A busy highway in North Yorkshire, England, was completely blocked for more than four hours in June 2014 after a truck spilled its load of instant mashed potatoes. Cars skidded dangerously on the liquid mash, which was eventually removed by plowing it with a tractor to make it easier to clear and then washing it away with freezing chemicals and high-powered hoses.

DEAD HEAD

Students at the Puchenii Mosneni elementary school in Romania's Prahova county learn human anatomy by studying the real-life skeleton of a former school principal. Alexandru Grigore Popescu worked at the school for half a century until his death in the 1960s. Since then his skeleton has been put on display for biology lessons.

EYE GOUGING

Gouging was an 18th-century North American backwoods sport that was used to settle arguments, the aim being to gouge out your opponent's eyes. Fighters would grow their fingernails extra long.

FLYING TOILET

A group of rocket enthusiasts launched a portable toilet 2,000 ft (600 m) into the sky from a field in Three Oaks, Michigan, and watched it land safely by parachute. The Michiana Rocketry club's aluminum-frame rocket stood 10 ft (3 m) tall and had seven motors and a portable toilet bolted on to it. The contraption weighed a total of 450 lb (204 kg) and was lifted with 2,865 lb (12,744 N) of thrust, compared to a NASA space shuttle's 7.8 million lb (34.7 million N).

CROCODILE BRIDE

Joel Vasquez Rojas, mayor of San Pedro Huamelula, Mexico, "married" a small crocodile in a special ceremony. According to tradition, the crocodile is a princess and the wedding ritual guarantees plenty of seafood for fishermen to catch along the Pacific coast. Before the nuptials, the wedding party walked through the town with the crocodile bride dressed in white with its jaws wired shut, and afterward the guests danced with the reptile.

DELAYED DEATH

A Swedish man, Johan Johansson, was finally declared dead in 2013—more than a century after he probably died. His family requested that the National Tax Agency should pronounce him dead, as he had not been heard from for 102 years.

PERFECT MATCH

Married couple Mel and Joey Schwanke, from Fremont, Nebraska, have worn matching clothes every day for more than 35 years. They own around 150 custom-made matching outfits, which they wear whenever they go out together—ensuring that his tie always matches her dress.

FREAK INJURY

While celebrating England's goal against Italy at the 2014 World Cup, national soccer team physiotherapist Gary Lewin fractured and dislocated his ankle—an injury that ruled him out of the rest of the tournament because he had to fly back to the U.K. for surgery.

LONG WILL

The last will and testament of Frederica Evelyn Stilwell Cook, who died in London, England, on January 9, 1925, at age 68, was 1,066 pages (95,940 words) long and occupied four leather-bound volumes.

OWN GOAL

During a tense overtime clash, Phoenix Coyotes' hockey goalie Mike Smith unfortunately decided the game in favor of the Buffalo Sabres with a freak goal against himself after the puck lodged in the back of his pants. When the puck looped up into the air and disappeared from view, confused players skated around searching for it, and Smith retreated into his goal—a fatal move as a replay showed he had unknowingly carried the puck with him. The goal was awarded to the Sabres, marking the end of the game.

TATTOOED SANTA

Vitor Martins, who has been dressing as Santa for more than 15 years in the Brazilian city of São Caetano do Sul, has 94 percent of his body covered in tattoos, many with a Christmas theme, including Santa himself, a reindeer, an elf helper, and a Christmas tree.

Most of Vitor's tattoos are covered when he wears his Santa robe.

INDEX

INDEX

INDEX

INDEX

INDEX

INDEX

INDEX

ACKNOWLEDGMENTS

COVER (t, b) © Alhovik/Shutterstock.com; (bkg) © Slanapotam/Shutterstock.com 7 (c) WGBH Educational Foundation / American Experience; © Aleksey Bakaleev/Fotolia.com 15 Angus James Tackle Tactics 16–19 www.burghleyimages.com 20–21 Caters News Agency 22 (sp) Bournemouth News/Rex 23 (t) Bournemouth News/Rex; (b) Bournemouth News/Rex 24 Adam Pacitti 25 Paul, Andrew & Sophia Hung 27 Circus World Museum, Baraboo, Wisconsin 28 Eric J. Eakin 29 William Rice 30 (tl) Newsflare.com 30–31 (tr) Newsflare.com 31 (t) Newsflare.com 32 AP/Press Association Images 33 © Europics 35 (t) Courtesy of Ugly Models 36–37 Collection of the John and Mable Ringling Museum of Art Tibbals Digital Collection 38–39 Brett Kern 40 Patrick Page-Sutter 41 Kirstin Mercer 42–43 Mikeal/Rex 44–45 Geoff Robinson Photography 46–47 Angus James Tackle Tactics 49 Zafer Kizilkaya 50–51 Sergey Krasnoshchekov 53 Sameer Ashraf/Barcroft India 54–55 Villa Escudero Plantations & Resort, Inc. 56 Reuters 57 Reuters/Damir Sagolj 58–59 Bruce Black 60 (t) © Andy Marshall/Alamy; (bl) SWNS.com; (br) SWNS.com 61 (r) Rex; (l) Rex 62 (t) ASSOCIATED PRESS; (b) Michael McGurk/Rex 63 Rex 64 (r) © Eddie Linssen/Alamy; (bl) © Eddie Linssen/Alamy 65 Reuters 66 (b) AFP/Getty Images 66–67 (dp) AFP/Getty Images 68 Michael Nichols, National Geographic Creative 69 ChinaFotoPress /Stringer/Getty 70 Arkaprva Ghosh/Barcroft Media 71 Arkaprva Ghosh/Barcroft Media 72 Rex/HAP/Quirky China News 73 David McQuinn/Janet Potter 74 (br) Caters News Agency 74–75 (dp) Caters News Agency 76 Public Domain 77 © Chaiwat Subprasom/Reuters 78 (l) Getty Images; (tr) Getty Images 80 Cedric Favero/Solent News/Rex 81 Janae Copelin/Barcroft USA 82–83 Caters News Agency 84–85 Reuters 86 PA Wire/Press Association Images 88 (b) Supplied by Wenn.com 88–89 (dp) Supplied by Wenn.com 90 Photograph by Barcroft India 92–93 © Miguel Vidal/Reuters 94 (tl) "Wieliczka" Salt Mine archives/Rafal Stachurski, Wieliczka Salt Mine 95 Irene Becker/Contributor/Getty Images 96–97 Zafer Kizilkaya 98–99 Getty Images 101 National News & Pictures 102–103 © Florian Schulz/visionsofthewild.com 104 Don Cooke/Cuddle Clones 105 Goodman, Brett A.; Johnson, Pieter T. J. (2011): Effects of limbs malformations on the locomotory performance of Pacific chorus frogs (P. regilla) in laboratory trials. Figure_1.tif. PLOS ONE. 10.1371/journal .pone.0020193.g001. 106 Cats Protection/SWNS.com 107 Gianfranco Gómez 108 Caters News Agency 109 © 2004 MBARI 110 (tr) Well Animal Clinic/Bournemouth/Rex; (bl) Well Animal Clinic/Bournemouth/Rex 111 John Birkett/Solent News/Rex 112–113 Getty Images 116 Stephen Hopkins/Rex 117 (tr) Reuters/Oscar Martinez; (cl) Reuters/Oscar Martinez 118 © Enrique Marcarian/Reuters 119 © Reuters Photographer/Reuters 120–121 Getty Images 122 AndreeSiwadi/BNPS 123 Matt Rudge/SWNS.com 124–125 (b) ASSOCIATED PRESS 125 (t) ASSOCIATED PRESS 126 Ingo Arndt/Minden Pictures/FLPA 127 (tl) Caters News Agency; (b) Caters News Agency 128 The LIFE Picture Collection/Getty 129 Photo courtesy of Monica Beckner and Roy Beckner 130 National News & Pictures 131 Caters News Agency 132–133 Sherry Lemcke Photography 134 Debra Mayrhofer/Lort Smith 135 Caters News Agency 136 Robertus Pudyanto / Stringer / Getty 137 Peter Roosenschoon & Dubai Desert Conservation Reserve 138 © Alex Mustard/naturepl.com 139 Barry Bland/Rex 142 (c) Caters News Agency; (bl) Caters News Agency 143 Sam Ireland 144 Library of Congress 145 Snap Stills/Rex 146 AFP/Getty Images 147 Caters News Agency 148 (l) Caters News Agency; (r) Caters News Agency 149 Caters News Agency 150–151 © The Natural History Museum/Alamy 152–153 Circus World Museum, Baraboo, Wisconsin 154 Matt Writtle/Barcroft Media 155 ASSOCIATED PRESS 156–157 Macchina anatomica – Donna (Giuseppe Salerno, 1763-64) © Massimo Velo 158 National Archives of Australia: A1336, 4890 159 Meredith Cahill, Cherryhill NJ 160 ASSOCIATED PRESS 161 ASSOCIATED PRESS 162 Alinari Archives/Contributor 163 TT News Agency/Press Association Images 164–165 ASSOCIATED PRESS 170 HAP/Quirky China News/Rex 171 © Europics 173 Richie the Barber 175 ASSOCIATED PRESS 176 ASSOCIATED PRESS 176–177 (br) ASSOCIATED PRESS 179–185 Leon + Lilly Mackie/cardboardboxoffice.com 186 (tl) Reuters; (b) Reuters 187 Alex Dodson/Solent News/Rex 188 Reuters/Sergei Karpukhin 189 Kim Kowalski of Clever Kim's Curios 190–195 Courtesy of Derin Bray American Art & Antiques 196–197 Tom McShane/Solent News 198 Hoang Tran 199 Maor Zabar Hats moarzabarhats.etsy.com 200 (tl) Ji Tan www.wildlifemalaysia.com www.pixelsdimension.com 200–201 (b) Supplied by Wenn.com 202 (t) Rex; (b) Rex 204–205 Angela Rossi 206 © Pictorial Press Ltd/Alamy 207 © Hulton-Deutsch Collection/CORBIS/Corbis via Getty Images 208 Mary Evans / SZ Photo / Scherl 211 David McHugh/Rex 212 Supplied by Wenn.com 213 Supplied by Wenn.com 215 (tl) Caters News Agency; (b) Caters News Agency 216 Science & Society Picture Library/Contributor/Getty Images 217 Science & Society Picture Library/Contributor/Getty Images 218 Wang jiayu - Imagine China 219 SAPOL 220–221 Supplied by Wenn.com 222–223 David McHugh/Rex 224 Hubcap Creatures 225 (t) Laurent La Gamba/Solent News/Rex; (b) Laurent La Gamba/Solent News/Rex 226–227 Austral Int./Rex 228–229 AFP/Getty Images 231 Quirky China News/Rex 232–233 (dp) Hou wei zk – Imaginechina 233 (tr) Hou wei zk – Imaginechina 234 SWNS.com 235 Reuters/Jason Lee 236 © Europics 237 © Darren Staples/Reuters 238 facebook.com/ITTFWorld/Remy Gros 240 Collection of the John and Mable Ringling Museum of Art Tibbals Digital Collection 241 Underwood Archives/Contributor/Getty Images 242 Cornell Capa/Contributor/Getty Images 243 © Bettmann/Corbis via Getty Images 244 (t) Quirky China News/Rex; (b) Quirky China News/Rex 245 James Cheadle/Solent News/Rex 246–247 (b) Rex/Tom Dymond 248–249 Barcroft India 250 (c) © Europics 250–251 (dp) © Europics 252 (l) Mike King/Rex 252–253 (dp) Mike King/Rex 254–255 (dp) Mike King/Rex 255 (c) Mike King/Rex 256 Caters News Agency 257 Caters News Agency 259 Jason Mecier 260–263 Bordalo II 264 BODILY CANDLES BY ANNA STERNIK, PHOTO COURTESY OF THE PHOTOGRAPHER, ANNA STERNIK 265 http://www.wahahafactory.com/ 266 www.margauxlange.com 267 www.margauxlange.com 268 (l) Barcroft India; (r) Barcroft India 269 Supplied by Wenn.com 270 Véronique Vedrenne 271 Photo by Gregory Halili 272–276 Bradley Hart bradley@bradleyhart.ca 278 Caters News Agency 279 (l) Jonty Hurwitz/Rex; (r) Jonty Hurwitz/Rex 280 Woolff Gallery, London 282 www.carolmilne.com/Rex 283 Jason Mecier 284–289 NaTalica www.natalica.com 290 (tl) Reuters; (tc) Reuters; (tr) Reuters; (b) Reuters 291 Getty Images for Ascot Racecours 292 (tl, tr) Ted Lawson/Rex; (bl) Ted Lawson/Rex 293 BNPS.co.uk 294–295 (b) Xiao junwei sh- Imagine China 295 (l, r) Shdaily - Imagine China 297 (t) Caters News Agency; (b) Caters News Agency 298 Reuters 299 Emanuel Pavao 301 Absente Semba (per DEAN 3.5.15) 302 © Cavendish Press 303 ChinaFotoPress via Getty Images 304 YOSHIKAZU TSUNO/AFP/Getty Images 305 Sutton Seeds/Bournemouth News/Rex 307 (l) Arkaprava Ghosh/Barcroft India; (r) Arkaprava Ghosh/Barcroft India 308 Morkes Chocolates 309 (l) Solum, Stian Lysberg/Scanpix Norway/Press Association Images; (r) Solum, Stian Lysberg/Scanpix Norway/Press Association Images 310 Mayumi Ishikawa 311 Clive Cooper - www.sparksflydesign.com 312 ASSOCIATED PRESS 313 Reuters/Kim Kyung-Hoon 314–315 Caters News Agency 316 Michael Lee and Fine Cheeses Ltd. 317 Jonathan Hordle/Rex 318 Absente Semba (per DEAN 3.5.15) 319 (tr) Reuters; (cl) Reuters 320 © Europics 321 (l) swns.com; (r) swns.com 323–327 Nikki Shelley - The Painting Lady 328 Tekniska museet, Stockholm 329 (t) Sun jinbiao - Imagine China; (b) Sun jinbiao - Imagine China 330 © Europics 331 Mike Drake 332 (t) meatcards.com; (b, bl) Laurie Cadman Creative (http://www.lauriecadman.com) 333 HAP/Quirky China News/Rex 334–335 A cure for rheumatism; Bob Wiles in the carcass of a whale, Twofold Bay, [1] [picture], Charles Eden Wellings, National Library of Australia, C.E. Wellings collection 336 Matt Austin/Rex 337 AFP/Getty Images 338 Allison C. Meier 340 SWNS.com 342 Mmuseumm 343 Haney Inc. - www.haneyprc.com 344 Marvin Muller/Barcroft India 345 Marvin Muller/Barcroft India 346 © Europics 347 © Europics 348–349 Lieske Schreuder 350 Jon Kent/swns.com 351 Thomas F. Wilson 352–353 Reuters/Nacho Doce MASTER GRAPHICS (halftone dot pattern) © Arts Vector/Shutterstock.com

Key: t = top, b = bottom, c = center, l = left, r = right, sp = single page, dp = double page, bkg = background

All other photos are from Ripley Entertainment Inc.

Every attempt has been made to acknowledge correctly and contact copyright holders and we apologize in advance for any unintentional errors or omissions, which will be corrected in future editions.